Satanic Killings

First published in Great Britain in 2006 by
Allison & Busby Limited
13 Charlotte Mews
London W1T 4EJ
www.allisonandbusby.com

Copyright © 2006 by FRANK MOORHOUSE

A catalogue record for this book is available from
the British Library.

10 9 8 7 6 5 4 3 2 1

ISBN 0 7490 8232 1 (Hardback)
ISBN 0 7490 8155 4 (Trade paperback)

Printed and bound in Wales by
Creative Print and Design, Ebbw Vale

Satanic Killings

FRANK MOORHOUSE

For the unquiet dead

Chapter One

⁓

𝕶illing 𝕵or 𝕾atan

Please allow me to introduce myself...

Killing for Satan is, of course, as old a tradition as the Devil himself. Despite being a minority sport when compared to the history of killing for God, it never loses its power not only to shock but to reflect precisely the moral climate of society. We say that we have banished superstition with the white light of science, yet still we keep inviting Old Nick across the threshold. Invoke his name and you can still send a shiver down the spine of 21st century communities and have them reaching for their Bibles.

The cases dealt with in this book are cautionary tales spanning the last 30 years. Each reflects the mood of a particular era, many interlink to form a much wider picture and, having read them all, you may come to the conclusion that rather than having advanced in our thinking, we are still clinging tightly to medieval mores. All of them hinge upon our modern perception of who the Devil is and on the ambassadors who came to spread his word. Often they say more about the rest of us than we care to admit.

Serial killers

The book falls into three fairly distinct sections, as if, in a grotesque funfair mirror distortion of society, the crimes themselves are following trends. Covering the years between 1976 and 1985, the bloody reigns of David 'Son of Sam' Berkowitz, The Chicago Rippers and Richard Ramirez introduce the phenomenon of the serial killer.

Reflected back through popular culture in the years since the citizens of New York, Chicago and Los Angeles actually had to live with these terrors, the serial killer has become an omnipresent staple of movies, books, and heavy metal, Gothic and industrial music. Reaching its apex in the frankly unbelievably urbane Dr Hannibal Lecter, portrayed as a demonic luvvie by Sir Anthony Hopkins, the serial killer has now morphed into a cartoon character, far removed from the depraved reality of the true crimes themselves.

Yet when David Berkowitz first stole into the hot New York nights of the late Seventies, if Hell actually was a city it would have been the crumbling, partially lawless Manhattan of that era, where the extreme poverty of the Lower East Side rubbed up against the hedonistic Uptown party encapsulated by the infamous Studio 54. That Berkowitz came for the beautiful people only heightened his bogeyman aura; that he emulated Jack the Ripper by playing cat-and-mouse with an all-too-eager press set a modern standard of press fire-stoking that interferes with the police investigation itself. The media play a big part in these stories and with the arrival of the Internet, an unregulated borderless press has sometimes helped to make these criminals into outsider heroes.

In his invaluable *Whoever Fights Monsters*, FBI profiler Robert Ressler identified the patterns that make a serial killer, and his thesis is vindicated time and time again. Abusive childhoods are the starting point and Berkowitz was deserted by not one but two sets of parents, before being abandoned completely when still only a teenager. The problem the tabloid press foster is to ignore the background and treat all killers as monsters, utterly detached from the rest of the human race. The Devil is their willing and best accomplice in reducing complex and far-reaching cause-and-effects into simple good versus evil, so that the rest of us may feel justified in washing our hands of the culprits.

Berkowitz used the Devil as his defence, but Ressler soon broke the truth out of him – the killer was taking his frustrations out on the carefree young he felt had spurned and reviled him. He was killing the people society would never allow him to be.

Satanic Panic

The next two cases are more complex, bloody and terrifying still. But it seems no coincidence that they happened at a time when America was deliberately starting a moral outrage of its own: the notorious 'Satanic Panic' fanned by the book *Michelle Remembers* and the subsequent nationwide publicity generated by its coverage on Geraldo Rivera's immensely popular TV chat show.

This book told America that there was a parallel universe going on behind the white picket fence. That legions of young children were being used in horrific sexual orgies and sacrifices by covens of Satanists up and down the land – and it could be going on in your own back yard. The movement was given wings not just by Rivera, but by the extreme evangelical and fundamentalist Christians, who to this day wield immense power in the US. From 1979 to 1985, when the book was discredited and Rivera forced to publicly admit that everything he'd been claiming was 'a bunch of crap', scores of innocent people were arrested and even imprisoned for crimes they didn't commit. Meanwhile, so-called 'experts' on Recovered Satanic Abuse (RSA) memories were spreading the panic to Europe.

At the same time, a scrawny, much-picked-upon kid from Chicago called Robin Gecht had grown into a manipulative, misogynistic sadist with enough charisma to convince three other men into abducting, mutilating, raping and butchering 18 women as part of a self-styled Satanic ritual.

Gecht's Chicago Rippers and their successor, Richard 'The Night Stalker' Ramirez, who laid siege to Los Angeles between 1984 and 1985, committed the most stomach-churning crimes of this collection and it is impossible to find any degree of empathy for them. Yet childhoods full of neglect and violence, Ramirez's two debilitating head injuries and copious amounts of narcotics taken in the teenage years mark out Ressler's road to ruin in both cases. Rather than Berkowitz, who constructed his demonic fantasies after the fact, the glorification of Satan was part of the myth that Gecht, and even more so Ramirez, fashioned in their own minds to justify their appalling deeds.

And what does it say about our society that the unattractive Gecht and his crew are seldom remembered while the devilishly handsome Ramirez became a poster boy for Satanism and had women fighting for his hand in marriage?

Modern-day witch trials

The next study, the Brisbane Lesbian Vampires led by Tracey Wigginton, anticipates the spate of crimes that come later in the book, spanning the late Nineties to the present, in which troubled young women identify with vampires and are treated as witches. The twist in Tracey's tale, however, is that the group of women she took up with, including her girlfriend Lisa Ptaschinski, very probably made up the stories about her being a vampire in order to try and save themselves from being implicated in the murder she committed. However, in an extremely patriarchal, rural and repressed part of Australia in 1989 they had no chance of casting off their image as deviants, both in dress and sexuality.

It is interesting to note though that Tracey Waugh, the youngest member of the group who was less outrageous in her attire and came from a respectable, middle class home, was acquitted. Without exception, all the criminals in this book come from working class backgrounds, often ones of extreme poverty and hardship, which tends to make them look even worse in the eyes of the juries that have tried them. Seldom articulate or attractive, you will find no Hannibal Lecters here.

The shadow of the Nazis

Chapters 6, 7 and 8 take us into different territories: continental Europe in the years 1993 and 1994 and three young men who used Satan as a cover for their real motivations – extreme racism, homophobia and nascent neo-Nazism.

Varg Vikernes, who called himself Count Grishnackh, was at the vanguard of a new strain of music called Black Metal that gradually made the progression from rock-standard Satanism to exploring the 'pagan' past of the Norse lands, and finally arriving at out-and-out admiration for the Third Reich.

Vikernes began his criminal career by torching ancient Stave churches and ended up murdering his former best friend, who had become a business rival. Along the way he courted the press feverishly, both locally and nationally, and as a result became even more infamous after his incarceration, partially through the best-selling book *Lords of Chaos* by Michael Moynihan and Didrik Sønderland. Thanks to Norway's liberal prison regime, Vikernes was able to run his own record label from the inside, fronting the lucrative Black Metal label Cymphane that one American neo-Nazi in particular was keen to get his hands on.

William Pierce, leader of the far right National Alliance, was an expert in youth culture and he chose the subject of the next chapter, murderous German schoolboy Hendrik Möbus, as a conduit to Vikernes' riches. A fellow Black Metal fan, Möbus, along with the other members of his fledgling Black Metal band Absurd, had been jailed at the age of 17 for killing 14-year-old Sandro Beyer. Prison was to prove a useful workshop for Möbus too, who put out records and raised his profile via an appearance in *Lords of Chaos* and various Internet outlets. Upon his release in 1999, Möbus headed straight to America and attempted to establish a global Black Metal empire. He was arrested near Pierce's home in 2000 and deported back to Germany, where he was sent straight back to jail for parole violation.

Vikernes and Möbus' cases are stark warnings of an underground network of neo-Nazism spreading its tentacles across the globe, hiding its true intentions behind Satanic metal, gothic and industrial music. The fall of the Berlin Wall and the subsequent tidal wave of Western pop culture that poured into the formerly communist East Germany seems to have helped to exacerbate the process of turning standard juvenile delinquents into something more sinister.

Without the help of the Internet and various people involved with the Black Metal scene it is unlikely that we would have even heard of Nico Claux, or, as he would prefer to be known, 'The Vampire of Paris'. But thanks to these networks, this homophobic killer was able to re-style himself as Dracula with a paintbrush and is now at liberty, with a cult following willing to pay good money for his technically unaccomplished canvases of fellow killers. The collecting of such 'murderobilia' has become a thriving industry and like his two predecessors, Claux was able to weave a myth around the sordid reality of his crime that has completely eclipsed what he actually did – shooting dead, then robbing, a gay man in Paris, using a prototype of the Internet to select his prey.

Vampire clans

As we proceed into the late Nineties and back to America, the line between cult fiction and reality becomes ever more blurred. The cases of Rod Ferrell and Natasha Cornett have haunting, tragic similarities that were completely overlooked as a new Satanic panic about vampire clans rose up around them. Both were from the dirt poor, utterly deprived areas of Kentucky that have long been the outposts of evangelism and race hatred. Both had terminally unfit parents and were sexualised far too early by abusive members of their own families. Both sought refuge in fantasy worlds that combined gothic novels with schlock-horror music, while indulging in rampant substance abuse and self-harm. Both became the focus of murderous mini-cults.

The German husband-and-wife team of Manuela and Daniel Ruda were admirers of Hendrik Möbus and vampire S&M culture. They shocked the world with their 2002 court appearances for the ritualistic murder of their friend Frank Hackert in a ceremony they claimed to have thought would bring them eternal life. With multi-coloured hair and multiple piercings, they deliberately provoked the press with their hammy theatricals. It was as if they couldn't tell the difference between fantasy and reality.

As was the case with our penultimate killer, Scottish loner Allan Menzies, a severely disturbed young man who sought to blame the vampire movie *Queen of the Damned* for his savage butchery of his own best friend in 2002. Menzies too was under the impression that by killing he would become immortal – even though he repeatedly, and eventually successfully, attempted to commit suicide.

The last and most recent case, the 2003 murder of Jodi Jones, crystallises our current fearful attitude towards youth gone wild and the 'Satanic' influence of popular culture. When the 14-year-old schoolgirl was found frenziedly hacked to death in a lane near her Scottish home, her boyfriend Luke Mitchell took the full brunt of society's rage. Because there was no physical evidence to use against him, Mitchell took the dock alongside all our modern bugbears – drug abuse, the breakdown of family and traditional morals and Marilyn Manson. It is unlikely he will see daylight again for a very long time.

The trouble with teenagers...

So how did we get here? Firstly it is important to consider that all these criminals, with the exception of Robin Gecht, were extremely young when they committed their crimes. They were teenagers with more to rebel against than most. Reared in atmospheres where there was no sense of morality or decency, shunned by normal society, they sought solace in the popular culture that has fostered the image of Satan as the ultimate rebellious outsider since teenagers officially began – in the Sixties.

In recent years, especially since the Columbine high school massacre in 1999, popular culture has been repeatedly blamed for its bad influence on criminal kids – usually by commentators who have little knowledge of what they are talking about. Oliver Stone's *Natural Born Killers* and Marilyn Manson are the prime folk devils, despite, or perhaps because, of the fact that both the film and the musician in question present savage satires on modern mores. Both are more concerned with the breakdown of society and the power of the mass media than they are with glorifying evil, and both could be said to have been wilfully misconstrued. A more in-depth evaluation is sorely overdue, and to do that, we have to look back to where it all began.

Youth culture, kickstarted by Elvis and his rebellious pelvis in the Fifties, seemed to take over the Western world in the next decade. As memories of World War II, the Empire and rationing receded, the bright young things of the Sixties seized the day from the dowdy adult world. It was the prime time for Satan to make his comeback. The establishment was rattled by the birth of the permissive society, the Pill, the hippies and the Beatles getting the MBE – and perhaps they had reason enough to think that dark forces were abroad. For a connecting group of hip filmmakers, musicians, actors and occultists had indeed begun to see the Devil as in the words of the Rolling Stones, 'a man of wealth and taste', the epitome of counter-culture cool. And their dabblings would eventually reap a whirlwind that none of them had bargained for, that would come crashing down in the final, fatal year of 1969.

What happened in those years has a direct bearing on the cases covered in this book and the social and cultural histories examined alongside them. Those who acted as Satanic ambassadors then have left an enduring influence on successive generations of young people since, a fascination which, rather than fading nearly half a century later, has endured and strengthened into anti-hero worship. We shall encounter the same names time and time again.

You could say that no sooner was the teenager born, than the Devil was there to tempt him.

Welcome to the Six-Six-Sixties

The mark of the beast

The roots of what happened in the Sixties stretch out long behind them, to a man born into Victorian wealth, who made it his mission to fly against the strict yet hypocritical morals of that era and attempted to establish his own counter-culture: Aleister Crowley. He is the predatory, abusive Godfather of all this book's delinquent children.

'The Great Beast 666' was the son of a wealthy brewery heir, Edward Crowley, who was also a lay preacher in an extreme puritanical sect called the Plymouth Brethren. As a child, Aleister used to enjoy watching his father stoking up believers into a righteous frenzy. But all that changed when Edward died, leaving his pre-pubescent son in the charge of his morally uptight mother Emily. As his great biographer Lawrence Sutin has pointed out, despite its anti-Christian stance, everything Aleister did next would be propelled by the same messianic zeal that his father had inspired in his converts.

In 1888, Crowley joined one of the many esoteric societies that had sprung up at the *fin de siécle*, the Hermetic Order of the Golden Dawn. A blend of Hinduism, Buddhism, spiritualism and Egyptian mysticism, devotees included the poet WB Yeats and author Arthur Machen. Crowley rose swiftly through the ranks, before deciding that his powers were destined for greater things. He developed his own occult philosophy, which he called Thelema, in homage to a profane 16th century novel. François Rabelais' *Gargantua* tells the story of a warrior monk and his abbey, Thelema, in which every conceivable sin of the flesh is indulged. The maxim of the abbey is: 'Do what you will'.

Crowley's ambition was to create his own abbey, and in 1903 he claimed to have received his orders to do so – from an ancient Egyptian god. While honeymooning in Cairo with his first wife Rose Kelly, Crowley performed a ritual that summoned Horus, who began speaking directly to him through the medium of his wife. For three days, Crowley took dictation from the disembodied deity and the resulting tome, *The Book of The Law* became the central core of Crowley's philosophy. He believed he was on the cusp of a new aeon, where the old religions would be swept aside and he would lead mankind into the Age of Horus.

But Crowley was a little ahead of his time. The three central tenets of the Law would not become widely recognised for another 60 years. By then, to the movers and shakers of the Swinging Sixties, they would make perfect sense:

Do what thou wilt shall be the whole of the Law

Love is the Law, Love under Will

Every man and every woman is a star

As far as the concept of 'love' itself went, Crowley was sadly lacking. He soon dispensed with Rose and his first daughter, Lola Zaza, abandoning them both on a mountaineering trek in Vietnam. When his daughter promptly died of typhoid, Crowley blamed this on Rose's 'alcoholism' and divorced her. His next lover was a man, the writer Victor Neuberg, with whom Crowley travelled to the Sahara Desert to perform a ritual. It left Neuberg a mental wreck, but confirmed to Crowley the power of 'sex magick'. In 1910, he was approached by a German occult order to which such rituals were essential rites, the Ordo Templi Orientis, usually referred to as The OTO. Crowley was soon the head of the English-speaking branch.

The First World War interrupted his reverie. Rejected by the British intelligence service, he spent the duration of the conflict in America, writing reams of anti-British propaganda for the Germans. Once the War was over it was impossible for him to return to his native land. So instead he sought refuge in Sicily, where, with his American mistress Leah Hirsig, he had a second daughter Poupee and at last set up his longed-for abbey of Thelema in a farmhouse near the town of Cefalu. He was soon joined by a coven of converts.

By this time, Crowley was a raging drug fiend, taking cocaine and heroin in massive quantities. Thelema was a sordid, unsanitary hellhole where unspeakable practices soon led to deaths. Poupee died there; Hirsig had a nervous breakdown; and Crowley's protégé Raoul Loveday followed Crowley's second infant daughter into the grave after performing a ritual where he drank the blood of a cat.

Loveday's wife Betty May fled to Britain and sold the whole sorry story to the *Sunday Express*, splashing the headlines that sealed Crowley's reputation as 'the wickedest man in the world'. Italy's Fascist dictator Benito Mussolini had The Great Beast deported in 1923, whereafter the remains of Crowley's sect were left to their own devices – most of them to insanity and early death.

Returning to Britain as a figure of hate and ridicule, Crowley was a broken man. He ended his days in typical English ignominy – in a guesthouse in Hastings in 1947. Crowley got off lightly. His wealth and influence spared him from any legal responsibility for a lifetime spent abusing others. Once he was gone, the legend around him swiftly grew.

Exactly 20 years later, his face would reappear on the cover of The Beatles' *Sergeant Pepper's Lonely Hearts' Club Band*. The Age of Horus would finally begin.

Scorpio Rising

In the year of Crowley's death, a precocious 17-year-old from Santa Monica, California made his first movie. A landmark in both experimental, ritual and gay film-making, the 14-minute-long *Fireworks* would introduce the world to the talents of Kenneth Wilbur Anglemyer, who had already changed his name to the more appropriate Kenneth Anger.

Although his career has been beset with every kind of trouble, his output limited to only nine completed movies, Kenneth Anger is one of the 20th century's most visionary filmmakers. And he is at the centre of Satan's web of the Sixties.

Anger's initiation into the world of film had come at an early age. His grandmother was a wardrobe mistress in Hollywood and through her contacts he was chosen to play the changeling prince in Max Reinhardt and William Dieterle's 1935 version of *A Midsummer Night's Dream*.

His next awakening took place at high school, where he first discovered the works of Aleister Crowley. *Fireworks* demonstrates how adroitly Anger digested the Great Beast's theories and used them to make his own initiation ceremony, both into Thelemaic magick and cinema history. Alone amongst film directors, Anger claims that cinema *is* a force that can be used to exert control over people and events, and that his movies are made with precisely that intention in mind. Imagine the uproar if Oliver Stone had said any such thing.

Anger was also the first director to use pop music as an ironic commentary on his imagery – a debt which Martin Scorsese has acknowledged on his soundtrack to *Mean Streets* and without which David Lynch's *Blue Velvet* could not have used the ballads of the Fifties to such stunning effect. Anger first used the song 'Blue Velvet' in his 1963 homage to the motorcycle and the perfect male, *Scorpio Rising*. Now a soundtrack to a Hollywood film that doesn't contain a plethora of knowing pop or rock songs is virtually unthinkable.

Fireworks took him straight to the heart of the avant garde. Jean Cocteau invited the youthful Anger to come over to Paris and Crowley's young disciple spent most of the Fifties hobnobbing with Edith Piaf, Jean Genet, Coco Chanel, Federico Fellini and John Paul Getty II. When his money ran out, Anger struck on another brilliantly innovative idea and wrote the book *Hollywood Babylon*, a wickedly witty catalogue of scandal and vice in America's sacred dream machine, prefaced archly with the Crowley dictum: *'Every man and every woman is a star'*. Although his French publisher Jean-Jacques Pauvert was delighted with the tome, which he published in 1959, Anger immediately faced trouble from the English-speaking word – it would take until 1975 for the book to come out in America. Like his master Crowley, Anger was just too far ahead of his time.

Anger returned to America in 1964, where he completed probably his most famous film, *Scorpio Rising*, whose fast-edit sequences, fetishistic imagery and pulsating pop soundtrack provided the blueprint for MTV. He called it 'a death mirror held up to American culture'.

Following 1965's camp classic *Kustom Kar Kommandos*, Anger hopped back over the Atlantic to Britain, where he met the Beatles and the Stones. Nothing would quite be the same again.

Sympathy for the Devil

London was in the grip of strange days, rather similar to those that Crowley had known at the end of the 19th century. Britain's two biggest bands had already had a brush with the dark side before Anger arrived in town, through the charismatic personas of Mary Ann and Robert De Grimston, founders of the Process Church, a breakaway group of ex-Scientologists.

Robert, a highly intelligent former military officer, and Mary Ann, a former Madam who had been involved in the Profumo Affair, were an odd but charismatic couple. Mixing Scientology's principles with the ideas of Freudian psychologist Alfred Adler, they formed the Process Church of the Final Judgement and, dressed in black turtle neck sweaters and capes, courted the leading lights of Sixties London from their 24-hour coffee shop, Satan's Cave.

In the Indicia bookshop on the King's Road, the De Grimstons met Peter Asher (brother of Paul McCartney's girlfriend, Jane) and John Dunbar (then husband of pop singer Marianne Faithfull, soon to be Mick Jagger's most infamous consort). It was 1966 and the two bands' exposure to these budding occultists meant they were eager to receive the wisdom of the De Grimstons' friend Anger.

Anger's first meeting with the Stones was with their founder Brian Jones and his then girlfriend, Anita Pallenberg. Pallenberg was fascinated by the occult and Anger soon found himself at the centre of a new magic circle, perhaps the most influential one of all time. By the time of the 'Summer of Love' in 1967, The Beatles had included a picture of Crowley on the cover of *Sgt Pepper*, which was closely followed by the Stones' *Their Satanic Majesties Request*. Anger's influence can also be found on the Stones' 'Sympathy For The Devil', although the song was actually inspired by a copy of Mikhail Bulgakov's novel *The Master and Margarita*, given to Jagger by Faithfull.

Installed in his Swinging Set, Anger returned to work he had begun in San Francisco, a filmic paean to the hippy revolution, *Lucifer Rising*. However, this movie had already got off to a bad start. When work resumed with the Stones onboard, everything started to go horribly wrong.

Invocation of my Demon Brother

Anger's intentions with *Lucifer Rising* were to restore the fallen angel of Christian teaching back to his gnostic status as 'bringer of light'. The original Lucifer was to have been a 5-year-old boy, but the chosen actor died in an accident before filming began. Not heeding this omen, Anger cast around for a suitable replacement and was struck by the name of the guitarist in the emergent San Francisco band Love, Bobby Beausoleil. In French, *beau soleil* means 'beautiful sun'. What could possibly be more perfect for Anger's bringer of light?

It didn't turn out that way. After a prolonged argument, Beausoleil was fired from the film, whereupon, according to Anger, Bobby seized the majority of the footage and buried it in the desert. For this crime, Anger cursed Beausoleil – with forthcoming spectacular results.

In London, Anger worked the remains of the original footage into a new film that incorporated scenes with the Stones and a Mick Jagger original soundtrack, *Invocation of my Demon Brother*. Happy with the results, Anger asked Jagger to be his new Lucifer.

But bad vibes were brewing in the Stones' circle. Pallenberg had decided to ditch an increasingly drug-addled Jones for guitarist Keith Richards in the middle of a Moroccan holiday in 1967. This precipitated Jones' mental deterioration and his eventual sacking from the band in 1969, weeks before his own suspect death in the swimming pool of his Sussex mansion.

In the initial stages of their relationship, Anger planned a pagan marriage ceremony for Richards and Pallenberg. In preparation for the event, he allegedly painted the inside of their front door gold – while supposedly out of the building. Whether this tale is true or merely a testament to the amount of drugs the couple were taking at the time, it freaked them out enough to cancel their nuptial plans and phase out Anger from their inner circle.

After the death of Jones, Jagger too felt the need to withdraw from the *Lucifer Rising* project, although his brother Chris, Faithfull and the filmmaker Donald Cammell did accompany Anger to Egypt to begin shooting. An on-set row led to Chris Jagger's dismissal and Lucifer ended up being played by a Middlesbrough steel worker called Leslie Huggins. Cammell, who as a child had been bounced on Aleister Crowley's knee, would also come to a bad end. The co-director of the era-defining *Performance* alongside Nic Roeg, he would cast Jagger and Pallenberg as dissolute swingers at the burnt-out end of the Sixties to stunning effect. And, in 1996, would commit suicide in an exact replica of the ending of that film.

With Jagger out of the picture, Anger asked another rising star and Crowley obsessive, Jimmy Page, to take over soundtrack duties. Initially, this seemed like an astute move – genius guitarist Page was on his way to forming a band that would eclipse even the Stones; rock behemoths Led Zeppelin.

What came next for the Stones themselves was another disaster. At a gig at the Altamont Speedway on 6th December 1969, the Hell's Angels hired as the band's security stabbed to death a young black man, Meredith Hunter, as the Stones finished playing 'Sympathy For The Devil'.

The Sixties were over, in a collision of dark forces. *Lucifer Rising* forms stage centre for a further cast of Satanic emissaries to make their entrance. To consider them, we must rewind back to San Francisco in 1966.

The Black Pope

For it is on the Satanic festival of Walpurgisnacht (1st May) in that year that a former carny barker and crime scene photographer named Anton Szandor La Vey founded the Church of Satan in the city by the bay.

La Vey's brand of Satanism was very different from the Eastern-inspired theologies of Crowley and the Lucifer perceived by Kenneth Anger. As a young man working in the American sideshows of the 1940s, La Vey had not found mystical enlightenment but an entrepreneurial insight into the capitalism of carnal pleasures. He watched men lusting after the showgirls on a Saturday night and then taking their penance with the tent-show evangelists at the other side of the field on a Sunday morning.

For deeper insight into the dark recesses of the human mind, La Vey enrolled at San Francisco City College in 1949 to study criminology. This led to his employment in the city's police force as a homicide photographer and later promotion to the department that investigated unexplained phenomena. La Vey lived in a Black House, dressed in black and even acquired a black panther as a pet. He became a local semi-celebrity.

Kenneth Anger first came into contact with La Vey in the early Sixties when Anton began hosting gatherings at the Black House that were known as the 'Magic Circle'. The man who the press would dub 'The Black Pope' would also appear in *Invocation Of My Demon Brother*, though not as famously as his 1968 cameo in the Satanic thriller *Rosemary's Baby*.

As the counter-culture converged on San Francisco looking for a hippy heaven in 1966, so La Vey decided that the time had come to establish his own church that would stand against everything these flower children believed in. He wrote down his Nine Satanic Statements, shaved his head and declared himself Head of the Church of Satan. With members of his original Magic Circle established as the ruling Council of Nine, he threw open the doors of the Black House to a curious press and an American-style swinging set of new recruits very keen to see La Vey's naked altar girls.

His most high profile converts were Sammy Davis Jr and Jayne

Mansfield. The former, the sole black member of Frank Sinatra's Rat Pack, was drawn to investigate the Church after playing Mephistopheles in the comedy film *Poor Devil* – and was no doubt delighted to discover that La Vey shared with him a penchant for buxom, blonde, white women.

Mansfield, probably the most pneumatic exemplar of this type, had found stardom in the rock'n'roll movie *The Girl Can't Help It*. By the time she met La Vey in 1966 she was also embroiled in a volatile relationship with her attorney, Sam Brody, who was becoming increasingly jealous and possessive as Mansfield's star ascended.

Jayne looked to Anton for protection but her very public cavorting with the Black Pope only served to enrage Brody further. After a series of rows, La Vey placed a curse on his rival, with appalling results. Jayne Mansfield was killed in a car crash on the night of 29th June 1967, while travelling in a car with Sam Brody. Though La Vey's foe was killed instantly, so was his beloved High Priestess – and to add insult to injury, the beautiful Mansfield was decapitated.

Meanwhile, in the Haight Ashbury district of San Francisco, amid the counter-culture La Vey so despised, another charismatic young man was out recruiting himself a Family. Among the acid-tripping teens, this recidivist drifter had already formed a close circle of young women to make up for the circle of his own kin he had never known. Most of them were also from broken homes, and high on the vibes of the Summer of Love, came to think of themselves as disciples of a guru.

When Kenneth Anger's fallen angel Bobby Beausoleil crossed paths with Charles Manson and his Family, they unleashed their own Summer of Hate. And all Hell was well and truly let loose.

Meet the Family

Charles Manson was born on 12th November 1934 in Cincinnati, Ohio, to a 16-year-old alcoholic prostitute called Katherine Maddox. At some point afterwards, she got married to a man called Scott Manson in order to give her son a surname, but he disappeared soon after the wedding and Charlie never knew him. 'So from birth,' he would often say, 'I'm a five-and-dime bastard'.

Manson was soon parted from his mother too; she was sent to jail when he was four years old for assaulting and beating a man she was trying to hustle. The infant Charlie was sent to live with his God-fearing grandparents in West Virginia, but shortly after that his grandmother fell ill and he was moved again, to an aunt and uncle in Illinois. It was not a happy home, situated in a rundown neighbourhood, and the boy was often a bone of contention between his strict aunt and more indulgent uncle.

After his mother's release from prison, Charlie was entrusted back to her custody, something she strongly resented and did her best to shirk as soon as she could get enough money together to go on another bender. Manson's childhood consisted of being left in a series of dingy apartments and rooming houses, intermittently punctuated by bouts of drunken remorse from Katherine, who would nonetheless be out of the door again once she had sobered up. Charlie was often forced to watch his mother carry out her trade, with members of both sexes. Once she even tried to sell him for a pitcher of beer.

As we shall see, this is a text-book example of how to breed a killer.

Juvenile delinquent

Charlie responded in the text-book manner by beginning to steal in order to keep something for himself. His transient lifestyle enabled him to get good at it before he was first caught, at the age of nine, and sent to a reform school. Three years later he had graduated, on another theft charge, to the Gibrault School for Boys in Indiana, where he was declared a 'delinquent'. When he graduated from this establishment at the age of 13, he decided he was never going back to his mother again. He became a hobo, trying to eke a living off the streets. By 14 he was back inside the Marion County Juvenile Center. The pattern would continue all his teenage life – a few months on the outside swiftly followed by a few more in a hopeless 'reform school' until he was old enough to be put into an adult prison.

Manson had spent most of his twenties inside California prisons, on charges as wide-ranging as rape, possessing illegal narcotics, pimping, theft and fraud, when another inmate gave him a different idea of how he may be able to make life work outside the joint. Alvin 'Creepy' Karpis was the sole remaining member of the Ma Barker gang, a veteran of Alcatraz and an accomplished musician who could play a mean blues guitar. When Charlie heard him play, he begged Karpis to teach him some musical secrets. By the time of his release in 1967, the 32-year-old Manson was nurturing a new dream. He wanted to be a rock star.

Out come the freaks

In order to get in with the right crowd, he followed the hippy trail to San Francisco. He liked what he saw there. A young, would-be folk singer called Nancy turned him on to the acid being brewed by legendary 'head' Owsley. Already a speed freak, Charlie enjoyed the sensations of this new, mind-altering substance – not only on himself, but more importantly on younger, more gullible people. In Haight there were plenty to pick and choose from. Manson started developing his own riff on the peace 'n' love vibes that were permeating the San Francisco air. He started collecting a 'family'.

'There's no good or bad,' he would tell them. 'There is no difference between you and I. There is only one thing, and that thing is everything.'

Charlie was an expert conman, and these new drugs were a handy aide. Other kids who had been brutalised by circumstance soon gravitated into his orbit and stayed, hypnotised, by this mini would-be messiah. He called his tribe 'the Garbage People'.

Bad vibrations

On his own trajectory to San Francisco came bad boy Bobby Beausoleil. Like Charlie, he had a traumatic childhood, leaving home at the age of 12 to escape continual sexual abuse from an aunt and uncle, and proceeded to duck in and out of the law's hands ever after. Rebelling against the prettiness of his own good looks, he cultivated a biker image and fantasised about Nazis and Vikings. He wandered into a gathering on Haight Ashbury where Kenneth Anger was presenting a Winter Solstice ceremony. The filmmaker strode towards him through the crowd and proclaimed: 'You are Lucifer!'

Bobby, like Anger and Manson, was a Scorpio. He was born in 1947, the year of Crowley's death and *Fireworks'* release. The portents were ominous.

'Kenneth brought it all to a head,' he would later tell John Gilmore, author of the essential Manson biography *The Garbage People*. 'He made me the star of *Lucifer Rising* and I was rising, and he made me believe that I had this power inside of me and it radiated out of me.'

In April 1968, Manson and his group left San Francisco in a stolen school bus with the aim of travelling to Los Angeles to make Charlie a rock star. They pitched up in Topanga Canyon on the outskirts of Los Angeles, where there was an unofficial hippy camp. Living just nearby, in the basement of his friend Gary Hinman's flat, was Bobby Beausoleil. Inevitably, their paths crossed.

Hinman was a music teacher and a friend of Beach Boy Dennis Wilson. Full of rock star dreams, Charlie engineered a meeting with the easygoing surf superstar and played him some of his songs. Dennis liked what he heard. He got Manson a development deal with Brother Records and the Beach Boys even recorded one of his ditties, the ominously named 'Cease to Exist', which they retitled 'Never Learn Not To Love'. He was even more impressed with Manson's female entourage and invited them all to stay at his Malibu beach house.

Inevitably, things went bad. Terry Melcher, the producer assigned to work with Manson, was not taken in by the scruffy hippy prophet with the unnerving eyes and dropped him from the label. The other Beach Boys had a similar nervous reaction and Manson fell out with Dennis Wilson when he altered the lyrics and title of 'Cease to Exist'. Worse for Wilson, the syphilitic, glass-eyed Manson girls began to freak him out. He ordered the Family out after they had spent almost a year living off his hospitality.

It's coming down fast

Parasitic Charlie found another sugar daddy to tap: George Spahn, an elderly ranch owner whose property in Chatsworth, in the mountains outside LA, had been used as a set for countless cowboy movies. Lonely and hard-up, Spahn was tempted by promises of sexual fulfilment from the Manson girls and let the entourage move into the surreal prop ghost town on his land. Here the Garbage People existed on a diet of food taken from the bins outside supermarkets, and drug deals struck between Manson, Beausoleil and local motorcycle gangs.

Manson's mania increased out on the Spahn ranch. As race riots flared across America, he began to preach to his circle that it wouldn't be long before the black man rose up and took over the country, making the whites his slaves. At the same time, The Beatles had released their double album with a plain white cover, which though eponymous was soon referred to as *The White Album*. Charlie, who believed the Beatles were divine messengers, scoured the lyrics for meaning. In Paul McCartney's 'Helter Skelter' he thought he heard a clarion call for the forthcoming apocalypse: *'It's coming down fast from miles above you'*. In George Harrison's 'Piggies' he heard how the rich must die.

Or so Manson would have us all believe. Having spent his life within the American prison system, he was already racist to the core. Beausoleil was obsessed by Herman Goering and the Nazis and at times thought he was a Viking berserker. And what led to the most infamous murders in American history was actually triggered by a quarrel over money.

Bloodbath in the Big Nowhere

Beausoleil's long-suffering friend Gary Hinman had come into an inheritance and the hard-up Family decided they needed to call in a favour. Beausoleil and one of the girls, Susan Atkins, decided to pay him a call on 27th July 1969. Four days later, Hinman was found stabbed to death with the words *'Political Piggy'* daubed all over the walls in his blood.

In the various tales that twist around the actual events, Beausoleil killed Hinman in a rage when he denied that there was any inheritance; Beausoleil held Hinman down while Susan Atkins did the stabbing to impress him; Manson gave the order to kill and Beausoleil decided on the worldly flourishes to confuse the police. Whatever the truth, they didn't fool anyone for long. Beausoleil was arrested seven days after Hinman's body was found.

According to the later testimony of his followers, after Bobby's arrest, thoughtful Manson worked out an ideal way to stop his friend from going down. He would have his Family kill yet more people, and leave their bodies in a similar state to Hinman's, to throw the cops off the scent. Charlie already had a target. Terry Melcher, the man who shut down his recording career. He'd even visited Terry's mansion on Cielo Drive with Brian Wilson.

Only Terry no longer lived at Cielo Drive. He had sold his property to the agent Rudi Altobelli, who in turn had leased it to the film director Roman Polanski and his young, pregnant, actress wife, Sharon Tate. On 9th September 1969, while her husband was away in Europe working on a movie, Sharon hosted a party with her friends Abigail Folger, a coffee heiress, and her boyfriend Voytek Frykowski; and celebrity hairdresser Jay Sebring. The next morning, all four of them, along with teenager Steve Parent, who had dropped by to visit the Polanksi's caretaker William Garrettson, were found slaughtered in and around the grounds of the house.

The scene was horrendous. Steve Parent had been shot in his car, the rest had been beaten and stabbed repeatedly. Worst of all, heavily pregnant Sharon had been hanged from a noose before being slashed to ribbons, her body then tied up to Sebring's similarly mutilated corpse. Blood was everywhere. Someone had daubed the word *'PIG'* onto a wall in it.

The next night, another, similar crime scene was discovered. Businessman Leno LaBianca and his wife Rosemary had been bound, strangled, suffocated and stabbed, the walls of their home covered with slogans: *'DEATH TO PIGGIES'*, *'HELTER SKELTER'* and *'RISE'*.

All were the work of Manson's Family. Charles 'Tex' Watson, Patricia Krenwinkel and Susan Atkins had been despatched to Cielo Drive. Charlie had not, apparently, been pleased with their work and the following day had accompanied them, along with fellow Family member Lesley Van Houten, to the La Bianca's residence. He had tied Leno and Rosemary up before leaving them to the mercy of his killer protégées.

At the subsequent trial all manner of motives were put forward by the prosecution, from Manson's belief in a coming Armageddon to the 'orders' supposedly encoded in Beatles songs on *The White Album*. However, all the killers were adamant that they had committed these atrocities to protect Bobby Beausoleil. Because they loved their little Lucifer 'like a brother' they were willing to risk the Death Penalty to clear his name.

Yet even after all of this, Kenneth Anger still hadn't had quite enough of Bobby Beausoleil.

The wages of sin

After meeting Jimmy Page at an auction of Crowley memorabilia at Sotheby's, Anger had asked the Led Zeppelin guitarist to work on a new soundtrack for *Lucifer Rising*. Initially, Page said he was honoured to take on the work, which he began in 1973. But work on the project was intermittent, with Page flitting between Led Zeppelin engagements and Anger commuting back and forth from London to New York to oversee the publication of *Hollywood Babylon*.

Things finally came to a head in 1976, when Anger was working on the film editing equipment in Page's Kensington mansion and was either thrown out of the house by Page's girlfriend or locked in to the cellar by Page himself, depending on whose story you believe. The bottom line was that Page had only provided 23 minutes of music in six years. True to form, Anger went public with his displeasure, denouncing Page as a heroin addict and a dried-up musician. It was rumoured that Page had been hit with one of Anger's legendary curses and, soon after, Led Zeppelin were indeed assailed by tragedy.

In 1976, singer Robert Plant and his wife Maureen were involved in a car crash which nearly killed her; a year later their young son Karac died from a stomach infection. Then, in September 1980, drummer John Bonham choked on his own vomit after an alcohol binge. Led Zeppelin, the band that defined the Seventies, would not outlast the decade.

Anger, meanwhile, had returned to the source of his own fixation. The eventual soundtrack for *Lucifer Rising* was written and performed by the incarcerated Bobby Beausoleil in 1980. He had finally completed his life's work, but what rewards came at the end of Kenneth Anger's rainbow?

Currently he lives in poverty in an ignominious quarter of Los Angeles, having made no further films and unable to secure a publishing deal for *Hollywood Babylon III*. In 1973, he gave a remarkable interview with Jonas Mekas in which he admitted that the making of *Lucifer Rising* had plunged him into unforeseen chaos:

'Frankly, it's taken me into some very strange corners...You see, I didn't think it was about demons or hell, really. I was trying to make a film about the Angel of Light. That was his first name. The Son of Morning, you see. But now I almost believe what the Bible says.'

But Anger, all things considered, is one of the luckier ones. He is still alive, at liberty and sane.

Manson and his followers will spend the rest of their lives in prison, which probably suits Charlie just fine, as he continues to bask in the attentions of subsequent generations fascinated by his crimes. He receives the most mail of any prisoner in the United States, four letters a day, has had countless books and films made about his exploits and is never short of new acolytes to preach to. When the young Brian Warner decided to name himself after America's twin obsessions, beauty and death, Marilyn Manson gave the old devil a fresh lease of notorious life.

Robert and Anne Marie De Grimston wandered off into obscurity in the mid-Seventies, after successfully suing author Ed Sanders for connecting them to the Manson gang in his 1971 book *The Family*. It is rumoured that he is now a postal worker while she works in a magic shop in Utah.

Anton La Vey died on 29th October 1997, two days short of his beloved Halloween, in a Catholic hospital in San Francisco. He was 67. After his death, his neo-Nazi daughter Zeena, who we shall be hearing more of shortly, denounced her father's work as a sham. Rumour had it, she was horrified to have discovered he was actually a Jew.

Having turned his back on the Devil, Mick Jagger was knighted in 2003, much to the disgust of Keith Richards. Jimmy Page remastered Led Zeppelin's back catalogue in the Nineties and successfully resold their music to successive generations of appreciative teenagers. Both have become, like the music business itself, the new Establishment.

The legacy of the Sixties

The extreme and explosive events of those few brief years form a dramatic microcosm of all the elements contained in this book. For a moment in the Sixties, it seemed like any man or any woman truly *could* become a star. It was the first time the class boundaries had ever really come down, leading the high and mighty to mix freely with the down and dirty. Troubled, working class boy John Lennon was on one end of the spectrum, Charlie Manson on the exact other. But thanks to the notions of arty, middle class boys like Kenneth Anger and Mick Jagger, everybody somehow connected. Add mind-bending new drugs and the Pill's sudden liberating effect on the teenage population and you set up the great morality shift of the 20th century.

The Sixties ended in extreme ugliness: Vietnam, American student protesters being set upon by the National Guard, Paris in flames, the Manson murders and Altamont. For the guardians of decency, it became imperative that young people must never be allowed such power again.

For the smart young minds of that era, the future had been revealed and hippy entrepreneurs like Bill Gates and Richard Branson would reap the benefits of the new 'youth culture' commodity. Dreams of being able to change the world through the power of youthful enterprise lingered, like a hangover, until the end of the 1970s, when a new global power was on the rise.

Margaret Thatcher in the UK and Ronald Reagan in America wanted to bury the idealism of the Sixties once and for all, and return us all to the mythical nirvana of right wing 'traditional values'. God and the State grew powerful again.

Against this increasingly repressive backdrop, all these stories unfold. As we shall see, the tighter our moral guardians squeezed, the more holes Satan had to slip through. Society in America, and increasingly in Britain, has been polarised with the biggest gap in history between the haves and have-nots. Yet while the disintegration of the welfare state and the education system have made the egalitarian meritocracy of the Sixties nothing but a distant dream, 'celebrity' culture has been shoved ever further in our faces, dangling unattainable riches over those at the very bottom of the pile.

Our fear of youth crime has spiralled, as the age of the perpetrators has plummeted. Because the one truth that nobody in power ever seems to want to acknowledge is that wherever there is poverty, injustice and want shacked up next door to obscene riches and vacant celebrity, the Devil will always have a fertile recruitment ground.

Chapter Two

David Berkowitz: Dogged by Demons (1976-7)

Hell is a City

In 1977, New York City was under siege: sweltering under the hottest summer in living memory, experiencing electricity blackouts which shut down whole areas of the city, plunging the streets into darkness.

In downtown Manhattan the disco craze, carried on the wings of John Badham's Brooklyn-based film *Saturday Night Fever*, was at its apex. It seemed like the youth of the city were all coming out – black, white, straight, gay – to wear satin flares and be seen at the celebrated Studio 54, or revel at the swingers' palace Plato's Retreat. These disco emporiums were shrines to hedonism: flamboyant clothes dressed up a world of cocaine, sex, transgender experimentation and general excess in all areas, soundtracked to Sylvester's 'Mighty Real' or Chic's 'Good Times'.

At the same time, another revolution was taking place at the grottier end of Manhattan's social scale. In a tiny club called CBGBs (Country Blue Grass Blues) on the notorious skid-row, The Bowery, teenage hustlers and glue freaks were turning their frustrations into the sounds of punk rock. These, mainly white, working-class kids had rejected the disco party in favour of aggressive, confrontational self-expression. The Ramones, who included in their number a former male prostitute and a singer who had done time in a mental institution, epitomised the bonding nature of this new music – dressed in black leathers and baseball boots they pretended to be brothers and played three-minute-long machine gun bursts titled 'Teenage Lobotomy' and 'Sheena Is A Punk Rocker'.

Whichever of these crazes your child had got hooked on was likely to be a nightmare for the concerned parent. It was a time of social change, and all the attendant fear that brings with it.

Then into this world of teenage dreams, with the shattering speed of a bullet, a figure exploded out of nightmare. A lone man stalked the streets of The Bronx and Queens, shooting beautiful women and their amorous beaus down in their prime. As if he was waging war on youth and beauty and the 'Good Times' themselves.

The crimes had begun in 1976, but it wasn't until April '77 that the killer formally introduced himself in a letter to Captain Joseph Borrelli, chief of investigations into what had up until then been called the '.44 Handgun Killings'. New York City now had a name for its very first serial killer.

Postcards from the edge

If it was in some way reminiscent of the calling cards sent to the Victorian press in London by a man calling himself Jack The Ripper then, well, that was the idea.

I am deeply hurt by your calling me a wemon hater, the writer said to Borrelli. *I am not. But I am a monster. I am the 'Son of Sam'. I am a little brat.*

He was killing, he said, for his father 'Sam', who needed the blood of his female victims to 'keep him young'. He complained that his father kept him locked up for long times in the basement and the attic, until his thirst became too strong and he commanded his charge to, 'Go out and kill'.

Rambling, misspelt and alternatively boastful and self-pitying, the letter went on to say:

I am the 'Monster' – 'Beelzebub' – the chubby behemoth.

I love to hunt. Prowling the streets, looking for fair game – tasty meat. The wemon of Queens are prettyist of all. It must be the water they drink. I live for the hunt – my life. Blood for papa.

It ended with a taunt to the NYPD:

Police: let me haunt you with these words:
I'll be back!
I'll be back!
To be interrpreted as – bang, bang, bang, bang, bang – ugh!!
Yours in murder
Mr Monster.

The demon dogs call

Two days after Son of Sam had sent his message to Capt Borrelli, Sam Carr, a retired city worker from Yonkers, NY, received a strange letter about his black Labrador dog, Harvey.

I have asked you kindly to stop that dog from howling all day long, yet he continues to do so, the note began. The tone rapidly descended from thin politeness into threats. *Your selfish, Mr Carr. My life is destroyed now… I can see that there shall be no peace in my life, or my families life until I end yours.*

Carr called the police and showed them the letter, though there was not much they could do at the time. Then, ten days later, someone shot Harvey in the Carrs' back yard. Rushing to the scene, Sam Carr saw a man in blue jeans and a yellow shirt running away. He managed to save his dog's life, and again called the cops over to his house, but at the time no connection was made between the Harvey letter and the Son of Sam.

However, in being so bold with his missives, this poison pen writer had begun to provide the clues for his own undoing. And what began with a bang, would end with a pitiful whimper.

Shots in the dark

Son of Sam fired his first shot in the early hours of 29th July 1976.

Two friends, Donna Lauria, 18, a medical technician, and Jody Valenti, 19, a student nurse, were sitting talking in Jody's Oldsmobile near the entrance of Laura's apartment building in The Bronx.

Both young, attractive Italian-Americans, they were everything the killer was looking for.

Donna's parents, returning from a night out, passed them at about 1am and knocked on the car window to say goodnight and remind their daughter not to be too much longer. But as they entered the building and turned the key in the door of their own apartment, the night was shattered by the sound of shots and screams.

A lone man had walked up to Jody's car, pulled a gun out of a brown paper bag and opened fire on both women. Donna was killed immediately. Wounded in the thigh, Jody survived but was unable to give a description of her attacker. It had all happened too fast.

The arbitrary nature of the murder suggested to the police that they were after a thrill killer, a man who hated women and stalked them at random in order to kill them for pleasure. It was an idea that few liked to contemplate. For the citizens of The Bronx, this was the beginning of a two-year siege of fear.

No one's safe

Three months later, on 23rd October 1976, young couple Carl Denaro and Rosemary Keenan, both 21, were sitting in his car near her home in Queens, kissing goodnight. It was about 2.30am. Suddenly, their peace was shattered by several loud bangs and the smashing of glass, as a bullet entered their rear windscreen. A man had walked up to the car and fired on Carl five times.

Acting on instinct, Rosemary managed to drive away and get Carl to hospital in time to save him, but again, neither could give a proper description of their attacker. All the police had to go on was the .44 bullet they found on the floor of the car.

One month later, on 26th November, Donna DeMasi, 16, and Joanne Lomino, 18, were shot as they walked home from a movie through the Floral Park section of Queens. It was half past midnight when a man approached them and started to ask for directions. Before he could finish his sentence, he pulled out a gun and began shooting.

Both survived but the bullet that lodged in Joanne's spine left her a paraplegic. When other shells were dug out of a front door and mailbox near the scene of the crime, they were revealed to be of the same type as those that killed Donna DeMasi and injured Carl Denaro.

It seemed as if the police could have a serial killer on their hands.

The Omega men

The press thought so, and soon became awash with stories about the '.44 Caliber Killer', frequently mentioning Captain Borrelli as the man on his tail. As the waves of fear swept across the city, the special taskforce that had been assembled were given more money and resources to go hard into the investigation.

Operation Omega consisted of 200 men, headed by Deputy Inspector Timothy Dowd, assisted by the original head of enquiries, Captain Borrelli, alongside Sergeant Joseph Coffey and Detective Redmond Keenan – the father of Rosemary, who had so bravely managed to save Carl Denaro from the scene of Son of Sam's October rampage. As 1976 drew to a close, these men were at the nerve centre of operations, working long, nerve-shredding hours that ran on a steady diet of alcohol and coffee. It didn't look like it was going to be much of a happy Christmas.

When two sevens clash

But, as if giving New York a festive respite, Christmas 1976 passed without incident. In fact, it wasn't until the end of January 1977 that Son of Sam was back in business.

In the early hours of 30th January, another good-looking young couple, Christine Freund, 26, and her fiancé John Diel, left The Wine Gallery bar in Queens and made their way to Diel's car. They were engrossed in conversation and so never noticed the man following them down the street, watching them open the doors and get inside. They never even noticed him standing in front of the vehicle until two bullets burst through the windshield.

Struck by both bullets, Christine keeled over in John's arms, never to regain consciousness. Neighbours, hearing the shots, called the police, while John desperately tried to flag down help from the street. It was all to no avail. Christine died a few hours later in hospital.

From ballistics tests on the evidence left behind, Capt Borrelli and Sgt Coffey were at least able to ascertain that Freund had been killed by a man using a .44 Charter Arms pistol. Coffey was certain all the shootings were the work of the same man, but there was no link that they could find between any of his victims that would help them any further – only that they were all young, attractive and happy. Which convinced Coffey still more that he was dealing with a psycho.

Portrait of a serial killer

It would take another death before the police got anything like a description of him though.

On 8th March, Barnard College student Virginia Voskerichian was walking home in the Forest Hills area and had just turned towards her home in Dartmouth Street, when a man approached her in the opposite direction. When he was almost eye-to-eye with her, the man raised a pistol up to her face. Virginia instinctively held up her books to cover her face, but the man shot her point blank nonetheless. They were standing only 300 yards from where Christine Freund had been likewise attacked just over a month earlier.

A man in the street witnessed the whole thing. As he stood there in a state of shock, the killer stopped and said, 'Hi mister,' before running off. There was even a patrol car in Dartmouth Street that also clocked the running man, but the cops had just been called to the crime scene and were unable to follow him. With luck on his side, the killer made good his escape.

However, with a match on the bullets used and a witness, the police were able to issue a description of the suspect at a press conference the next day. New York's Mayor Abraham Beame announced they were looking for a white man, about five feet ten inches tall and 25 to 30 years old, who was well groomed, with his dark hair slicked back.

Beame later admitted that he had dreaded giving out this news. 'The killings were a horror. The police were under terrible strain. Everyone was beginning to question his ability to capture the gunman. The letter fused everything together. It was a man against an entire city. He had written to this one policeman, but I knew it wasn't that captain he was writing about. It was every cop who was after him, all 25,000 of them.'

Deputy Inspector Dowd was given more men and more resources as virtually every cop in the city put forward their name for selection.

The killer's calling card

But all the Mayor's men could not come soon enough to save aspiring actress Valentina Suriani, 18, and her boyfriend Alexander Esau, 20, a tow truck operator. As the two sat kissing in their parked car near the Hutchinson River Parkway at 3am on 17th April, another car glided silently up alongside them.

The driver leaned out and shot both of them twice. Valentina died immediately, Alexander later at hospital.

This time, however, the killer had not just left his signature .44 bullets. He had also dropped a letter at the scene, the one that proclaimed his name and intentions to Captain Borrelli.

Forensic psychiatrists, headed by Dr Martin Lubin, former head of forensic psychiatry at Bellevue, worked on a mental profile of the suspect to go with the physical description. Police were looking for a paranoid schizophrenic, a loner who had difficulties forming relationships with women. But after the Son of Sam letters, there was an added twist. The psychiatrists believed that the man the police were seeking was likely to consider himself possessed by demons.

Paper trail

Omega Force was flooded with calls from a city in the grip of fear and paranoia. Every oddball in every neighbourhood was fingered by neighbours who held a grudge or disapproved of a lifestyle. In The Bronx and Queens, neighbours formed vigilante squads to patrol the streets at night and woe betide anyone who looked a little strange. With thousands of calls to check out, the cops were further taunted by the killer's next move.

Son of Sam became emboldened. He sent his next letter to Jimmy Breslin, a reporter on the New York *Daily News*.

The tone of the letter now seems eerily reminiscent of the monologues of Travis Bickle, in Martin Scorsese's *Taxi Driver*. The 1976 film cast Robert De Niro as a Vietnam vet struggling to make a living in New York as a cabbie, while trying to fight the urge to kill the junkies, pimps and pushers that line the streets. Bickle dreams that 'some day a real rain will come and wash all the scum off the streets' before turning vigilante and becoming an unlikely hero. Similar imagery fills Son of Sam's letter:

Hello from the gutters of NYC, which is filled with dog manure, vomit, stale wine, urine and blood. Hello from the sewers of NYC which swallow up these delicacies when they are washed away by the sweeper trucks.

Some portions of the letter were kept from publication, because they were deliberate taunts to the investigating officers – a list of names *to help you along.*

Duke of Death. Wicked King Wicker. The 22 Disciples of Hell. And lastly, John Wheaties, rapist and suffocator of young girls.

He had been writing other letters too.

'Please be careful...'

A man called Jack Cassara from New Rochelle received a strange get-well card from a man purporting to be Sam Carr of Yonkers.

Sorry to hear about that fall you took, it read. *Please be careful next time*. The card had on it a picture of a German Shepherd dog.

Cassara had neither had an accident nor heard of Sam Carr. But a German Shepherd dog in the area had recently been shot.

Feeling something was badly amiss, Cassara contacted Sam Carr and told him his story. Recognising the tone immediately, Carr invited Cassara over to his house so that they could compare the weird notes they had both received. There was only one conclusion they could possibly come to – they were from the same person.

Carr's daughter Wheat was a dispatcher for the Yonkers police and he had her contact Officers Chamberlain and Intervallo there to begin an investigation, while Cassara called the cops in New Rochelle.

Later, when he heard the news, Cassara's son Stephen offered an idea as to who the letter writer could be: a strange tenant who had rented a room from them in 1976 and complained about their dog. His name was David Berkowitz.

Nan Cassara, Jack's wife, called the Carrs back and got them to pass on the information to Yonkers police. She also called New Rochelle again, but the officers there waited two months before they called her back. When they did, a detective mentioned that a neighbour of Berkowitz, Craig Glassman, had also reported a strange letter to them that mentioned the names Carr and Cassara as part of a group of 'demons'. But, the detective mused, all that proved was that Berkowitz was probably nuts, not that he was Son of Sam.

Never mind what the psychiatrists had said…

Summer of Sam

At least Yonkers police were running the name David Berkowitz through their files. Unaware, Son of Sam had shown no intention of slowing down.

The killer's activities were by now thinning out crowds of young people across the city that were scared to go out and have a good time, lest Son of Sam put an end to their fun for good.

In fact, it was his name that was on the mind of Judy Placido, as she left the near-empty Elephis disco in Queens on 26th June 1977 with her boyfriend Sal Lupo.

'This Son of Sam is really scary,' she said to him. 'The way he comes out of nowhere. You'll never know where he'll hit next.'

No sooner had they got inside their car than a sudden booming noise echoed through the vehicle. The couple looked at each other in shock, before Sal got out and ran back to the disco for help.

When he came back, he realised Judy was covered in blood. She had been shot three times in the right arm, although as she was later to recall, she had felt no pain, just dizziness and disorientation. Similarly, Sal also had a gunshot wound in his forearm, which he had yet to register.

Their attacker had melted back into the night without either of them seeing him. Compared to what was to come next, they had both been very lucky.

Happy anniversary

The anniversary of Son of Sam's first killing was rapidly approaching. Omega Force were convinced he was ready to strike again and the newspapers fanned the heat of the summer with incendiary headlines, prophesising there would be another murder on 29th July.

The police were by now desperate. Detective Coffey, who had been in the vicinity of the Elephis disco just 15 minutes before the Placido/Lupo shootings, even considered luring out the killer with mannequins placed in bullet-proof cars. Tensions were at breaking point throughout New York as the day passed into night. But nothing was heard from Son of Sam.

That was, until the early morning of 31st July, when Stacy Moskowitz sat with her boyfriend Bobby Violente in his car, in a quiet spot near Gravesend Bay, Brooklyn, close to the river's shore.

They had been out to a movie, and Bobby was still in no mood to go home. He suggested a walk in the park, but like Judy Placido, Stacy was spooked by the idea that Son of Sam might be watching and refused to leave the car. She pleaded with Bobby to take her home.

Bobby tried to silence Stacy's protests with a kiss. It was to be their last embrace.

'All of a sudden,' Bobby later recalled, 'I heard a humming sound. Then I heard glass break. Then I didn't hear Stacy any more. I didn't feel anything but I saw her fall away from me...'

Both Stacy and Bobby had been shot, he in the face, she in the head. He hit the car's horn and then dragged himself out of the car to try and yell for help. Emergency services were there quickly, and the couple rushed to hospital. Bobby survived the ordeal, losing his left eye and 80 per cent of the vision in his right. But tragically, after 38 desperate hours of surgery, Stacy became Son of Sam's final victim.

Hunting the hunter

While Son of Sam's reign reached its crescendo, the two beat cops from Yonkers that Wheat Carr had called were getting ahead of their superiors. Unlike the cops from New Rochelle, these were convinced that Stephen Cassara was onto something.

Having run his details through their files, Officers Chamberlain and Intervallo had begun to amass some facts about David Berkowitz. From the details on his driver's license, he appeared to fit the general description of Son of Sam. So they went to the apartment block at 35 Pine Street, Berkowitz's given address. The rental agent told them that their man always paid on time and that he had written on his rental application that he worked at IBI Security in Queens. This, the policemen reckoned, could indicate some knowledge of firearms.

Checking in at IBI, they discovered that Berkowitz had given in his notice in July 1976, and had left to work for a cab company. Here the officers hit a brick wall. Of the hundreds of firms they called, none had any knowledge of their suspect, but that still left a few hundred more to go through. The task seemed insurmountable – until Omega Force got another break.

At the time of the Moskowitz/Violante shootings, a woman out walking her dog had noticed two policeman putting a parking ticket on a Ford Galaxie, parked near a fire hydrant on Bay 17th Street, close to Gravesend Bay. Only minutes later, a man had come running towards the car, jumped in and driven away.

Only four parking tickets had been issued in that area that morning, and only one for parking near a fire hydrant. The Ford Galaxie belonged to David Berkowitz.

'True, I am the killer'

Over in Yonkers, Officer Chamberlain had another call about Berkowitz – the man seemed to be popping up all over the place. This time the call came from a male nurse named Craig Glassman, to report a suspected arson at Berkowitz's apartment, which he lived above on 35 Pine Street.

Glassman was the same neighbour who had called New Rochelle about the weird letters he had received.

He showed Chamberlain where the fire had been set and had failed to catch light. Then, when asked more about his neighbour, Glassman showed Chamberlain the letters that New Rochelle had taken such little notice of.

Threatening and rambling in tone, the contents and the writing itself looked exactly the same to Chamberlain as the letter that Sam Carr had received. But they went further. *True, I am the killer*, said one, *but Craig, the killings are at your command.*

Carr, meanwhile, was not resting either. Aggrieved by what he saw as police inaction from Yonkers, he related his story to the Omega Force.

'I'm Sam'

It took a few days for all the mounting evidence about David Berkowitz to come together. Chamberlain and Intervallo called Omega Force with the Glassman evidence, but their information wasn't passed on for two days.

Meanwhile, the cop who had given out the fire hydrant ticket to

Berkowitz, Jimmy Justus, called Yonkers and got Wheat Carr on the other end of the phone. She gave the cop an earful about David Berkowitz and everything her father had tried to impress upon the cops days earlier.

When Chamberlain and Justus compared notes and called Omega Force again, things finally started to happen. Pine Street was put under surveillance on 10th August 1977. Day turned into night, and there was almost a false move when Craig Glassman inadvertently strolled into a posse of police at 7.30pm. It wasn't until 10.15 that another figure finally emerged from 35 Pine Street. A thickset man with dark hair, carrying a paper bag, he walked slowly towards the Ford Galaxie parked nearby.

The assembled police waited for him to get in the car before they made a move. Closing in on his car, the cops drew their weapons and gave the order: 'Freeze! Police!'

The man inside the car turned his head slowly and smiled at them. The nearest officer to him, John Falotico, instructed Berkowitz to get out of the car and asked him, 'Now that I've got you, who have I got?'

'You know,' came the reply. 'I'm Sam. David Berkowitz.'

The Wicked King

The spectre that had terrorised the streets of New York for two long and bloody years was not, in the flesh, so much to look at. A pudgy little man with doughy features and a beaming smile, he gave off the impression of a backwards child.

Nothing like the dreadful Demon Killer he'd conjured up in his many letters.

Inside his apartment, all police found was a lone mattress, a bare lightbulb and a littering of empty cartons and bottles. On the walls were scrawled the stuff of Berkowitz's interior fantasy world. *In this hole lives the Wicked King. Kill for my master. I turn children into killers.* Now he was caught it seemed pitiful, rather than frightening. This view was later reinforced by Sergeant Joe Coffey, after the first interview Berkowitz gave him.

When he emerged from his session with the killer, who calmly and politely admitted to everything, the veteran detective was clearly taken aback.

'When I first walked into that room I was full of rage,' he told reporters. 'But after talking to him? I feel sorry for him. The man's a fucking vegetable.'

What was it about the man who had set himself up as a modern day demon, spooking an entire city by using techniques pioneered by Jack the Ripper and leaving a trail of beautiful young people dead or maimed in his wake, that reduced the hardened cop to this shocking conclusion?

Who was David Berkowitz and what had made him kill?

Unwanted child

Berkowitz was the product of an unhappy relationship between desperate people, an unwanted bastard from the get-go. His mother, Betty Broder, grew up in Brooklyn to a dirt-poor family who had struggled to survive the Great Depression of the Thirties. She married an Italian, Tony Falco, to the dismay of her Jewish parents, and started up a fish market from their meagre savings in 1939.

Betty gave birth to a daughter, Roslyn, only for Tony to leave her for another woman. The fish market went bust soon after this, and, exiled from her parents, Betty faced an uncertain future, struggling to bring up a baby alone.

In her loneliness, Betty took up an affair with a married man. But Joseph Kleinman was no more supportive than Falco had been before him – when he got Betty pregnant, he threatened to leave her and refused to pay any child support. Faced with little choice, she gave up the boy she gave birth to on 1st June 1953.

At least, Betty thought, the baby was going to a good Jewish family, Nat and Pearl Berkowitz from The Bronx.

The Berkowitz Family

Pearl and Nat were unable to have their own children, and so doted on little David. Not particularly sociable themselves, they brought the boy up in something of a bubble, away from the rest of the world. As a result, David was always a loner.

He was also big for his age, making him clumsy and not popular with other children. He, in return, was not comfortable around them. His neighbours remembered him as a nice looking child, but with a violent streak. Because of his size, he found it easy to bully other neighbourhood children, often for no reason at all. As he got older he displayed signs of hyperactivity and was sometimes difficult for Pearl and Nat to control.

Berkowitz later told the FBI profiler Robert Ressler that he had started torturing animals when he hit adolescence, lending his life the classic pattern of a serial killer. The first thing he had ever killed was his mother's goldfish – to get back at her for 'ignoring' him.

David's time as part of a normal family unit was destined not to last for long. When, for the second time in her life, Pearl was stricken with breast cancer in 1967, Nat didn't take time out to really explain to David what was happening. Assaulted by the swift deterioration of his mother, through chemotherapy and the disease itself, David could only watch in horror as Pearl rapidly slipped away. By the autumn of that year, it was just him and Nat.

High-rise Hell

To add to David's misery, shortly before the cancer had struck, Nat and Pearl had decided that their part of The Bronx was no longer a safe area to bring up a child, and had bought an apartment in the new high-rise development called Co-Op City, in the northeast section of the borough.

David was faced with life under a distant father in a scary new place he didn't know at all.

His school grades dropped and his faith in God was shaken. Showing the first signs of paranoia that would later grow into full-blown schizophrenia, David began to believe that Pearl's death was part of a plot to destroy him. He spent more and more time alone, brooding.

Nat Berkowitz was not the sort of person that relished the 'woman's work' of bringing up a teenage boy alone. Or maybe it was the sort of teenager David had become that he couldn't stomach. Whichever, he was not exactly an ideal father and had little time or sympathy for his disturbed charge.

When he remarried in 1971, to a woman who intensely disliked his adopted son, Nat more or less washed his hands of David. The couple moved to a Florida retirement community and left him behind in New York. Without family or friends, David was alone in the Big, bad Apple.

Present arms

With not many other options open to him, 18-year-old David enlisted in the US Army in the summer of 1971. In his three-year tenure, which included a year's stint posted in Korea, he proved an excellent marksman, who was particularly good at aiming a rifle. During this period he also converted from the Judaism that he considered had failed him into the Baptist faith – but this change of ideology would not sustain him for long.

Desperate for some kind of identity other than that which Nat and Pearl had provided him with, David tracked down his real mother. With his biological father long dead (in 1965, from cancer), Betty and his sister Roslyn welcomed David with open arms. For a while it seemed they could rebuild what had been lost to the past. David made many visits to see Roslyn, her husband Leo Rothenberg and their young daughters Wendy and Lynn, often bringing them gifts. But then he drifted away from them too. Maybe, by then, dealing with a real family was too much like hard work, something he just couldn't feel comfortable with. Or maybe reality was no match for the fantasy world he was constructing in his head.

When he left the army in 1974, David went back to the streets that had spawned him and started a new, secret career in parallel to his various occupations as a security guard and postal service worker – as an arsonist.

Hot in the city

Each of the fires Berkowitz started was recorded meticulously in a diary he kept. If they hadn't been, even an FBI agent like Robert Ressler, who interviewed Berkowitz in 1979 while setting up his profiling system for serial killers, admitted he would have found the numbers hard to believe. Berkowitz had set 1,488 fires, going back to the scene to revel in the panic he had caused, the deployment of fire engines and police, the very chaos he had unleashed into the night.

But even these fireworks only provided temporary respite for a mind already tortured to the point of unspooling. In perhaps a last recognition of his own vulnerability and culpability, David wrote a letter to his estranged father Nat in November 1975 that was a real cry for help.

It's cold and gloomy here in New York, he wrote, *but that's okay because the weather fits my mood – gloomy. Dad, the world is getting dark now. I can feel it more and more. The people, they are developing a hatred for me. You wouldn't believe how much some people hate me. Many of them want to kill me. I don't even know these people, but still they hate me. Most of them are young. I walk down the street and they spit and kick at me. The girls call me ugly and they bother me the most. The guys just laugh.*

Anyhow, things will soon change for the better.

After writing the letter and receiving no response, David locked himself in his apartment for a month, leaving only for food. He began writing his *Wicked King* slogans across the walls, because, he would later tell psychiatrists, he had become possessed by demons. When he emerged from his chrysalis, in Christmas 1975, he wasn't David Berkowitz any more. He was Son of Sam.

The demons speak

According to his testimony to psychiatrists, it was Christmas Eve 1975 that David was first ordered by his demons to kill. Tortured by the voices in his head, he took out a long hunting knife and drove around, searching for a victim. The demons would tell him when he had found the right person.

But it was more likely the ghosts of his past that compelled him to take his car to Co-Op City, where the bleakness of his life without Pearl had begun. And more likely the fact that Pearl had left him there – just like Betty had left him with Pearl, in a world where women were unreachable and untouchable – determined his choice of victim.

David saw a woman leaving a grocery store. He claimed that the demons commanded him to stab her, which he did, plunging the hunting knife into her back.

'I stabbed her and she didn't do anything. She just turned and looked at me,' he claimed. Then she started to scream and he took flight.

His blood up, David wasn't going to stop there. He got back in his car and continued to drive around until he saw another likely young woman. Creeping up on her, he attacked her from behind, stabbing her in the head. Michelle Forman was only 15, and, although severely injured, she fought back, screaming. The noise panicked David, and she was able to escape him, surviving her ordeal despite six wounds from the hunting knife.

The howling

In the New Year of 1976, Berkowitz returned to the job he had at IBI Security and moved into an apartment owned by Jack and Nan Cassara. But his stay in Yonkers was far from a pleasant one.

The Cassaras had a German Shepherd dog that was noisy and howled long into the night. Other dogs called back, and the nights became a cacophony. David told psychiatrists that the demons' voices were contained in the howling of dogs, that they were baying for blood – and ordering him to do the killing.

The image of a talking dog proved the most genuinely chilling moment of Spike Lee's 1999 movie *Summer of Sam*, which recreated some of the events of 1977 and how the killings affected the community in The Bronx. Interestingly, the dog Lee cast as tormenting Berkowitz was not a German Shepherd but a Rottweiler, a more frightening-looking beast that was probably first introduced to the public consciousness as the demonic protector of the child Satan in Richard Donner's 1976 horror classic *The Omen*.

Berkowitz claimed that there was no difference between such movie imagery and what was going on in his mind.

'I'd come home to Coligni Avenue like at 6.30 in the morning,' he recalled under questioning. 'It would begin then, the howling. On my days off, I heard it all night, too. It made me scream. I used to scream out begging for the noise to stop. It never did.

'The demons never stopped. I couldn't sleep. I had no strength to fight. I could barely drive. Coming home from work one night, I almost killed myself in the car. I needed to sleep...The demons wouldn't give me any peace.'

Got a hellhound on my tail

Whatever the truth of the matter, David left the Cassaras after three months, never asking for the $200 deposit he had left for what was to have been a two-year tenancy.

'When I moved in the Cassaras seemed very nice and quiet,' he explained to psychiatrists. 'But they tricked me. They lied. I thought they were members of the human race. They weren't! Suddenly the Cassaras began to show up with the demons. They began to howl and cry out. "Blood and death!" They called out the names of the masters!'

He moved in to 35 Pine Street, where he still wasn't safe from the hellhounds on his tail, because on this street lived Sam Carr and his black Labrador, Harvey.

David first tried to kill this dog with a Molotov cocktail, but it didn't go off properly. So then he shot the animal. Harvey must have been made of stern stuff though, because he survived both assaults.

As Harvey's owner, Sam Carr became the next person for the unhinged Berkowitz to fix his fantasies on. When he called himself 'Son of Sam', it was this Sam he referred to. He claimed later that at the time he believed Sam Carr to be the Devil.

In real life, Berkowitz had had two lousy dads, both biological and adoptive, who had both rejected and deserted him. Maybe that's why he had to blame what came next on a fantasy father figure.

The Bad Son

Clearing his decks for the night freedom of the city, David quit his job at IBI the day before he murdered Donna Lauria and went to work as a taxi driver. From then on, he had the freedom to travel as he pleased and do his demons' work. Like the fictional Travis Bickle, he could roam the city at night behind the wheel of his cab, staring out of his windscreen at the mean streets full of lowlifes and human filth and fantasising about what he could do to them.

Berkowitz even claimed that he had not wanted to kill Donna or her friend Jody, but that the demons, led by Sam, had forced him to shoot. They had tricked him too – promising that Donna would rise from the dead and become his bride.

But once he had killed her, he felt pleasure and relief, the satisfaction of a job well done.

The defence psychiatrists who had heard his testimony classified David a paranoid schizophrenic. They believed that the alienation he had suffered as a child and a vulnerable teenager had forced him into a fantasy world of his own making. Gradually, the fantasies took the place of reality, and David lived in a world populated by demons.

As his state of mind deteriorated, he became more and more tense, and could only release the pressure by successfully attacking someone else. For a time, he felt better, but then the pressure to please his masters would grow more urgent and he would be forced to kill again. The cycle repeated itself with increasing frequency.

However, the demons were not going to get David out of facing a criminal trial for what he had done. The prosecution's forensic psychiatrist Dr David Abrahamsen stated: 'While the defendant shows paranoid traits, they do not interfere with his fitness to stand trial…the defendant is as normal as anyone else. Maybe a little neurotic.'

Realising he wouldn't get any lenient treatment by reason of insanity, David Berkowitz offered no further defence and pleaded guilty as charged. He was sentenced to 365 years in jail.

The cult of Sam

In the years after Berkowitz's incarceration his case was increasingly pored over by journalists and criminologists, and even – in the pages of William D Tatum and Brian McConnell's book *Multiple Murder and Demonic Possession* – those with a conviction that David was, in fact, genuinely possessed by demons.

Eminent theologians concurred with the theories advanced by this book. Malachi Martin, whose book *Hostage to the Devil* had been a strong influence on author Tatum, stated that: 'The presence among human beings of a non-human power could in certain cases be the only adequate explanation of the aberrant behaviour of such criminals.'

The legend of Berkowitz taking orders from talking demon dogs passed into infamy.

But Robert Ressler was having none of all that. In the first of his 1979 interviews at Attica Prison, the profiler was on a mission for the truth.

Ressler's first question went straight to the sexual content of the crimes, the fact that Berkowitz had vented his rage on the young, beautiful and in love. From the interviews given to the police at the time of his arrest, Ressler could ascertain that David's sole sexual experience had been with a prostitute, during the year the army had stationed him in Korea. The end result of the encounter was a case of venereal disease.

Berkowitz began to reel off his demon dog shtick to order, but Ressler told him he wasn't interested in that. Once they had that established, it didn't take long for David to slip out of his parallel universe and admit the sorry truth.

Mad or bad?

David admitted that his primary reason for killing was the resentment he felt towards his mother(s) for deserting him and his inability to form any kind of relationships with women.

Because his initial knife attacks on Christmas Eve 1975 had failed to produce the result he sought – they had left him covered in blood and the women still alive – he drove all the way down to Texas with the sole intention of purchasing a gun.

He bought the Charter Arms .44 pistol and bullets. This was grim premeditation, not the work of someone tortured out of his mind by demons, for the reason David went to Texas was that he thought New York police wouldn't be able to trace bullet casings from there.

Furthermore, Berkowitz admitted to Ressler, the process of stalking and then shooting his victims was what actually turned him on. After the shootings, he would masturbate. He roamed the streets almost every night, looking for the perfect victims. Only when he thought they were right would he stop and shoot. On the nights when there was no one to kill, he would revisit the scenes of his previous triumphs, ogling the chalk marks on the pavements left by the police, and get his rocks off that way. David revelled in the chaos he had caused, in a similar way as he'd reacted to the scenes of his earlier arsons.

Infamy, infamy

When the press had picked up on the fragment of Berkowitz's letter to Borrelli in which he proclaimed himself 'Son of Sam', a whole new identity was created for this angry misfit that endowed upon him the aura of mystery and terror he had longed for all his lonely life.

David was happy to stoke the press's fire. The very idea of leaving the note in the first place, he admitted, had come from a book he had read about Jack The Ripper. That the first self-publicising serial killer had addressed his letters: *'From Hell'* added the necessary demonic inference.

Further favoured reading matter was Anton La Vey's *Satanic Bible*. With all its notions of brutality being noble and most of the human race being nothing but trash, La Vey's dictum presented the sort of ideals that would appeal to an alienated young man, suffused with rage against the world.

He would become the noble killer on his mission from Lucifer. His victims deserved what they were getting, and society did too.

So Berkowitz baited Jimmy Breslin, and Breslin responded as primed. He wrote columns about 'Sam' and published maps of the killing grounds, wondering if he would hit the city borough by borough. This was an idea Berkowitz hadn't actually considered, but which gave him food for thought, so he switched from trawling The Bronx to Queens to Brooklyn.

After confessing that his earliest fantasies had revolved around violence towards women, Berkowitz finally told Ressler what his inquisitor had suspected all along. The demon fantasies were all nonsense.

Honour my father

David Berkowitz's case last came before a court on 11th June 2004. He was denied parole in a hearing lasting less than ten minutes.

'You caused irreparable harm to many victims and society was gripped in fear because of your acts,' stated the summary of the hearing. Although David has behaved himself in jail while serving his six consecutive 25-year sentences, it is unlikely that any parole board will let the 51-year-old killer ever leave his maximum-security cell in the

Sullivan state prison in Fallsburg.

Berkowitz himself believes he should never be allowed to step free either.

'People are suffering today because of my actions,' he had told his previous hearing on 9th July 2002. 'I know they have a lot of pain and hurt that will probably never go away. I wish that I can go back and change the past. I can't, so I have to come to terms with this and realise that I'm here in prison.'

If this sounds like a very different David Berkowitz to the one that wrote all those Son of Sam letters, then that's because while in prison, David has come back to God. He has his own website, on which his thoughts are posted, including this one from the month before his last parole hearing, May 2004:

I would love to undo my horrible past and have the chance to relive my life, this time never doing wrong, he states. *If I had a chance to live my life over again, I would make sure that I honor my parents. I would never again be a source of grief and heartache to them.*

But David Berkowitz is never going to be the Good Son.

Chapter Three

The Chicago Rippers: Lucifer's Hirelings (1981-2)

'Indescribably evil'

With its towering Art Deco skyscrapers, red lights winking on top of the Sears' Tower and downtown strips of bars across Damien and Division still offering Irish whiskey with their original neon signs, Chicago still looks very much like the city of Al Capone. This has always been a city knee deep in sin – the term 'Chicago lightning' was first coined in the 1920s to describe the sound of machine gun fire.

The Windy City has always been, as its finest writer Nelson Algren described it, a 'city on the make'. But it isn't just Mobsters who've cast their long shadows over the settlement on the banks of Lake Michigan. Ghouls have made history here too: from HH Holmes, who erected a house of death while the city hosted the World Fair in 1983, to John Wayne Gacy, the 'Killer Clown' who slaughtered 33 young men in the late 1970s, keeping their remains in the crawl space under his Des Plaines home.

But when police were called, on a rainy day on 1st June 1981, to investigate the remains of a young woman found at the Moonlit Hotel in the neglected suburb of Villa Park, it was the start of something that would put even those cases in the shade. A catalogue of carnage began in this unloved part of the city and Chicago police had never witnessed anything like it.

Between 1981 and 1982 the bodies of 18 women would be found in the environs of the Windy City, tortured, raped and dismembered. What they had suffered was worse than anything the city's most notorious crime bosses could ever have dreamt up.

As the body count grew, and women were snatched audaciously from their cars, from their places of work, from seemingly out of thin air, the press began to summon again their favourite bogeyman, Jack the Ripper. In light of the horrors that had been inflicted upon these women, and the fact that some of them were prostitutes, this was understandable. Only, this time, there wasn't just one Ripper on the loose – there were four of them.

In a lonely place

Villa Park was not a salubrious suburb. The Moonlit Hotel was situated on North Avenue, amongst similar low-rent crash-pads, fast food joints, used car lots and bars and hock shops frequented by junkies. The area had a reputation for a quick fix and an easy lay and the Moonlit itself was frequently the scene of all-night revels that more often than not descended into knife fights and worse. Detective John Sam of the DuPage County Sheriff's office referred to it, fittingly, as 'the Bates' Motel'.

A hotel maid first noticed a terrible odour outside the hotel that was seemingly getting worse by the day. The Moonlit's manager, Hank McGinnis, made a foray into the rubbish-strewn field that backed onto his premises in search of a likely source – probably a dead animal, he reckoned. What he found in that lonely place was the badly decomposed remains of a young woman.

John Sam and his partner Warren Wilkosz arrived at the scene at 11.15 and quickly realised that they were looking not at the remains of an expired junkie, but at a murder site. The woman's body was badly deteriorated, lying face-down in the field. But her wrists had been clamped together behind her back with handcuffs before she'd been dumped and she had cloth in her mouth, a primitive gag. She still wore her sweater and panties, but they'd been pulled down to her thighs. Inside her socks, John Sam found a small roll of bills and change – thirteen dollars and a couple of cents. This sad amount, left in place, indicated that robbery had not been a motive.

They had no reports of missing persons that fitted the general description, which told the cops that the body had not lain here for too long. The only thing that could be accurately surmised before the coroner made his report was that the practice of keeping rolled bills inside socks was common to Chicago prostitutes – but that in itself made the task even harder.

Severed

It took two weeks of searches until the dental records and fingerprints matched up with an ID. The victim was 21-year-old Linda Sutton, a black woman with two children who had a long history of prostitution.

The last person who had seen Linda alive was her boyfriend, who had argued with her over her reliance on prescription cough syrup, a common cheap fix for the girls who worked this particularly hard beat. She had left him to go and get some and he'd never seen or heard from her again.

But something else nagged at detective Wilkosz when he finally got the coroner's report. By the state of the body he had seen in the field behind the Moonlit Hotel, it had seemed to this experienced detective that Linda must have been dead for weeks. But according to the details in front of him now, she had only lain there for three days.

He called the Deputy Coroner, Pete Siekman, who had carried out the autopsy. He duly explained the discrepancy.

The advanced state of her decomposition was due to the fact that parasites had not had to burrow their way in steadily, the way they do normally. Linda had had two massive wounds inflicted on her body that gave them immediate access and allowed the body to be stripped in record time.

Both her breasts had been severed.

Wilkosz reeled as he heard it. The level of brutality inflicted upon this woman suggested that Linda Sutton had unwittingly walked into hell.

The bodies pile up

Another five bodies turned up at the morgue bearing the scars of such torture. Firstly a 19-year-old, identified only as 'Molly', who was reported missing by her parents in June 1981. Then, a 35-year-old cocktail waitress was abducted from her car on the early morning of 12th February 1982. The petrol gauge showed that her tank was empty – had she left to seek help, only to find herself in the worst kind of company? It seemed so – her purse was still on the passenger seat, her keys still in the ignition.

There was no ID left inside the rifled handbag, however. The waitress' car was shown on the late-night news. Her boss identified it and reported her missing. Police and public combed the area around the abandoned motor for nearly two miles. They found her body just outside the city limits, on an embankment by the side of the road. She had been raped, tortured and mutilated – one of her breasts had been severed. The police asked the press to keep this last fact secret. It was their most vital piece of evidence in establishing the identity of the actual killer from the regular round of cranks who confessed to such things.

A few days later, the body of a 40-year old Hispanic woman was discovered. She had also been raped, stabbed and strangled some time over the previous two days. While her breasts had not been amputated, they had been badly bitten, and someone had masturbated over the body.

Police didn't formally acknowledge the links between Linda Sutton and the next five bodies found in a similar condition, unwilling to let loose the devastating cry of 'serial killer'. It had only been three years since John Wayne Gacy had been brought to justice, and no one wanted to stir up a panic on that level unless it was solidly based in fact.

But they did draft in the FBI to examine hair and fibres found at the dump sites and to establish a likely profile of who they were looking for. Psychiatrists pegged the killer as a local man, with good knowledge of the geography of the city. He not only knew where to prey upon the vulnerable, but where to leave the remains of his crimes undisturbed for days. There was an impression that this was not a loner, but a family man living a double life.

The vanishing

On 15th May 1982, 21-year-old Lorraine Borowski, known to her family as Lorry Ann, was due in early to open up the real estate office in Elmhurst where she worked. She parked her car in her usual place and even got as far as putting her key in the front door. But when her fellow employees turned up, they found the key still dangling there, Borowski's shoes and the scattered contents of her handbag strewn outside the door.

A woman on her way to work told police that she had seen a car filled with people going past her on the way out of town. She didn't recognise anyone in it, but felt the woman in the back seat was being held against her will. When she heard about Lorry Ann's abduction, the full horror of what she probably saw dawned on her.

A massive search began but it wasn't until five months later that Borowski's remains were found, hidden in the Clarendon Hills cemetery, too decomposed for an exact cause of death to be given. However, she had been left in the same area as Linda Sutton.

It seemed that this killer could not be sated. Only two weeks later, on 29th May, Shui Mak was abducted as she returned home from her family's Ling-Ling restaurant in the suburb of Streamwood. She had been travelling in her brother Kent's car, but they were in the middle of a furious row over their sister's desire to marry an American man. At around 1.30am, the argument had reached such a peak that Kent stopped the car and ordered Shui out. He thought their parents were following behind and would pick her up. Instead, they had actually overtaken and were waiting further up the road, thinking that Kent must have had a breakdown.

None of her family ever saw Shui alive again. It was as if she had disappeared from the face of the earth. Detective Larry Troka was in charge of the investigation and had been canvassing the baffled Chinese community for months when Shui's broken body was eventually found on 30th September, buried in a construction site in Barrington, one of the most exclusive suburbs in the state.

Shui's skeleton was in pieces, but the jade dragon pendant that she wore for good luck was still around her neck. Several pieces of sharp wire lay around her body. The Cook County medical examiner Dr Robert Stein found she had suffered extensive head injuries. A deep, horseshoe-shaped crack on the back of her head had almost pierced the thick bone. It was an image that would haunt Detective Troka for the rest of his life.

Angel on the sidewalk, devil in a red van

Detectives from across Chicago were now entwined in their operations, making connections that seemed to establish their worst fears – that there was indeed a serial killer at work here. Area Five detective Phil Murphy shared his files with Wilkosz of DuPage and they made a crucial link.

There was a report from 13th June from a young black prostitute called Angel York who had been hideously assaulted just off the strip on North Avenue, a teeming thoroughfare of streetwalkers.

A red van had been cruising her for a while, and 19-year-old Angel was keen to get off the strip and avoid any patrol cars. She ducked down an alley and the van followed. When Angel opened the door to talk money, she found herself staring down the barrel of a gun.

The .45 was wielded by a short, skinny white man with greasy, shoulder-length brown hair and icy blue eyes. He told her to sit still and shut up as he drove away from the strip to a deserted industrial estate in North Cleaver.

Once the man was satisfied he'd found an isolated enough location, he gestured for Angel to get into the back of the van, which had been partitioned off from the cab with a plywood door. There, he made her strip off and kneel down while he handcuffed her wrists behind her back and wrapped duct tape around her mouth. He then produced a pair of tights which he quickly and expertly wound around her torso so that her breasts protruded. When he was satisfied by her appearance, he took off his own clothes – and reached for a huge knife from one of the shelves in the back of the van. He uncuffed her left hand and ordered her to cut into her left breast.

When at first she refused, the man smacked Angel round the head with his .45 and began shouting at her. Hyperventilating with fear, she made a small nick at the side of her breast, the pain from which made her almost pass out. Screaming and ranting, the man snatched the knife away from her and ripped the wound wide open.

He went on to torment her for over an hour, before slapping duct tape over the wound he had made and dumping Angel headfirst into an alley. She was found, bleeding and hysterical, on Grand Avenue by a security guard, who took her to hospital in enough time to save her.

Doctors reported there was semen inside her wounds.

Since making her report, Angel York had seemingly fled Chicago in terror of what had happened to her there. Certain that the man who had attacked her was the man they were after, Murphy had tried in vain to find her again, to no avail. But her statement would prove crucial in tracking down the red van man.

Frenzy

Despite this crucial information, the killer was still out in the Chicago night, cruising for victims and showing no signs of slowing down. The next victims' bodies paid tribute to his increasing frenzy.

Teenage prostitute Sandra Delaware was found stabbed and strangled to death on the bank of the Chicago River on 28th August. Her wrists were bound behind her with a shoelace and her left breast had been severed with piano wire. The coroner estimated the time of her death to be just six hours earlier.

Then the battered body of marketing executive Rose Beck Davis, 30, was found in an alleyway behind the salubrious North Lake Shore apartment building on 8th September. A black sock was tied around her neck, another around her left wrist. Her clothes had been pulled away from her torso and abdomen, left tangled around her wrists and ankles. She lay in a pool of blood, and great arcs of it had splattered the surrounding walls up to two feet high and nine feet around. Her face had been battered in, her breasts carved up and there were pieces of wood from an axe inside her vagina.

Just three days later, 42-year-old Carole Pappas, wife of a Chicago baseball player, disappeared without a trace from a department store in Wheaton, Illinois. By now it was apparent that there wasn't a woman in Chicago who was safe. Although the killer had started his work and continued to prey on vulnerable prostitutes, he was obviously completely opportunistic.

There was no distinct type of woman that he singled out. Black, white, Asian, Hispanic, middle-aged, teenage – absolutely anyone who strayed unwittingly into his path would do.

Robert Ressler was asked for his opinion. He threw another idea into the mix. Any man who attacked women in this way was likely to be uncertain about his sexuality, he opined. He expected the killer to look effeminate and be bisexual or gay, but not openly so. He was probably, Ressler thought, a small, skinny guy.

Back from the dead

It was a long four months from Angel York's description of the small, skinny guy until detectives got another such break. In October 1982, another prostitute, Beverly Washington, 20, had been found stripped and savaged by a railway track. Her left breast had been severed, her right deeply slashed – but she was breathing. Emergency treatment saved her life.

And even in her brutalised state, she was able to give descriptions that provided significant details for the police to work on.

Beverly, too, had been cruised by a red van driven by a slender white man of about 25, dressed in a flannel shirt and square-toed boots, with greasy brown hair and a moustache. He had offered her significantly more money than she'd asked for and seemed to Beverly to be unaccountably nervous.

Inside the van had also been red, with tinted windows and a wooden divider partitioning off the back. Beverly even noticed there were feathers and a roach clip hanging from the rear-view mirror.

As he led her into the back of the van with him, the man pulled out a gun. He ordered her to strip and then handcuffed her, forced her to fellate him and then threatened her with violence if she didn't swallow the handful of pills he crammed into her mouth. At that point she passed out, her last memory being of her attacker standing over her, holding some kind of cord. At this point, Washington thought she was about to die.

Once he had done his worst, the man threw Beverly into a dumpster in an alleyway in North Maplewood, where she was discovered the next morning by an elderly vagrant who was rooting for scrap metal. His screams for help brought paramedics to the scene quickly enough to save her.

And now it was the police's turn to go out hunting.

Killer clowns

Within three weeks, detectives Phil Murphy and his partner Tom Flynn from Chicago Five pulled over a van that matched Washington's exact description.

The driver did not, however – he had a shock of fuzzy, bright red hair that made Murphy immediately think of Bozo the Clown.

The man acted as if he wasn't all there. He stammered and shouted as the two men asked him to get out of the van and answer their questions. He told the police his name was Eddie Spreitzer and that the van belonged to his boss, Robin Gecht, with whom he was working on renovating a house on North Linder.

The officers told Spreitzer to drive to this house and beckon Gecht outside, so they could take a good look and see if the clown's boss would turn out to be the greasy-haired, hillbilly type Washington had described.

Ambling towards them as if he had all the time in the world, 28-year-old Robin Gecht was even wearing the same plaid shirt and work boots. Yet, while Spreitzer made his unease plain, virtually hopping up and down on the spot when confronted by two detectives telling him that his vehicle had been implicated in a recent crime, Robin Gecht acted completely calmly.

'We want to co-operate fully,' he smiled when Murphy and Flynn suggested a further chat down at the station. 'Don't we, Eddie?'

For Robin Gecht was that most dangerous of types: a psycho with charisma.

'Monster is right here'

Murphy and Flynn went back to Beverly Washington's hospital bed to show her a sheaf of photographs that now included a picture of Robin Gecht. She pointed to him without hesitation. 'Monster who cut me up is right here.'

Then things became more complicated, because the next thing they needed to do was put Gecht into a line-up. Because her injuries were so severe, there was no way Beverly could come to the police station to do this. They had to bring the men to her.

Still in a wheelchair and breathing through tubes, Washington faced the man who had destroyed her life. Murphy could see her fighting back her panic.

'It's him!' she pointed to Gecht and then fainted.

As Murphy and Flynn moved to arrest him, Gecht was the picture of outrage.

They took him straight back to Area Five, where his wife Rosemary was waiting for him. The profilers had been right. The suspect was a married man with children. A man who had been stirring up trouble for a long time now, with a past and a predilection for the company of young girls that bore strong similarities to another man who'd started a death cult in San Francisco in the late 1960s.

Robin Gecht looked like Chicago's answer to Charles Manson.

Beginnings

He was born on 30th November 1953 at the Illinois Masonic Hosptial, the son of an unmarried couple, Jacob and Ruth, who brought their baby home to live with Jacob's parents, Rubin and Sara Gecht. The old couple took care of infant Robin while Jacob and Ruth went out to work. Soon he was joined by a brother, Everett, and a sister, Rachelle.

He had been a happy little boy until Rachelle came along, replacing him as the centre of his grandparents' attentions. Their house was small and the new baby's arrival meant Robin now had to sleep on the floor. With Sara and Rubin's time stretched looking after Rachelle, Robin was left in charge of Everett, a task that he spectacularly failed at. At the age of three, the younger boy ran out into the street and was knocked down by a car. Severely brain-damaged, Everett was taken away to an institution.

By 1961, another sister, Julia, had arrived and the Gechts had moved to a slightly larger house on the northwest side of Chicago. By then, Robin was hardly at school, but staying at home with his grandparents to help look after his siblings. Not that he had enjoyed school much anyway.

Smaller and shabbier than his contemporaries, he was bullied constantly for being poor and Jewish. Although Rubin had not been orthodox enough to actually get married or observe any other religious holidays, he would not allow his children to celebrate Christmas, a source of much mirth to his Christian classmates.

In 1964, Ruth gave birth to another girl, Joann. That same January, Grandma Sara was diagnosed with stomach cancer. Jacob also became ill, and as a result, Ruth was left as the sole breadwinner. It was down to 11-year-old Robin to take care of the rest of the family. When Sara died that March, the young kid began to come really unstuck.

Constant fighting

Robin was in trouble with school authorities for his constant fighting. He began to steal and start fires. When he was at home, he was frequently beaten by his harassed father, Jacob. He ended up at Montefiore school for troubled juveniles, where he was bullied even more by the hardened older boys.

Finally, he was sent to juvenile court and remanded to live in the Parental School for eight months. By the time he came out, his beloved Grandpa Rubin had died.

But around this time, he discovered he had a talent for carpentry and electrics. He set up a workshop in his basement and began fixing things around the house. By the age of 15, he could repair a television and was on his way to establishing his own business.

Yet he couldn't stay out of trouble for long. He started a relationship with a girl who already had a jealous boyfriend. When the two fought, he was threatened with another stay in Parental School. So Robin didn't return home. Instead he went to stay at the apartment of a family friend, who Jacob and Ruth probably didn't realise was also a homosexual. Maybe Robin felt some relief staying with a man who was unafraid of his own sexuality, but to the outside world, he kept up his straight demeanour.

At 18, he had his first serious partner, a girl from the neighbourhood with whom he fathered a child. But things didn't last and the girl left him shortly after the baby was born. Gecht's attempts to set himself up in business also came to nought. He was caught operating without an electrical licence and fined $200. After that, he got a job at an auto-repair shop and kept his electrical work on the side.

Gecht shuttled between the apartment of the family friend (who wished to remain nameless) and various women until everyone was utterly fed up with him and kicked him out. Unwilling to return home to his father's disapproval, Gecht ended up with his Uncle Rodger, his mother's youngest brother. For a while, there was a period of calm. He got on well with Rodger, and they were able to work together, enabling

Robin to make savings for the electrical repair business of his dreams. He even made things up with his former flatmate and moved back in with him.

Then in early 1975, Robin Gecht met 17-year-old Rosemary McCaffrey. They hit it off immediately and were married on 23rd August. By January 1976, their first child was born.

Girls, girls, girls

But Robin's marriage to Rosemary was never straightforward. It wasn't long before he was cheating on her, and openly too. Teenage girls descended on the Gechts' first house at all hours of the day and night. At one point, he was accused of raping a 15-year-old at gunpoint in his daughter's bed, but the girl later dropped the charges.

Rosemary was always threatening divorce, but it never happened. The couple had two more children, a boy and another girl. And, perhaps in an attempt to make sense of what her husband was doing to her, Rosemary began to make friends with his numerous girlfriends. She needed to compare notes on a few of Robin's quirks.

She showed them the six hatpins that Gecht forced her to wear skewered inside her breasts, feeding her drugs to numb the pain and stop the wounds from going septic. She told them about the way he forced her to watch him having sex with her parents' dog in their front room. The weapons he made as sex aids – sticks with pins in them and axes.

The friend with whom Gecht roomed as a teenager later told police that a profound change had come over Robin when he split with the mother of his first child. He apparently got into drugs in a major way and had a source giving him all kinds of prescription uppers and downers. He also began boasting about how many women he had conned out of money and began to amass a stockpile of guns.

Rosemary Gecht also showed this man the wounds her husband had inflicted on her. He tried to make her go to the police, but Rosemary refused.

Catalogue of carnage

The cops had Spreitzer and Gecht in custody, but getting anything out of them was a different matter. The latter retained his cool under intense questioning, never deviating from his line that he had never seen Beverly Washington before. But Eddie Spreitzer was a different matter.

It soon became apparent to Wilkosz and Murphy that Spreitzer, 22, was very afraid of the older Gecht. Keeping them apart, they worked on Eddie until he began to crumble. The weight of what he had seen and done eventually came tumbling out.

The sweating, stuttering Spreitzer first admitted that he had been at the wheel of the red van when Gecht committed a drive-by shooting on two Puerto Rican men. His story checked out – one of the men had been killed, the other left paralysed. After this little prelude, Gecht then ordered him to drive to Villa Park where it was easy to pick up prostitutes. Spreitzer said that Gecht disappeared down an alley with a black woman and came back alone. But he had a little trophy to show Eddie, which he threw on the floor of the van. It was the woman's left breast.

Spreitzer was crying as he spilled out these details, claiming that he couldn't bear the sight of all the blood.

After that night, he said, Gecht became insatiable. Spreitzer had witnessed him killing, mutilating and carving up woman after woman to get his diseased sexual kicks, which were all fixated around breasts. Sometimes he would masturbate in front of Spreitzer with the freshly severed organ. One time he 'forced' Eddie to do likewise.

By the time he had finished his testimony, Spreitzer had furnished his interrogators with the details of seven murders and one aggravated battery. The officers were profoundly disturbed by what they'd heard and only hoped it would give them something to break down Gecht with.

But when they went in to show him the photos of the known victims, Gecht reacted as if they were simply boring him – he knew nothing about these women and had never met them before in his life.

The cops tried another tack; moving Gecht into a room where he could clearly see Spreitzer co-operating with police and showing them something.

Gecht didn't even flicker.

But when the officers reversed the scenario, Eddie's reaction was extreme.

Seeing his accomplice again, Spreitzer began to panic and immediately changed his account, saying that Gecht had not murdered anyone. His testimony became so chaotic that it was near impossible to follow what he was going on about. It seemed that the very nearness of Gecht had turned Spreitzer into a gibbering wreck.

Spreitzer now claimed that there was another man involved in all this carnage, who was the real ringleader and killer. A man called Andrew Kokoraleis.

The third man

Spreitzer led Warren Wilkosz to the Kokoraleis' townhouse in Villa Park. The area was rundown and shabby. Rents were cheap and the parking lot at the rear of the buildings had become a hangout for teenage stoners.

Twenty-three-year-old Andy Kokoraleis was at home when Wilkosz called. He seemed oddly unsurprised when he was asked about Spreitzer and Gecht.

In the interview room, Tom Flynn began the questioning. 'Eddie Spreitzer has implicated you in a string of murders,' he said.

'You mean all 18 of them?' asked Andy.

Kokoraleis was vastly more lucid than Spreitzer. He began by describing what he, Gecht and Spreitzer did to Shui Mak. How they pulled her off the side of the road and silenced her screams of protest with repeated punches to her face. Then they took her to a deserted construction site and punched her some more, Gecht slamming her head into the van door, causing the horseshoe crack that Larry Troka was so disturbed by.

Then Gecht had started cutting her, while Eddie held a wire to her throat. Each man took turns inserting himself into the wound.

By the time he had finished his interview, Andy had admitted the murders of Lorraine Borowski, Rose Beck Davis, Sandra Delaware and 15 other women.

Kokoraleis could remember the hideous detail of each woman's fate. He told police that he had shoved a rock into Sandra Delaware's mouth to stop her from screaming, forced a wine bottle into her and stabbed her with a knife. The autopsy report confirmed that everything he said was true.

Wilkosz went back to the Kokoraleis house in an attempt to find out how and why this young man had got himself involved with Robin Gecht.

The sign of four

Andy Kokoraleis was the son of Greek immigrants. His mother had died when he was fairly young, and his father was a patriarch with old country ways, a man who seemed scornful of indulgent American society. He had a sister, Elizabeth, and a younger brother, Tommy. It was Tommy who Wilkosz wanted to question.

Almost as soon as the detective arrived at their home, Tommy K began to look nervous. He had a low IQ anyway, but it wasn't just that that sent Wilkosz's instincts prickling. It was the way he squirmed around on the couch, acting guilty without being accused. It soon became clear this interview would be best conducted down at the station.

What Tommy explained there put a whole new complexion on Gecht's obsessions. Gecht, he said, had wanted to put his 'mark' upon the world. The women had died so that Robin Gecht could make sacrifices to Satan at the altar he had in his house.

The Satanic Panic

Two years before the Chicago Rippers began their bloody reign, a book had come out that had spread panic across America.

Michelle Remembers was purported to be the 'recovered' memories of a young girl called Michelle Smith who had been subjected to years of sexual abuse by a Satanic cult while she was a child. The group, she said, were also involved in ritual sacrifice and cannibalism.

Michelle Remembers was sold as the factual work of a patient and her psychiatrist Dr Lawrence Padzer (whom she later went on to marry) and was followed by a spate of copycat books on the same theme. The contents of these tomes were furiously discussed on every radio and TV show going, and an industry quickly sprang up to 'help survivors of Ritual Satanic Abuse (RSA)' – more often than not headed by evangelical and fundamentalist Christians.

The omnipresent talk show host Geraldo Rivera summed up the mood of the nation when he announced on his influential TV show that: 'Estimates are that there are over one million Satanists in this country...The majority of them are linked in a highly organised, very secretive network. From small towns to large cities, they have attracted police and FBI attention to their Satanic ritual child abuse, child pornography and grisly Satanic murders. The odds are that this is happening in your town.'

Rivera's odds were way off the mark, in fact they were completely fictitious. But, stirred up by panic, rumour and teenage rebellion, things were happening in Chicago.

Teenage Black Magic rituals

While Wilkosz had been digging into Spreitzer and Gecht's background he had uncovered a world rife with such rumours as could be found between the pages of *Michelle Remembers*.

Spreitzer had shown up at a school prom with blood all over his mouth. Other students were appalled, much to Eddie's delight. He refused to wash off the blood and spent the night bragging about how he had been taking part in Satanic animal sacrifices out in the woods. The other kids believed him – Spreitzer had been considered a weirdo all of his school life.

The more people Wilkosz talked to, the stranger the stories became. There was talk of ceremonies, orgies, involving Gecht's sister-in-law and a circle of friends.

The student counsellor at Eddie's alma mater, Willowbrook High, confirmed that a Satanic fad had been sweeping through the school. Kids were scratching Pentagrams and 666 signs on their desks and schoolbooks and drawing inverted crosses in pen on the back of their hands. She had witnessed students whispering arcane oaths to each other, telling tales of witchcraft and secret ceremonies. Indeed, in the area behind the school, which backed onto a forest, teachers had found the smouldering remains of fires, stone circles and sometimes even the skeletons of cats and dogs.

Kids are always susceptible to tales of voodoo and witchcraft. But at this particular time in American history, so was the rest of the adult population.

Rivera hosted show after show on the subject, linking his 'Satanic network' to Charles Manson and Anton La Vey and featuring many guests who claimed to have recovered memories of RSA.

It wasn't until 1985, after *Michelle Remembers* had been thoroughly discredited, that Rivera himself did a *volte face* and apologised for the hysteria he had helped to unleash.

'I am convinced that I was terribly wrong,' he admitted, 'and I am equally positive [that the] Repressed Memory Therapy Movement is also a bunch of crap.'

But by then, scores of innocent people had been hounded, arrested and even sent to prison for crimes they did not commit and quack psychiatrists had made a fortune implanting RSA memories into vulnerable patients.

Probably no one who was profiting from the panic had ever stopped to think whether the sensationalist material they were spreading about was giving real psychos some bright ideas. For in Chicago, Tommy Kokoraleis was about to relate a true story that had all too many echoes of this lurid fiction.

Temple of doom

Robin Gecht had a shrine in the attic of his Northwest Side home, Tommy told Commander John Millner, John Sam and Warren Wilkosz at Elmhurst police station. It was painted with six red and black crosses and there was a red cloth placed across a home-made altar. Here the killers would take the severed breasts harvested from their victims, cut up the flesh and then devour it as part of an ancient ritual honouring Satan.

They did this most nights, while Rosemary Gecht was out working as a barmaid.

Tommy K described how the four men would kneel together around the altar and Robin would produce and divide the flesh of their victims in a mockery of the act of Communion. He would then recite passages from the Bible as each man masturbated into his portion. When each had finished, they would consume the flesh.

Gecht kept a trophy box to keep the skin of the breasts in. Tommy said he had once counted 15 of them in it.

From what Kokoraleis confessed, he had been more active at Gecht's 'church' than he had at the actual killings, although he had witnessed two of them, including the attack on Lorry Ann Borowski.

The appalled officers asked him how he could have brought himself to do such things. Tommy replied seriously. Gecht, he said, had the power to make the other three comply exactly with his wishes. 'You just had to do it,' he emphasised, firmly.

Tommy believed Gecht had a personal connection to his infernal master and was afraid of what Satanic powers would be unleashed if he refused to obey his commands. He also furthered the information that Gecht was bisexual, a story that would be backed up by other friends and acquaintances of the four killers. Various people claimed that both Eddie and Andy K were Gecht's sometime lovers and every expert asked vouched that such extreme sadism could only have been the work of a man or men at raging odds with their sexuality.

All this tied in with the way Eddie Spreitzer dissolved when faced with Gecht, and the calm demeanour of the ringleader himself. Maybe Robin Gecht, lord of his comrades' bodies and minds, had even convinced himself he was actually diabolically protected.

When the cops went to check out Tommy's story they found the attic as he had described it – complete with altar, empty trophy box, books on Satanism and a recently fired rifle.

Lord of lies

Still, Satan's little helper tried every trick he knew to keep himself away from facing trial. His power over his followers was still strong – they all refused to testify against Gecht, despite repeated assurances that he would never be out of custody to get to them ever again. When finally faced with a trial, Spreitzer, Andy and Tommy K all tried to recant their testimonies and blame each other – anyone but Gecht.

All this meant was that they alone could be tried for murder. With no physical evidence against him – Robin had always been very careful to wash and clean his van after every night on the town – and no confession, Gecht could only be tried for the physical attacks, kidnappings and rapes of Beverly Washington, Angel York and 16 other dead women.

He first attempted to plead insanity, but his psychiatric assessors found him competent to stand trial, as well as being of sound mind at the time his offences took place. Lurid stories in the press caused his first hearing to be deemed a mistrial. It wasn't until 20th September 1983 that he finally took the stand.

Beverly Washington was brave enough to give evidence against him. She described what Gecht had done to her, and the months of reconstructive surgery she had undergone as a result.

Then there was the testimony of Angel York, read out to the court, along with the graphically detailed victim reports, in which the murderers' *modus operandi* was detailed for the jury.

Against this, Rosemary and Ruth Gecht professed Robin's innocence and his lawyers tried to insinuate that Eddie Spreitzer had acted alone in the attacks. Gecht had only one course of action to take. Deny everything.

When he took to the stand to speak in his own defence, he began by saying that he had killed and raped no one. He was utterly innocent of the crimes, and furthermore had not even made the acquaintance of his co-defendants at the time the attacks took place.

The jury was not taken in by this pious act. They found him guilty of all the crimes he had been charged with: attempted murder, rape, deviant sexual assault, aggravated battery and armed violence. He was sent down with a 120-year sentence.

Bad lieutenant

One by one, the rest of Gecht's sect fell down. With realisation dawning all too slowly, Tommy Kokoraleis made a futile attempt to get his confession blocked from his trial. He lost. He was convicted in 1984 for his part in Lorry Ann Borowski's murder, and sentenced to 70 years.

The next trials, those of his brother Andy, were going to prove a great deal more complicated.

Andy K was being tried separately on two counts. The first was for the murder of Rose Beck Davis. In his confession, Kokoraleis said that he had abducted Davis along with his accomplices, forced her into the van and beaten her to death with a hatchet. The jury deliberated for three hours before returning their verdict of guilty of rape and murder. He was sentenced to life imprisonment.

Andy had never been so much of a stooge as his dim-witted brother and Eddie Spreitzer. His first recollection of events to the police had indicated that he was more like Robin Gecht's bad lieutenant, a man who took part in the extreme sadism the gang meted out with as much gusto as his commander. Now he was going to try using the same methods as Gecht to avoid taking any responsibility for his actions.

At his trial for the murder of Lorry Ann Borowski, Kokoraleis recanted everything he had confessed on four separate occasions previously. Instead, he claimed that the police had beaten his confession out of him, making false promises that if he admitted everything he would get off lighter, and even directing what they wanted him to say.

His line was even more audacious than Gecht's, and prosecutor Brian Telander was forced to go through each interrogation, the work of six separate detectives and two prosecutors.

Warren Wilkosz took the stand to describe how he interrogated Andy K. He said he had shown the defendant a line of photographs, from which he picked out the face of Lorry Ann Borowski.

'That's the girl Eddie Spreitzer and I killed at the cemetery,' Kokoraleis had said.

One angry man

When it came to convincing a jury, Andy wasn't half so clever as he thought. Sullen and angry, he stared with undisguised loathing into the courtroom. His claims of innocence sounded hardly convincing.

The deliberations didn't take long. Kokoraleis was found guilty of the murder of Lorry Ann Borowski and sentenced to death. The sight of his own impending mortality made Andrew angrier still.

At his sentencing hearing, he continued to deny his guilt, while his attorneys tried everything to get him out of Death Row. A prison chaplain and a counsellor testified that he was no danger to society and could be rehabilitated.

The court thought otherwise and upheld his sentence. So, nurturing his rage from a jail cell, he tried a different tack.

Kokoraleis' attorneys went back to appeal that their client was a schizophrenic who hadn't known what he was doing at the time of the murders. His trial lawyers should have submitted a defence of insanity, but instead they had not even had him psychiatrically evaluated, a significant error on their part. They argued that even if Andrew K's useless lawyers hadn't realised he needed such an assessment, the judge should have ordered one for court.

A prison psychiatrist had diagnosed Kokoraleis with a borderline personality disorder and found him incompetent to stand trial. Poor, weak Andrew had been under the influence of a much stronger personality, Robin Gecht, and therefore was not entirely responsible for what he had done.

What a sob story. Judge Edward Kowal went with it to those officials involved in the original trials. They told him that no pattern of aberrant behaviour had ever made anyone involved with the case suspect that Kokoraleis was suffering from a psychiatric disorder. That persuaded the judge that Andrew K's attorneys were wasting their time.

However, he still had one last glimmer of hope on the horizon. A movement had started in Michigan to overturn all death sentences in the state.

The ultimate penalty

In the late 1990s, a series of crusading articles in the *Chicago Tribune* had brought to light some serious miscarriages of justice within the local legal system. As a result, 12 people had had their cases overturned and been released from Death Row. The Illinois Governor George Ryan was under pressure to review all the cases of men currently sentenced to death.

One of those was Andrew Kokoraleis, scheduled to be executed on 17th March 1999.

But Ryan was not of the mind that there had been any miscarriage of justice in this case. Just hours before Andrew K was due to meet his destiny, the Governor issued a detailed statement setting out his reasons for refusing to reconsider the verdict of this case.

A jury, he said, had found Kokoraleis guilty by the law of the land. His 16-year campaign to appeal his verdict had failed to convince anyone. There was no reason why the execution should not go ahead as planned.

'Some crimes are so horrendous and so heinous that society has the right to demand the ultimate penalty,' he surmised.

The prisoner was sent to the maximum-security prison at Tamms, Illinois, where he spent his last hours praying – and not to Satan. When they strapped him on the gurney, he finally offered the Borowski family an apology and said the Kingdom of Heaven was at hand.

Wherever he ended up, he got there at 12.34pm.

After Kokoraleis had been safely dispatched, Governor Ryan announced a moratorium on all executions in the state. It seemed that he had bided his time just so the State's most reviled Death Row inmate could get the punishment he was awarded.

Not many people complained.

Every woman's nightmare

And what of Eddie Spreitzer, the stuttering goon who had first led the cops to the rest of the killers? Was he, like Tommy Kokoraleis, a dim-witted fool who had been led along for the ride by his fear of the controlling Robin Gecht? Or had Eddie enjoyed playing his part in those nights of terror?

Spreitzer too faced two separate trials, the first of which was fairly straightforward. He pleaded guilty on 2nd April 1984 to the murders of Rose Beck Davis, Sandra Delaware, Shui Mak and a drug dealer named Rafael Torado – the victim of the drive-by he confessed to. He was awarded life sentences for each murder, as well as time for deviant sexual assault and rape.

He was then tried for the Linda Sutton murder – and faced a possible death sentence for it. Which was when Eddie started to squirm.

On 25th February 1986, he admitted that he and his comrades had snatched Linda Sutton off the street as she walked near Wrigley field, taken her to the field at the back of the Moonlit Hotel and inflicted rape, murder and mutilation upon her.

Yet his attorney, Carol Anfinson, painted a picture of a young man who had lost his way, who was too immature and unsure of himself to resist obeying the dictates of his stronger-willed companions. Friends and relatives testified that Spreitzer was indeed a docile young man who had a history of being bullied. Anfinson asked the jury to spare his life.

However, the prosecution had a witness who testified that Spreitzer had bragged about the killings to him, referring to the women as 'broads' and happily admitting to slashing and killing along with the others.

Prosecutor Brian Telander summed it up. 'Eddie Spreitzer isn't a cute little boy who goes and delivers sugar to his neighbours...Eddie Spreitzer is every woman's worst nightmare.'

Spared the chair

The jury didn't take a lot of convincing. Eddie Spreitzer was convicted of kidnap and murder and sentenced to death.

He languished in Pontiac State Correctional Facility in Illinois, exhausting every attempt to appeal, including the old 'insanity' chestnut.

Until October 2002, when Governor Ryan's moratorium on Death Row inmates finally brought his case back up for consideration.

Spreitzer's attorney Gary Pritchard sought to appeal for clemency on the grounds that Eddie's low IQ (he scored only 76) made him an easy target for Robin Gecht to manipulate.

The victims' families moved *en masse* to try and block any change in the sentence, backed by prosecutor Michael Wolfe, who described Spreitzer's crimes as 'the worst of the worst'. But when George Ryan left his office in 2003, he pardoned four of the prisoners left on Death Row and granted blanket clemency to the rest. Spreitzer's sentence was commuted to life imprisonment.

No rest

For the families of the victims, however, there will be no such mercies. Three of the four killers evaded a death sentence, which for many of those involved was no justice at all.

From his prison cell, Robin Gecht still proclaims his innocence to anyone who will listen to him, most recently Jennifer Furio, who interviewed him for her book *The Serial Killer Letters* in 1998. His wife and family continue to stick by him.

Would Spreitzer and the Kokoraleis brothers have done such things if they had never met him? Probably not. Criminologist Edward W Hickey points out that 'the pathology of the relationship operates symbiotically', that once the moral restraints that bound them had been lifted, each was spurred on by his own excitement in reaction to the crimes. Not one of them had, at any point, attempted to stop Robin in his savage quest.

In the opinion of Warren Wilkosz, who chased them down the hardest, there are probably more bodies still out there that bear the

Robin Gecht hallmarks. Not just in Chicago, but in other states, in lonely places where bodies can lie undisturbed. For everyone unfortunate enough to be affected by them, the crimes of the Chicago Rippers have no end on Earth.

Chapter Four

⌒

Richard Ramirez: Satan Wants Me (1984-5)

Bad moon rising

It had been a long time since Los Angeles had felt this kind of fear. It was 16 years since the Manson girls creepy-crawled out of the desert to make their murderous journey through the Hollywood Hills. Eight years since the Hillside Stranglers, Kenneth Bianchi and Angelo Buono, began leaving the bodies of young women out on the slopes of Glendale-Highland Park.

But for a hellish six months in 1985, the entire city of dreams was at the mercy of a nightmare more intense than anything that had gone before. A bogeyman was abroad. He would break into people's houses while they slept, wake them up with a bullet and do unspeakable things to their corpses. He would rape and rob and leave the scene of his crimes covered in Satanic Pentagram symbols – carved in the flesh of his victims or smeared over the walls in their blood.

The man who headed the investigation of this case, Frank Salerno, had made his name bringing Bianchi and Buono to justice. He'd even busted a teenage Manson for drug dealing – you could say he was on first name terms with the city's most infamous ghouls. But now he was dealing with a kind of criminal he had never had to face before. This killer was indiscriminate about the age, gender or nationality of his victims. Far from just concentrating on the richest homes, or a particular racial enclave, he wandered far and wide across the city to make his calls. By August 17th he had brought chaos and death to a 40-mile radius of Los Angeles. No one could sleep easy at night. No one could afford to keep their window open as the temperatures soared. All they could do was invest in a fierce dog and a gun and say their prayers before bedtime.

For here was a man determined the world would know his name and his purpose, who would snatch at least 13 people from their dreams forever before his reign was over.

It was the season of the Night Stalker.

While you were sleeping...

Nobody knew it yet, but the first victim had actually been taken a year since, on another hot and sultry night, 28th June 1984. She was Jennie Vincow, a 79-year-old woman from Glassel Park, a small community mainly inhabited by low-income working class. On that fateful night, she left the window of her first floor apartment open because the heat was unbearable. The man who came into her home simply had to remove the screen in order to climb straight through.

Jennie was sound asleep and didn't hear the noise of him ransacking her room in search of valuables, hear his cries of frustration that the old lady had nothing that was worth as much money as he would have liked. Nor did she hear his gloved hand open her bedroom door. The first Jennie knew about it was when he launched himself upon her, knife in hand.

Jennie was found the next morning by her son, Jack, almost slashed to pieces. Her neck had been slit with such force she was virtually decapitated. Her apartment had been turned upside down and what little of value she had – a small, portable radio – was taken.

The autopsy report found something else. Sexual abuse had also taken place. The act of stabbing had aroused the killer so much he'd attempted to have sex with her mutilated corpse.

The police suspected a coke fiend, desperate to fund his next score, had carried out the brutal raid. Dr Joseph Cogan, who performed the autopsy, thought that the man was an experienced killer who enjoyed what he did. Forensics lifted some decent prints from the scene. But the investigation came to nothing. The killer had gone to ground. He wouldn't resurface again for another eight months.

Eyes of a maniac

It was 11pm on the evening of 17th March 1985. Maria Hernandez, 22, was just returning home to the condo she shared with her 34-year-old roommate, Dayle Okazaki, in Rosemead, an affluent, middle class town in northeast LA. She was tired and ready to put her feet up as she headed her car into the driveway and opened the garage with a remote control.

But as she got out of her car, she saw something in her peripheral vision. A man was rushing towards her, tall and dressed entirely in black, with a baseball cap pulled down low over his eyes. In his hand, he was holding a gun, pointed straight at her.

As he got up close, Maria began to beg for mercy. She tried to look away, so that he couldn't accuse her of getting a proper look at his face, thinking that might save her. But as he held the gun just inches from her nose she couldn't help but see into his eyes.

Dark pools of nothingness met her.

Hernandez continued to plead with him to spare her life. He squeezed the trigger. The sound of the gun going off in the concrete garage was deafening and she fell to the floor. She knew she was alive but was so afraid she acted dead. The man kicked her out of the way and went through the door that led into the condo.

After a while, Maria realised her hand was bleeding. When the man had shot at her, she had instinctively raised the hand that was holding her keys. By a miracle, the bullet had deflected off them, saving her life. Shakily, she got to her feet and made her way out of the garage.

She heard another shot, coming from the inside of the condo. Maria began to run, but as she did so, she collided with the gunman as he came out of the front door of the house. Convinced he would finish her off, Hernandez screamed: 'Please don't shoot me again,' and ran back into the garage on wobbling legs. No one followed. Her attacker shoved his gun back into his belt and fled the scene.

Fearing what had happened inside, Maria made tentative steps into her home. Dayle was lying face down in a pool of blood on the kitchen floor. The whole room was thick with gunsmoke and death, blood splattering the walls, surfaces and implements. Shot through the forehead at point-blank range. Okazaki hadn't had a chance.

Hernandez called 911 and Los Angeles sheriff's deputies John Powell and Anthony Dallas were first on the scene. They called the paramedics to take Maria to hospital, but there was nothing they could do now for Dayle. They called in Deputy Gil Carrillo, at 34, the youngest detective in their department, who retrieved the killer's baseball cap from the garage floor. Carrillo was the man who would go hardest after the Night Stalker, and was the first person to connect one man to the crimewave that would begin in earnest this night.

But even while the blue lights flashed outside Maria Hernandez's condo, the man who had killed Dayle Okazaki was searching for another victim. Something had gone wrong for him at Rosemead. His bloodlust had not been sated yet.

Carjacked

In nearby Monterey Park, Ron Endo from the Monterey police had just been dispatched to investigate a shooting. Resident Joseph Duenas had seen a man trying to pull a young woman out of her car while waving a gun and had immediately called 911. Bt the time his cousin Jorge Gallegos had got to the scene, the woman was lying critically injured in the street. Her assailant had fled into the night.

She was alive, but only just. Thirty-year-old Taiwanese Tsia-Lian Yu, known to her friends as Veronica, had been shot four times by a man who had been tailing her car. When officer Endo arrived, her empty yellow Chevrolet was still in the middle of the road with its engine running. He could see the woman lying on the pavement next to it. He ordered everybody back and took her pulse.

Ron Endo knew it didn't look good. He called for medical back-up while Duenas and Gallegos told him what they had seen. The policeman tried to get a statement from Veronica, but she was fading fast. He administered CPR until the ambulance arrived but it was not to be. The young law student died on her way to the hospital.

Carrillo studied hard what had happened at these two crime scenes. There had not been an overt sexual element to these crimes, but he still felt strongly that the man he was after was getting his kicks from killing. He had taken a course in sex crime, put together at the FBI's Behavioural Science Unit and, as soon as he had Maria Hernandez's composite of the man in black who had attacked her, he went over to the East LA station where he could study other sex crime cases. He wondered if there had been any other crimes perpetrated by a man fitting this description. He also went to see Sgt Frank Salerno, considered the 'absolute best' homicide detective in the city.

Meanwhile, the killer had re-thought his strategy. He had given up mainlining cocaine ever since he had decided to take up killing full time, thinking the drug would make him careless. Now he limited himself to marijuana and the odd beer, but ever since the night of Jennie Vincow, the need to achieve another, greater kind of high had been coursing through his veins.

He started following a pattern that he obviously revelled in – delivering death door-to-door.

Home invasion

On the morning of 27th March 1985, Peter Zazzara was visiting his parents at their home in Whittier, Californa. His 64-year-old father, Vincent, was a retired investment advisor who was now running his own pizzeria, while his mother Maxine, 44, was an attorney. Peter was expecting them both to be in, so he was surprised they didn't answer the bell. He had his own key, so he turned the lock and opened the door on a vision of hell.

Vincent was lying dead on the sofa. He had been shot through the left temple and had probably died instantly. In the bedroom, Maxine lay stretched out on the bed, naked and bloody. She had been stabbed repeatedly around the face, neck, abdomen and groin. There was a big, T-shaped incision in her left breast and her eyes had been gouged out. The sockets were empty.

The house had been ransacked, the couple's valuables taken.

Six weeks later, the killer returned to Monterey Park and the home of Bill and Lillian Doi. He woke the couple from a deep sleep by shooting 66-year-old Bill through the head. Then he started beating up 56-year-old Lillian, who had been confined to a wheelchair after a stroke two years earlier, demanding to know where she kept her money and valuables. Lillian could hardly speak clearly as it was, and in her panic her words were still more incomprehensible. He tied her up, locking her hands into thumb-cuffs, while he searched the house and collected the couple's valuables. Returning to the bedroom, he dragged the tiny woman to the side of the bed and raped her. Satisfied with his night's work, he left.

Mr Doi, however, was not dead. Despite his head wound, he managed to crawl to the phone and call an ambulance for his wife. Although brave Bill died later that night, Lillian was able to overcome her shock and grief enough to give the cops a description of a man in black with rotting teeth. Forensics found a footprint at the rear of the Doi house, of a type of training shoe called Avia Aeorbic, size 11½. It was a print the cops would be seeing again.

Foul of breath

Two weeks later, on 30th May, 42-year-old Burbank resident Carol Kye was rudely awakened from her sleep. A flashlight was shining straight into her eyes. A man had silently broken into her home and was holding a gun to her head.

Carol was a registered nurse who had experience in dealing with psychopaths. Realising she was face to face with one, she did everything in her power to keep him calm.

He ordered her out of bed, and into the next-door room of her 12-year-old son. There, he jumped on the boy's bed and warned Carol not to make a sound. Then he handcuffed the boy and locked him in a closet in the hallway.

'Don't look at me again!' he warned Kye. 'If you look at me again I'll shoot you.'

Carol assumed the intruder was a burglar, even though he seemed greatly agitated. So she offered the man her most valuable item of jewellery, a gold and diamond necklace, and led him to the dressing table in her bedroom where she kept it, hoping her co-operation would placate him. But it wasn't enough. After rummaging around the house still further, he ordered her to face the wall with her hands behind her back.

The man tied Carol's hands together with a pair of her tights and shoved her on the bed. Despite her pleading, he ripped off her nightdress and sodomised her twice. Up close, his breath was foul and his eyes, she later told police, 'were absolutely demonic'.

Despite all the trauma that had come rushing out of the night for her, Carol Kye remained calm. 'You must have a very unhappy life to be able to do this,' she told her attacker, once he had finished. The man replied that he thought she looked good for her age, so he would let her live, even though he had killed many others. When she complained that the binds around her wrist were hurting her, he loosened them and brought her a dressing gown to wear. Then he let her son out of the wardrobe and handcuffed the two of them together. He left them that way, and the son was able to reach a phone to call the police. Carol's description was good – they were after a tall, thin Hispanic man, dressed all in black with long black hair.

Mark of the Beast

Worse was yet to come. On the morning of 30th May, 78-year-old gardener Carlos Valenzuela went to call on one of his regular customers, Mabel Bell, who lived with her invalid sister, Nettie Lang, in the remote and beautiful enclave of Monrovia.

Mabel was the sort of person who left her front door unlocked at night, because she wanted to think the best of people. What poor Valenzuela discovered in her house that morning made a mockery of the old lady's faith.

Both women had been beaten with a hammer, with such force that the handle had split. Nettie was lying on her bed with her hands tied behind her back with wire. She was comatose and her hands had swollen so badly that they were black and bursting open. She lay under an inverted Pentagram, the symbol of Satanism, scrawled in lipstick on the wall. Tears around her vagina indicated she had been sexually molested.

Mabel was also trussed and in a coma. She had been hit so hard around the head that throbbing brain matter protruded from just above her left ear. An inverted Pentagram had also been drawn in lipstick on her inner thigh. The sisters had been left in this way for two days before they were discovered. Doctors were eventually able to revive Nettie, but Mabel died of her injuries without ever regaining consciousness.

When Detective Carrillo heard about the case he went over to examine the scene. A Satanic symbol had never been left at any of the Stalker's crime scenes before, so he was troubled as to what this meant. He talked it over with Salerno who agreed that, if they were looking at the same man for all of these attacks, then he was following a pattern they had never seen before.

Nightmare in Arcadia

One month later, on 27th June, the Night Stalker raped a 6-year-old girl in Arcadia. A day later, the body of 28-year-old Patty Higgins was found in her home in the same district, another well-heeled residential community at the base of the San Gabriel mountains. Her throat had been cut, the house ransacked. On 2nd July, 75-year-old Mary Louise Cannon was found in the same district and the same condition. And the killer hadn't finished with Arcadia yet.

On 5th July he made an audacious break-in at the house of Mr and Mrs Steve Bennett and beat their 16-year-old daughter around the head with a tyre iron. He had intended to rape and kill her, but something happened that night that the killer would later describe as an 'intercession' by Jesus. The girl woke up the next morning with a blinding headache, unable to remember what had happened to her. She would need 478 stitches to piece her head back together.

Forensics found the mark of a size 11½ Avia Aerobic shoe on her bedlinen.

Two days later, Joyce Nelson was found in her home in Montery Park, beaten to death with a blunt instrument. The mark of a 11½ Avia shoe was left clearly imprinted across her face. On the same night and in the same area, 63-year-old psychiatric nurse Sophie Dickman was woken up by a 'tall, bony man dressed in black' standing over her bed pointing a gun at her head.

He ordered her to go up and get into the bathroom and then stay there in silence, while he noisily ripped her house to pieces searching for loot. When there was nothing to satisfy him, he returned to the bathroom in a rage. He made her reveal to him where she kept her jewellery. But Sophie made the mistake of trying to hide her diamond wedding ring. It made the man furious.

Sophie was forced back into her bedroom and down upon her bed. Her attacker there attempted to rape and sodomise her, but he couldn't maintain an erection. Frustrated and humiliated he continued to scream abuse at her in such a manner that Sophie was sure she was about to be killed. But instead, he gathered up all her belongings he deemed worthy of taking, and disappeared back into the night. Sophie later told Gil Carrillo something he found very unusual for a description of a rapist. He was, she said, 'good looking'.

These two attacks had given the detective some important information, however. In the whole of the city of Los Angeles, there had only been sold one pair of Avia Aerobic trainers in size 11½.

When the press put it together that there was a serial killer in their midst a collective terror seized Los Angeles on a scale never seen before. The sales of alarms, guard dogs and guns soared. When they realised that Frank Salerno, of the Hillside Stranglers fame, was heading up the investigation, he and Carrillo were hounded.

And the press had found a name for their bogeyman, one that would stick. They called him the Night Stalker.

Killing couples

The killer now changed locale, leaving the environs of Montery Park for the middle class, suburban enclave of Glendale. On 20th July, he struck again, once more choosing a couple to vent his hellish wrath upon. Maxson Kneiling, 68, and his wife Leila, 66, were killed in their own bed, shot in the head and then slashed frenziedly with a machete. Maxson had been butchered so brutally his head was barely attached to his shoulders.

Even as the bodies of the Kneilings were discovered, the Night Stalker was striking again.

Over in Sun Valley, he broke into the home of Chainarong and Somkid Khovananth. He shot 32-year-old Chainarong dead instantly. Then he raped Somkid, 29, on the bed next to where her dead husband lay. He repeatedly ordered her to 'swear on Satan' as he then helped himself to a fortune in jewellery.

On 6th August, the emboldened Night Stalker tried out the same pattern on another couple, Christopher and Virginia Petersen. Under cover of the night, he broke into their Northridge home and shot them both in the head while they slept. But 38-year-old Christopher, a big, powerfully-built truck driver, got out of bed and chased the intruder off, despite having a bullet lodged inside his head. Miraculously, both the Petersens survived.

The next couple weren't so lucky. Two nights later, in Diamond Bar, California, Elyas Abowath, 31, was shot in the head and killed while he slept. His wife, Sakina, 27, was then set upon. Again, the attacker demanded the terrified woman repeatedly 'swear on Satan' and he set about gathering together her jewellery. He then raped and sodomised her, finally forcing her to give him oral sex.

Los Angeles was traumatised as the Night Stalker stepped up the frequency and brutality of his late-night callings. Record rewards were offered for information that could lead to his arrest. Carrillo and Salerno knew he would strike again. The only question was, where?

Jack the Knife

On 18th August, another couple were found lying in their bloodsoaked bed, in a suburb of San Francisco called Lake Merced. Both had been shot in the head. The Night Stalker had left his calling card above the scene: a Pentagram had been scrawled in lipstick on the wall, along with the words *Jack the Knife* – a line from the Judas Priest song 'The Ripper' that is written from the point of view of London's Saucy Jack.

These lyrics give a clue as to where the killer's head was that night.
You'll soon shake with fear
Never knowing if I'm near
I'm sly and I'm shameless
Nocturnal and nameless
Except for the Ripper
Or if you like Jack the Knife

Peter Pan, a 66-year-old accountant, was pronounced dead at the scene. His wife, Barbara, 62, had been shot in the head for trying to resist the Stalker's sexual advances. She survived but would be paralysed for life.

The San Francisco police were devastated. It seemed the LA nightmare had moved to their patch. They sent a bullet recovered from the scene to the LAPD's forensic department. It was an exact match for those found at two of the Night Stalker's Los Angeles crime scenes.

Carrillo and Salerno were soon on the scene, only to watch on in shock as the city's mayor, Dianne Feinstein, gave a live press conference telling her citizens that the Night Stalker was at work in the Bay Area. She even gave away the secret of the Avia shoes and the ballistics, things the LA cops had deliberately wanted the press to keep quiet about. Now the Stalker could get rid of the evidence. Which he did, tossing his sneakers off the side of the Golden Gate Bridge as soon as he read the reports of the Mayor's speech in the press.

He stole a car and headed back to a small town called Mission Viejo, 50 miles south of Los Angeles.

'Swear to Satan'

Here, 29-year-old Bill Carns, a computer engineer, and his 27-year-old fiancée Carole Smith had just drifted off to sleep when loud gunfire cracked through their bedroom. The woman reached out for her fiancé, but he lay, unmoving, in a pool of blood. Before she could assimilate all this information, she was hauled from her bed by the intruder, and pulled by her hair into the spare room. The intruder bound her wrists and ankles with neckties and asked her if she knew who she was dealing with.

'I'm the Night Stalker!' he said.

'Oh God, no,' wailed Carole.

'Not God,' leered the intruder. 'Say you love Satan.'

He hog-tied her, slapping and kicking her as he did so, and then proceeded to shakedown the house, searching for anything valuable. There wasn't that much to find, so he went back to Carole to rape and sodomise her, then tied her up again.

Terrified of what he would do afterwards, the woman showed him the drawer where her fiancé kept some spare money.

'Swear to Satan that's all there is!' he screamed in return.

She did as he asked. The Stalker found the money in the drawer where she said it was. He counted it out slowly, mocking her, telling her this was all she was worth, that this was what was going to save her. But still he wasn't quite satisfied.

'Swear your love for Satan,' he demanded.

Carole mumbled her affirmative reply, terrified of what was to come. He ordered her to say it again, over and over. Then, grabbing her by the hair, he forced her to fellate him. When he was finished, he stood back and stared at her.

This is it, she thought, I'm going to die.

But instead, her tormentor just laughed and left her there.

Working her way free from the ties, Carole got to the window in time to see him driving away in an orange Toyota station wagon. She immediately called the police.

Earlier that night, the same vehicle had been noticed by a teenager, James Romero, who had been working on his motorbike outside his parents' house. It was a small town and he'd never seen the car before, nor the creepy looking guy in black driving it. When he saw it go past a second time, he made a note of the number plate. When he heard the next day about the assault on Carole Smith, he rang Orange County police.

With the number plate, the police were able to track the vehicle. It had been stolen in LA's Chinatown the night before the attack and it turned up two days later, abandoned in the Rampart section of the city. The car was kept under surveillance for 24 hours in the hope the Night Stalker would return to it. He didn't.

However, the forensics team were able to get one good fingerprint from the vehicle. They sent it down to Sacramento for analysis. Hours later, they got a match. The print belonged to Ricardo 'Richard' Muñoz Ramirez. It was the same as a print taken from the Pans' house in San Francisco. At long last, the police knew who their man really was. And it didn't take the press long to make that name, and a corresponding mugshot, public.

The wrong neighbourhood

After the last attack, the Night Stalker moved north. He wanted to steal a car and chose to go 'shopping' in East Hubbard Street, a largely Hispanic area where he may have thought he wouldn't stand out. But he chose the wrong place and the wrong person to steal from.

At first, he was unaware that his photograph had just been plastered all over the newspapers. But when he heard two elderly Mexican women referring to him in hushed voices as '*el matador*' – 'the killer' and his eyes alighted on a newsstand, he realised he was in deep trouble.

He needed to find a car quickly.

Hopping over fences in search of an easy steal, Ramirez found a red Mustang unlocked in a driveway. He jumped in and began to start the engine, without realising that the car's owner was lying underneath, working on the car.

Faustino Piñon, 56, was incensed that anyone should touch his precious motor. He jumped up and grabbed the thief by the scruff of his neck.

'I've got a gun,' Ramirez warned, but Piñon was too angry to be scared.

The Night Stalker put the car into gear and tried to drive away, but

Faustino would not let go of him. The Mustang crashed into the garage and its owner hauled the driver out, throwing him to the ground.

Fear coursing through his veins, Ramirez jumped to his feet and ran across the road, to where Angela De La Torre was getting into her Ford Granada. Waving his gun at her, he screamed in Spanish for her to give him the keys, threatening to shoot if she didn't. Their combined yells brought Angelina's husband Manuel running from the backyard. He'd brought with him a length of metal fence post.

In the meantime, neighbour Jose Burgoin had heard the fracas and called the police. He ran outside to help Piñon and when he heard Angela scream, he called to his sons Jaime, 21, and Julio, 17, to help. As they saw the skinny stranger grappling with Angela, Jaime realised who he was looking at. It was the Night Stalker.

The men gave chase, and Ramirez must have thought he was running for his life. Manuel De La Torre was first to catch up with him, and whacked him around the back of the neck with his metal pipe. High on adrenalin, the skinny kid kept running, but the older man kept pace with him, hitting him repeatedly as he did so.

Jaime Burgoin drew level with Ramirez and punched him. He stumbled, got back on his feet and kept on running.

Then, unexpectedly, he stopped and wheeled around. His eyes flashed as he laughed and stuck his tongue out at them. For a moment, his pursuers where taken aback by this mad act. Then as he tried to run away again, they gave chase. Finally, a block away from where it began, De La Torre swung hard and belted his metal pipe round Ramirez's head.

He collapsed on the ground. Jaime and Julio kept him pinned down as the police arrived.

It was over.

The making of a serial killer

Richard Ramirez was born and brought up as a good Catholic boy in the town of El Paso, Texas. He was the youngest child of five: there were three other boys – Robert, Ruben and Joseph – and a girl, Ruth. At the time he was conceived, Richard's mother Mercedes had been working in a bootmaker's factory, where she mixed the pigments for shoe dyes with chemicals that, at the time, no one realised were toxic. Her pregnancy was hard and she was forced to give up her job when she was five months' gone for the unborn baby's safety.

Ruben and Joseph had both been born in Juarez, Mexico, near the atomic bomb test sites in Los Alamos. Ruben had been born with strange lumps on his neck, which later disappeared, but Joseph had an incurable bone condition called Collier's disease, which meant his bones grew at angles and he would be faced with a lifetime of operations. He had already undergone 15 such ops when Richard was born, while Ruben had become something of a rebel who was starting to get in trouble at school. Their father, Julian Ramirez, treated his errant son the way his own father had treated him – he gave him sound beatings. As Richard grew up, Ruben and Robert would both continue to get in more and more trouble, and Julian's rage increased with the size of their crimes. Sometimes he would get so angry he would turn his rage on himself. One time, in front of his entire family, Julian began to beat his own head with a hammer until blood was flowing down his face.

The infant Richard, by comparison, was a quiet and gentle child. His sister Ruth spent hours with him, treating him like a doll, speaking to him in Spanish and English, glad of the break from her rough-and-tumble older siblings.

When Richard was two he was almost killed when he was trying to turn on the radio and the dresser it was standing on toppled over, knocking him unconscious and deeply gashing his forehead. He was out for 15 minutes and it took 30 stitches to close the wound. He would suffer another head injury at the age of five, when a swing at a playpark slammed into his head. That wound needed five stitches, and could well have led to the temporal lobe epilepsy Richard began to suffer from when he started school. He was never treated properly for his condition, which stopped when he was a teenager, and would only be properly diagnosed when he was behind bars.

Seeing monsters

At the age of seven, Richard had already developed a liking for sugary food, and normally began his day drinking cola, eating sugar-coated cereal and watching horror cartoons on TV. Sometimes, as part of his pre-mal seizures, he would hallucinate that the monsters had come out of the TV screen and were running around in the yard outside. The fear he felt when experiencing this was dismissed as a wild imagination. Richard had always been good at amusing himself.

But other than his epileptic attacks, Richard was not a bad boy at school like his brothers. He was funny, popular and worked hard until 1973, when he reached 13. At this point, very much against the wishes of his father, Richard started hanging out with his cousin Miguel, also known as Mike.

Mike was a Vietnam vet, a Green Beret who had seemingly enjoyed his tour of duty a lot more than many of his contemporaries. He boasted to Richard about the many ways he tortured and killed the enemy out there – and had the photographic evidence to prove it. Among his Polaroids were pictures of Vietnamese women forced on their hands and knees, giving Mike oral sex with the barrel of his gun pointed to their heads. He kept eight shrunken heads, which he told Richard once belonged to enemies and now he used as a pillow. His stories and photos made an indelible impact on his younger cousin. They got him excited in a way he'd never felt before.

Pot was cheap in El Paso and Richard had been getting it from his older brothers since he was ten. Now he and Mike spend long hours smoking and talking about war and killing. Mike also taught Richard how to hunt, to become at one with his surroundings, so that he could kill with stealth and absolute certainty.

Yes, Mike was one of those psychos who flourish at a time of war. He just hadn't adjusted well to civilian life, as his wife Jessie was about to find out.

Fed up with watching her husband spend all day every day getting high and hanging out with his geeky cousin, she started to nag him to get his life in order. Mike's response was to shoot her in the face right in front of Richard. Then he made his cousin leave. 'Don't you ever say you saw this,' Mike yelled. 'Do you understand?' Richard said not a word to anyone.

Mike was ultimately convicted for this act of cold-blooded murder, but the judge went lenient on his sentencing, after his lawyer pleaded that the stress of his Vietnam experiences had unhinged Mike's mind. He was found guilty by reason of insanity and committed to a mental home.

Richard didn't stay long in El Paso after that. Without Mike to provide the highs, he started skipping school, stealing to fund his pot habit. Eventually, the restrictions of smalltown life got too much for him. He left El Paso and like so many dreamers before him, headed for the bright lights of Los Angeles, where his brother Ruben had already been blazing a trail.

Heavy metal thunder

Because of an earlier heroin habit, Ruben had already infiltrated the world of criminals who hung out at the city's bus terminal, fencing their goods, buying their drugs and pimping their women. In the neon wilderness of Los Angeles, he taught Richard the tricks he had learned about breaking into houses and bypassing alarms. Coupled with Mike's hunting skills, Richard soon became an adept cat burglar, able to blend in with the night, using the cover of trees and fences to hide while he cased out likely houses to burgle.

When Ruben and Richard fell out, over an argument about Ruben's wife, Richard carried on with his new profession. It wasn't just to keep himself alive though. There was something about being in other people's houses while they thought they were safe in their beds. Something about being able to stand over them while they were at their most vulnerable, knowing that in an instant he could take away their lives. Sneak-thieving was how his murderous fetishism began. And he had a soundtrack to score his fantasy world.

Heavy metal was big business in mid-Eighties America and two stadium-filling acts were favoured by the teenage Ramirez. One was the aforementioned Judas Priest. These Birmingham metallers went down particularly well in middle America, where they were vastly more successful then they were back in Britain. Lost on many of their American fans was the cartoonish aspect of the Priest, whose juvenile delinquent anthems like 'Breakin' The Law' combined classic Black Country rifforama with the theatrical, high-pitched singing of Rob Halford, a man dressed from head to foot in leather and spikes who usually rode onto stage on the back of a gigantic Harley.

Being the Night Stalker's music of choice wasn't the only time the unfortunate band landed themselves in trouble with Americans all too willing to confuse 'Satanism' with parental neglect. In 1989, a court case was brought against the band by the parents of James Varley, a teenager who tried to commit suicide by blowing his face off with a shotgun and was left with severe facial deformities as a result. Varley's parents claimed their son was 'driven' to this act by repeatedly listening to Priest's *Stained Class* album, which apparently contained backwards-masked messages urging him to 'do it, do it, do it.'

Actually, as the court found out, Varley was an extremely troubled teenager, who had a history of running away from home after conflicts with his step-father, a recovering alcoholic. He had no contact with his real father, and his mother admitted to hitting him frequently when he was small enough for her to do so. In the year leading up to the shooting, as a result of his increasingly violent nature, his school had asked his mother to put him forward for psychiatric help. He later admitted that at this time he had been taking reams of uppers like cocaine, speed and barbiturates along with the extreme hallucinogen, PCP. Judas Priest were completely exonerated.

Ramirez's other favourites were the Australian band AC/DC, who, while being a great deal less theatrical than Judas Priest, also laced their lyrics with comical images of Satan. Their first LP, and the only one to be recorded with original singer Bon Scott – a rock'n'roll bad boy who died choking on his own vomit after a drinking binge at the age of 34 – was called *Highway to Hell*. This was Ramirez's favourite, and it contained the track that would furnish him with his sobriquet 'The Night Stalker'.

The lyrics *Was that a noise outside your window?/ What's that shadow on the blind?/ As you lie there naked like a body in a tomb/ suspended animation as I slip into your room* provided him with an unfortunately fertile soundtrack. At his arrest, he told officer George Thomas: 'Of course I did it. So what? Shoot me, I deserve to die,' before humming the chorus of this song.

Judas Priest and AC/DC were merely providing a typical teenage outlet of hormones and hard guitars. Despite their macho posturing, Rob Halford was actually gay and AC/DC is Australian slang for bisexual, which perhaps gives a clue as to how unseriously their lyrics were supposed to be taken. But to the ears of Ramirez, these fantasies were the heroic acts of men who lived outside the law, black-clad outlaws who scorned society and never had to face the penalties of living within it. Men who were doing the Devil's work.

Hail Satan!

Ramirez, like David Berkowitz before him, was also a fan of Anton La Vey. He had first read *The Satanic Bible* when he was 18 and a cokehead burglar living in a flophouse in LA. He was so impressed he immediately stole a car and took off for San Francisco, where he hoped he could finally fit in with other people who felt the way he did.

He claimed that he had attended a ritual at La Vey's Black House in which the Black Mass was performed over the body of a naked woman. Ramirez said he felt the 'ice-cold hand of Satan' touch him, marking him out as a disciple. Anton La Vey confirmed that he had met the teenage Night Stalker. 'I thought Richard was very nice – very shy. I liked him,' he recalled.

We are legion

After that, Ramirez would always identify himself as a Satanist. At his arraignment in October 1985, he appeared in court flashing a Pentagram sign on his palm, shouting: 'Hail Satan!' When news of his arrest made headlines around America, Ramirez was deluged with letters from other self-styled Satanists praising his actions, often from women who wanted to get intimate with him. Zeena La Vey, daughter of Anton, went to meet him in jail as he awaited trial. Her father, she told him, was very proud of him and was praying to Satan for him. They made him an honorary member of their Church.

It took three years and over $1million to bring the Night Stalker to trial. During that time he dismissed a series of experienced public defenders and instead appointed two wholly inexperienced attorneys who were friends of his family, Daniel and Arturo Hernandez. To the chagrin of prosecutor Philip Halpin – who had been co-counsel on the Charles Manson case – the Hernandezes stalled for time at every step of the way. Ramirez had initially decided to plead guilty – he didn't want his family to know the details of what he'd been charged with; he'd convinced them he was an innocent victim of police racism, even though Detective Carrillo was as Mexican as he was. But the Hernandezes convinced him to change his plea to not guilty.

On his arrest, the 26-year-old Ramirez had been charged with 14 murders and 36 other serious related crimes, including rape, sodomy, burglary and attempted murder. By the time he actually came to trial, 18 charges, including three abduction-molestation counts and one robbery, in which the victim had since died, had been dropped. Richard saw that as a sign that Satan was watching his back. At every pre-trail hearing his legion of groupies grew in number. For those that could remember it, this was like the Manson trial all over again.

Trials and tribulations

Jury selection took six months and it wasn't until 10th January 1989 that the trial could finally begin. Judge Michael Tynan presided, Alan Yochelson joined Philip Halpin prosecuting, and public defender Ray Clark was ordered to assist Daniel Hernandez after Arturo stopped showing up regularly. The Hernandezes (who were not related but many took to be brothers) had taken on the case to attract attention to their fledgling business. They had no capital from the Ramirez family, other than an agreement that any money to be made from film or book rights about Richard's life would be turned over to them. In the years it had taken to get to court, they had lost, rather than gained, business, and Arturo was out trying to drum up new clients when he should have been working the Night Stalker case.

Halpin outlined his case in minute detail. He called upon 137 witnesses and 521 exhibits, including fingerprints and the Avia shoeprints taken from crime scenes. Jack Vincow, Maria Hernandez, Carol Kye, Sophie Dickman, Somkid Khovananth, Virginia Petersen and Sakina Abowath all testified, as well as a string of criminals who had fenced jewellery for Ramirez. When the first reward was offered for information about the Stalker, they hadn't been backwards in coming forwards.

The defence that the Hernandezes had prepared was simple, in every sense of the word. The witnesses, even Carol, Sophie, Somkid and Sakina who had all been viciously raped and beaten by Ramirez, had got the wrong man.

The trouble was, Lucifer's poster boy had been a bit too devout. He had asked his victims to swear allegiance to Satan. He had left the Pentagram, the mark of the Beast, not just at crime scenes – he'd flashed it at the courtroom as well. Towards the end of the hearings, when Zeena La Vey and a host of acolytes swept into the courtroom to lend Ramirez their support, the jurors couldn't help feeling intimidated. Nor could they help themselves from thinking back to their youth, when southern California had quaked at the weird powers of the Manson clan.

The jury had heard almost a year's worth of evidence when the summing up finished on 25th July. But they had only been retired a few days when their fears would seemingly be realised. One of their number, Phyllis Singletary, was murdered on the night of 13th August. Rumours spread like wildfire that one of Ramirez's groupies had committed the crime and that other jurors would taste the same Satanic justice if they didn't vote to acquit the Night Stalker.

In fact, Phyllis had been killed by her jealous boyfriend, 51-year-old James C Melton, who had long been abusing her both physically and mentally. After he had dispatched Phyllis with two gunshots to the chest, Melton shot himself through the head. He left a suicide note, which blamed a row over Ramirez for the killings. But that wouldn't be the end of the strangeness that overcame certain members of the Ramirez jury.

'See you in Disneyland'

On 20th September, the jury had completed their arduous task. They found Richard Ramirez guilty of every charge brought against him. Nineteen of those counts made him eligible for the death penalty, and next they would be asked to vote on that.

Daniel Hernandez and Ray Clark tried to get their client to work with them at this stage of the proceedings, for if he didn't offer any mitigating circumstances, they knew he would be condemned. But the Stalker had had enough of his attorneys. 'Dying doesn't scare me,' he told them. 'I'll be in Hell, with Satan.'

So, on 3rd October, when the jury unanimously voted for the death penalty, Ramirez smiled through the sobs of his coterie of admirers and said: 'Big deal. Death always went with the territory.' As he was led in shackles back to his cell, he told the swarm of reporters that surrounded him: 'See you in Disneyland.'

He would elaborate further at his official sentencing on 9th October, reading out a pre-prepared speech to the court:

'You do not understand me. I do not expect you to. You are not capable of it. I am beyond your experience. I am beyond good and evil. Legions of the night, night breed, repeat not the errors of night prowler and show no mercy. I will be avenged. Lucifer dwells within us all.'

Sobbing along with his groupies, juror Cynthia Haden was convinced she had made a terrible mistake. She had followed the word of the law and done her duty by sending this killer to Death Row. But she was tormented by the poor representation the Hernandezes had given, which had led her to this pretty pass. And something else. Cynthia would later confess that she had 'fallen in love' with Ramirez the moment she laid eyes on him. Nothing in the trial that followed, no act of depravity, sadism or cruelty had been too much to dissuade her heart. Cynthia was besotted. And she was not the only one.

The handmaidens of Satan

When Ramirez was transferred to San Quentin, the legendary big house that overlooks the aptly-named Bay of Skulls in San Francisco, two women uprooted their lives to be near him. One was Cynthia Haden, who was so consumed by her guilt at giving Richard the death sentence that she would re-train as a private detective, to try and ensure such 'miscarriages of justice' could never occur again. The other was a devout Roman Catholic virgin called Doreen Lioy, who had devoted her life to proclaiming Ramirez's innocence ever since she saw his arrest photos and 'knew in her heart' he was innocent.

Doreen had attended every day of Ramirez's trial, and visited him as often as she could while he was held in custody. She was on a mission to become Mrs Ramirez, and she had the blessing of the Ramirez family after forging a solid friendship with Richard's sister Ruth during the Los Angeles trial.

Doreen was disowned by her own family when she moved to San Francisco. But she didn't care. The former magazine researcher, who has an IQ of 152 and a Bachelor's degree in English, had more pressing worries than that. She had to get Cynthia, and Richard's other admirers, out of the way first. It was a long battle, but she won.

On 3rd October 1996, 41-year-old Doreen finally married 36-year-old Richard at a civic ceremony inside San Quentin. She was beside herself with joy. She had even been thoughtful enough to purchase her new husband a platinum wedding ring, because 'Satanists don't wear gold.'

It is probably very lucky for Doreen that Death Row prisoners are not allowed conjugal rights.

All in the Family

For detectives Gil Carrillo and Frank Salerno, Richard Ramirez was the worst criminal they had ever dealt with in their long and distinguished careers. He had eclipsed the Hillside Stranglers in their depravity and rivalled Manson in his ability to get inside people's minds using rock star imagery and the potent power of danger. Like David Berkowitz and Robin Gecht, Ramirez was a big fan of Jack the Ripper, and he more than any other killer has succeeded in becoming almost as big a pop culture icon.

The Satanism he professes is no pose but a genuine conviction. Ramirez told Philip Carlo, author of his most thorough biography *The Night Stalker*, that he believes that when he dies he will descend to the left hand of Satan, and sit amongst the people he most admires – Saucy Jack, Adolph Hitler, Ted Bundy and John Wayne Gacy.

Ramirez also presents perhaps the most perfect profile of a serial killer – the head trauma suffered as a child, his untreated epilepsy, the violence of his father and the overwhelming influence of his psychotic cousin at the moment he reached puberty. That the troubles he was already carrying around his head fused a soundtrack of heavy metal and a carnival barker's flashy doctrine of Satanism, that he dressed like a rock star and used society's worst fears to fuel his killing campaign, made him appear as a glamorous rebel to those disaffected enough to turn him into a pin-up.

But how many of his admirers would actually want him to appear on their doorstep at midnight? Would they welcome him over the threshold? Would they like the life of Virginia Petersen, who considers herself the 'luckiest woman' to survive a Ramirez attack, and testified thus at his sentencing:

'My daughter was four years old in 1985...I can still hear her screams of terror during the shooting and her crying "Mommy, please don't die, please don't die," while I was bleeding uncontrollably in front of her. When we were released from the hospital I reached for her, but she recoiled at my face, saying, "You're not my mommy, you are ugly." That wounded me worse than any gun could have... In kindergarten, she came to me one day to talk over something that was troubling her. She told me she could understand why people killed themselves because she hurt inside because of what the bad man had done.'

There is only one thing that could possibly hurt the Night Stalker so badly. The fact that he wasn't like Jack the Ripper, cunning enough to flee into the annals of infamy unmasked and untried. The fact that Satan let Richard Ramirez get caught.

Chapter Five

⟷

Tracey Wigginton and Lisa Ptaschinski: Daughters of Darkness (1989)

The Terror of Tiny Town

I n the late Eighties, Brisbane in Queensland was a place that could be accurately described as the Deep South of Australia. This was a state built on cotton and cane, worked on the backs of imported slave labour. And reactionary attitudes still lingered, malignantly, in the sub-tropical heat.

For over twenty years, the state had been ruled by a fundamentalist Lutheran peanut farmer called Johannes Bjelke-Petersen, head of the Nationalist Party, who was defiantly out of step with prevailing liberal attitudes in the rest of Australia. After a disastrous campaign to run as Prime Minister, Bjelke-Petersen had only just been unseated by the 1988 Fitzgerald commission into police and political corruption.

Dodgy insider dealing, union busting, hippy bashing and unaccountable, brutal policing were all hallmarks of the Bjelke-Petersen years, and earned Brisbane the succinct soubriquet 'Pig City' from the punk song of the same name by local heroes The Parameters.

There was plenty to rebel against in Brisbane, but you had to have a nerve to do it. Queensland was full of right wing gun nuts like the Confederate Action Party and the One Nation party, who even managed to get a representative in the Federal Senate on their immigrant-bashing ticket. But corrupt regimes can make for great art – Brisbane also spawned one of Australia's greatest ever bands, The Saints, who made the country's first punk rock record in 1977, the ferocious and self-explanatory *I'm Stranded*.

By 1989, punk rock had mutated into various alternative subcultures, represented by the freaks and heads that mingled around an area of Brisbane called Fortitude Valley, but generally referred to as the Valley. It was a busy stretch of clubs, illegal gambling dens, cafés, brothels and strip joints, all owned by a mixture of Italian mobsters and Chinese Triads, with the cops being paid off from both sides.

The most prominent customers in the clubs and gay bars were known as 'Swampies' – Goth/psychedelic crossbreeds named after the song 'Swampland' by Perth's The Scientists, a band who looked back to the acid-fried end of the Sixties for inspiration. Swampies were visions in paisley shirts and pointy boots, little round dark glasses and lots of hair to hide behind. Goths, who had further homegrown talent like Melbourne's Nick Cave and the Bad Seeds to look up to for style tips, came a close crimped-and-patchouli-oiled second.

These creatures of the night mingled in straight clubs like Mortitia's and gay bars such as the Set, Club Lewmors and Terminus on Brunswick Street, at the heart of The Valley. The gay clubs were safe havens for effeminate straights that were just as likely to get queer-bashed for not looking 'normal' in Brisbane. They provided an atmosphere of tolerance and cool music in which the city's more rebellious sons and daughters could mingle, drink, dance and conspire.

Only, over one night in November 1989, a coterie of young women met inside Club Lewmors and hatched a plot that would bring fear to the heart of Tiny Town. Individually, these women would probably have just remained oddballs on the fringes of society, who dressed weird and liked to make out that they dabbled in the dark arts. But when they got together, it was murder – mad, lesbian vampire murder.

Last orders

On the night of 20th October, 47-year-old Edward Clyde Baldock was doing what he usually did on a Friday night – having a drink and a game of darts with his mates at the proudly Scottish Caledonian Club. Baldock, a council road paver, was a father of five, who had recently celebrated his silver wedding anniversary. He worked on flexi-time so that he could spend his Fridays out with the lads, and though he was likely to roll home somewhat merry, he never stayed out much later than last orders.

Which was why, when she woke up alone in the early hours of the next morning, Mrs Elaine Baldock knew there was something very wrong. She was so sure of her instinct, she picked up the phone and called the police.

Her Edward was never to make it back home that night or any other. He had been intercepted on his way home, picked out by a group of young women out cruising in a green Holden Commodore Sedan, looking for a likely mark.

Someone to make a human sacrifice of.

A couple of early morning joggers and a solicitor out for a row at the South Brisbane Sailing Club found his body at 8am on 21st October in Orleigh Park, on the banks of the Brisbane river. He had been stripped naked and stabbed repeatedly around the head and neck, with such a frenzy that he was almost decapitated. What could this poor, unremarkable man possibly have done to inspire such a violent end?

But even as the police sealed off the area and television cameras moved in to hover over Baldock's blood-splattered corpse, one of those responsible for his untimely death was already hanging around the scene in the nervous certainty that she had done something terribly stupid to give herself away.

Tracey Avril Wigginton was right. For even as she watched, Detective Senior Sergeant Pat Glancy was plucking her bankcard out of the dead man's shoe.

Friday the 13th

The events that led up to Brisbane's most notorious murder began on Friday 13th October, when a full moon was riding high over the city and four young women with an interest in the occult came together at the lilac-fronted Club Lewmors.

Kim Jervis and her girlfriend Tracey Waugh, both 23, were regulars on the scene. Jervis, who worked as a photo processor by day, was a flamboyant Goth, dressed that night in black and purple satin with striking, back-and-white make-up. Kim had covered her skin in myriad tattoos and her wrists, throat and fingers were adorned with Pentagram jewellery and other magical symbols.

Waugh, an unemployed secretary, cut a much plainer, more subdued figure. She didn't dress up and she rarely drank, eschewed drugs and took a backseat in conversations. Not that she would have much chance of joining in on this particular night.

For dominating the discourse was six-foot-tall, 17-stone Tracey Wigginton, a 24-year-old student sheet metal worker the duo had met in August at the Set, when Wigginton was the new girl in town. With a shared interest in Satanism and witchcraft, Jervis and Wigginton had hit it off immediately. But perhaps to diffuse any sexual tension that might be lingering on this night, Kim had brought another friend along to meet with her.

Lisa Ptaschinski, 24, was another large, hulking character who had found it hard to fit in wherever she went. She had gone through a brief, unhappy heterosexual marriage before she came out as a lesbian, but even acknowledging her true sexuality had not seemed to bring Lisa any peace of mind. She was frequently depressed and had been admitted to hospital 82 times in the past five years for what seemed to be suicide bids – a heroin overdose and once even a stomach full of razor blades. Lisa was attracted to Tracey as soon as they met.

'She has a strange attraction,' Ptaschinski would later say. 'I don't know what. She dominated me more than anyone has in my life. She had some kind of inner power.'

They talked that night of the strange conjunction between a full moon and the ominous date, as if destiny had brought them together for some greater purpose. They talked of witchcraft and horror movies, delighted in the fact that they were of a similar mind, when all about them was so backwards, so safe and boring. When the Club closed for the night, Ptaschinksi left with Wigginton, to consummate their relationship while the hunter's moon still waxed in the sky.

Twisted sisters

The truth of what happened between the two of them over the next couple of weeks can probably never be properly ascertained. But Lisa's bizarre testimony of her brief but overwhelming relationship with Wigginton would form the basis of a modern Australian folk legend.

After they had made love for the first time, Lisa claimed that Tracey complained of being hungry. Only she wasn't about to do the usual thing of ringing for a takeaway pizza. She said that she didn't eat normal food. Instead she collected animal's blood from butcher's shops and sustained herself on that. Knowing Ptaschinski had been a heroin user, she asked her to wrap a tourniquet around her arm and pump up a vein. Then she nicked Lisa's wrist and feasted on her blood.

This was, Lisa would later claim, the first of four such bizarre meal requests.

'I wanted to keep the relationship going,' she would say in her defence. 'I wanted to keep in her good books. If you're going out with someone, you do what you can to please them.'

Jervis and Waugh would also add to these vampire stories, maintaining that during the brief time they knew her, Tracey refused to go out in daylight and avoided mirrors. 'Tracey has a mind power,' Waugh would claim. 'She has a hold on you. She is like a magnet. You can't stop yourself from doing what she tells you to.'

But all these pleas would be made later, in the cold light of day and police custody. For the time being, Lisa, Kim and Tracey Waugh were happy enough to be swept along by whatever claim to infernal powers Wigginton may have been making.

On 18th October, only five days after the quartet's initial meeting, the women convened at Jervis' flat in the suburb of Clayfield. Tracey had a plan to put to them that night, and though the other three would later paint a pretty grim picture of what that was, none of them appear to have recoiled from it at the time.

'Become the Destroyer'

Kim's flat was a good setting for a coven. A collection of dolls stared glassy eyed from walls adorned with pictures of cemeteries. A tombstone, filched from a local graveyard, rested in the fireplace. The four women sipped Sambuca as Wigginton revealed what she wanted them to do.

The Devil, she said, wanted her to become the Destroyer. In order to fulfil her destiny, she must find a human victim, kill them and drink their blood. She had thought of a foolproof and simple plan to carry out her mission.

Tracey Waugh and Lisa would pose as prostitutes and use their charms to lure a victim – a man or a woman, chosen at random – into one of Brisbane's parks. Once they had found a secluded enough spot, Wigginton and Jervis would drink the mark's blood.

When it was over, they would take the drained body to a cemetery and find a freshly-dug grave. They would toss their victim into the hole and cover the corpse with a layer of soil. That way, a coffin would be lowered over the top the next day and hide their dirty deed without anyone being the wiser. The person would simply have vanished into thin air.

They all agreed that the plan seemed foolproof. Indeed, Wigginton already had her murder weapon ready – a small, silver butterfly knife, bought from a martial arts shop. A few days later, Jervis bought herself an identical blade.

They met up again on the evening of 20th October, again at the Club Lewmors. Finding a secluded table at the back of the grim-looking, concrete bunker of a club, they toasted their plan with two bottles of champagne. Even that seemed strange to the manageress who served them. Bettina Lewis had been familiar with Kim and Tracey Waugh's usual drinking habits for the past two years. 'I found that unusual,' she said. 'I had never served them champagne before.' If they hadn't wanted to draw attention to themselves that night then they'd already made a bad start.

They finished their drinks and left at 11.30pm.

Night of the huntress

Just after midnight, Edward Baldock staggered out of the Caledonian Club. He was in his cups. He held onto a lamppost for support as Wigginton's large green car swept past and fixed him in its headlights.

She had been cruising through the Botanic Gardens and the New Farm Park for the past twenty minutes, on the lookout for likely prey, listening to Prince's 'Batdance' on the stereo as they crossed the Story Bridge and drove up River Terrace towards Kangaroo Point.

The pudgy, middle-aged drunk swaying in front of her now looked like laughably easy prey. Wigginton stopped the car.

She and Kim approached Baldock, asked him if he was looking for a good time. Their insinuation of what that might mean was clear. He got into the backseat of the car with Wigginton and held onto her hand.

Lisa took the wheel and the car drove on in silence, four miles to Orleigh Park in the West End, very near to where Baldock actually lived. Ptaschinski stopped the motor underneath a large fig tree at the deserted South Brisbane Sailing Club.

Wigginton repeated her offer.

'Do you wanna have a good time?'

Baldock responded in the affirmative and they walked together down to the riverbank.

Wigginton was back at the car five minutes later.

'I need some help,' she said. 'The bastard's too strong.'

Lisa didn't want to let her lover down. She took Kim's knife from her and went down to the water's edge.

To the slaughter

Their victim was sitting on the sand, naked except for his socks, wondering what was going on. The women crept up behind him, knives at the ready. But when it came to the moment she was supposed to plunge the blade in, Lisa could not bring herself to attack the vulnerable, confused old drunkard in front of her. Instead she collapsed at his feet, babbling incoherently.

Wigginton was not impressed. She would later describe to psychiatrists what happened next. 'I took my knife out of my back pocket. He asked me what I was doing. I said nothing and stabbed him...I withdrew the knife and stabbed him on the side of the neck. I stabbed him on the other side of his neck, and I continuously stabbed him. I then grabbed him by the hair and pulled him back, stabbing him in the front of the throat...at that stage he was still alive.'

Wigginton's attempts to kill became more frenzied. 'I stabbed him in the back of the neck again, trying to get into the bones, I presume, and cut the nerves. Then I sat...and watched him die.'

By then, Baldock was almost completely decapitated.

According to Ptaschinski, Wigginton then told her to get back to the car and wait while she drank Baldock's blood. This was something that Wigginton herself never mentioned to police or the many psychiatrists who later questioned her at length about her motives. But the other women would be adamant that Tracey had feasted on the corpse, then washed herself clean in the river. Waugh said she could smell the blood on Wigginton's breath as they drove back to Kim's flat. Jervis added that their friend had looked 'satisfied, like a person would if they had just sat down to a three-course dinner'.

But any air of composure would soon turn to panic, when, back at Jervis' flat, Wigginton realised she no longer had her bankcard. She made Lisa turn straight around and accompany her back to scene of the crime.

Yellow card, blue light

No one had yet chanced upon the ruined body of Edward Baldock when Wigginton and Ptaschinski returned to the scene. But though they scoured the area as best they could in the dark, they couldn't find the tell-tale piece of plastic anywhere.

That was because, drunk though he may have been, Baldock still had a reserve of his natural reticence. He had not entirely trusted the motivation of these girls to bring him out to the park for some no-strings sex, and somewhere at the back of his mind, he thought they would probably try to rob him. So, while Wigginton went back to the car, he had taken out his wallet and hidden it behind the metal swing doors of the Sailing Club. As he did so, he found a credit card lying on the ground. The yellow livery of the Commonwealth bank was familiar; he banked there himself, and must have assumed it was his own card that had somehow got dislodged from his wallet. A naturally fastidious man, Baldock slipped it inside his shoe, which he placed beside the neatly folded pile of his clothes.

Searching desperately in the dark, it was the last place Wigginton and her lover would have thought to look. After a while, Tracey convinced herself that she must have lost the card somewhere else on their travels that night. She ordered Lisa back into the car and they drove back along the eerie riverside road, a place where illicit lovers steamed up the windows of parked cars, and voyeurs hung out in search of them. Because of its seedy rep, patrol cars often cruised this lover's lane. Lisa and Tracey drove straight into a blue light.

It was just a police routine, checking for drunk drivers and stolen vehicles. But in their panic to retrieve Tracey's card from the murder site, the women had forgotten to bring their relevant papers back out with them. When Lisa was asked for her driving licence, she could only sit there in a cold sweat while the details of the car were taken down and she was breathalysed. Similarly, Tracey could not present her ownership documents.

It must have seemed like an eternity before the cops let them drive on, with the caveat that the relevant documents would have to be handed in at the police station first thing in the morning.

The women returned to Jervis' flat shaking and frightened. It had only taken hours for their 'perfect crime' to unravel into a nightmare and now they were sure the cops would connect their car to the murdered body such a short distance back down the river. In a blind panic, they began to cobble together the alibis they would give if they were taken in for questioning.

Body of evidence

By 8am, Elaine Baldock received the call she had been dreading when she had woken up alone at 5pm. Three detectives stood on her doorstep, with news that the body of a man matching her husband's description had been found at the South Brisbane Sailing Club.

Someone else had been unable to sleep. As she watched the sun come up, Tracey Wigginton's instincts kept screaming to her that the lost card was still somewhere out there, by the body. She could sense that big trouble was headed her way, the way it had been all her life. Tormented, and unwilling to bother the others any more, she slipped back out alone, hoping against hope she would get back to Baldock's corpse before anyone else did.

But the crime scene tape was already up and a crowd had accumulated around the body.

Wigginton knew as soon as she saw it that her time was up. But she wanted to warn her friends, have some time to get the crux of their alibis straight before the inevitable happened. She turned on her heel and stalked back to Kim's flat.

But already, the police had her Commonwealth card. And it didn't take them long to establish that the green Holden that had been stopped in the area in the early hours of this morning was registered to the same person.

By 1pm Tracey Wigginton was back at the Sailing Club for the fourth time in 12 hours. Only this time she was there to talk to detectives, who videotaped everything she said to them as she tried to defend the strange series of coincidences.

At first, she attempted to stick to her hastily-assembled alibi, but it came out so gabbled and strange it was hardly creditable.

Herself and Kim Jervis, she said, had been out at Orleigh Park the day before – but not in the night time. When asked if she had been anywhere near the vicinity of the body, she blabbed: 'Well, I can't remember exactly, but Kimmie and I were sort of racing around this area here...'

Wigginton couldn't stand up to interrogation. She admitted that she had been in the park the previous evening, and she had 'stumbled over' a body in the dark but had been 'too frightened' to report it to the police.

None of which explained what her bankcard was doing in Edward Baldock's shoe.

It was only a matter of time before she caved in and confessed.

The turn of the screw

Big, tough Tracey Wigginton was not the only one of the gang of four who was about to bow under the pressure of their fatal secret. Lisa Ptaschinski was out pacing the streets, not knowing what to do with herself. She was supposed to be handing in her driver's licence, but the memories of the night before and the pressure of providing an alibi were all too much for her frazzled, sleep-deprived brain to take. So instead, she handed herself in at the Ipswich police station, about 30 miles out of central Brisbane.

By 7pm that day, both women had been charged with the murder of Edward Baldock, with Jervis and Waugh soon to follow. Only Waugh was allowed bail.

Because she had confessed to the murder shortly after she'd been taken in, Tracey Wigginton was charged separately from her accomplices, who all denied they had acted willingly in any part of this sordid story. From what the investigating detectives and psychiatrists had already heard from Wigginton, they had quickly realised there was something badly wrong with this woman.

Facing the prospect of life imprisonment, Ptaschinski, Jervis and Waugh turned on their leader with ferocity. After all, Brisbane in 1989 was not the sort of enlightened place where three lesbians accused of murdering a respectable family man were going to get much in the way of sympathy from the general population.

But if there could be something worse than being gay, something more diabolical abroad in this fundamentalist heartland, then surely they could be seen as the victims they all insisted they were? When in Salem, it's better to cry witch. From the moment Wigginton's accomplices were brought in for questioning, the vampire legends began.

Meanwhile, the psychiatrists talking to Tracey Wigginton were hearing quite a different story.

Motherless child

Tracey Avril Wigginton was born in 1965, in the city of Rockhampton, Queensland – a place that grew up around vast cattle ranches, known as the 'Beef Capital of Australia'. Her mother, Rhonda, was the adopted daughter of self-made millionaire George Wigginton, which maybe should have foretold that Tracey had an idyllic childhood full of privilege. But her father, Bill Rossborough, was a drifter who had no intention of being tied down. He left Rhonda when Tracey was very young, and it wasn't very long before Rhonda had tired of the pressures of being a single mother. When Tracey was six years old, she was deposited into the care of her maternal grandparents.

George and Avril Wigginton were not your archetypal sweet old couple, although they already had two other adopted young girls, Dorelle and Michelle, entrusted into their care. Their genteel, moneyed exterior was a front that hid a house full of malice, jealousy and sexual and physical violence. George was a womaniser, and Avril was consumed by hatred for him because of it. What little affection the woman had left was lavished upon her three chihuahua dogs. Her bitterness and loathing was taken out on the three pretty young girls she was supposed to be taking care of.

Dorelle later described what went on behind closed doors. 'We were flogged with the ironing cord. It wasn't a normal flogging...the beatings went on and on...[Avril] tried to poison our minds, telling us men were bastards.'

As if that wasn't enough, Tracey would later tell psychiatrists that her grandfather began sexually abusing her when she was eight years old.

As she reached adolescence, Tracey's behaviour rapidly deteriorated. She was expelled from High School for molesting other pupils, and perhaps as an attempt to straighten her out, was sent to the strict Sisters of Mercy Range Catholic College. She didn't fare any better under the watchful eyes of the nuns; the other children thought she was a weirdo, and she decided to live up to that image by flaunting her lesbianism.

Tracey left College at 17, and began to call herself 'Bobby', dressing like a man and acting tough. She vandalised her grandparents' property and became physically violent towards her mother on the rare occasions that she saw her. By the time she was 21, both Avril and George were dead, and she inherited over £35,000 from their estate. Tracey took off to the Northern Queensland resort of Cairns, far away from her old life, and took up a job bouncing on the door of a gay club.

Bad girl Bobby

But Bobby went through her inheritance quickly and recklessly. As the money ran out, the woman she was living with deserted her, and she was left alone and confused. Thinking that a child of her own might fill the void, she asked John O'Hara, the owner of the club where she worked, if he would get her pregnant. He agreed, but just to prove she wasn't going all heterosexual, they had sex in front of an audience of 'close friends'. Bobby succeeded in getting pregnant, only to have a miscarriage.

Feeling more alone and alienated than ever, Tracey shed the image of Bobby and moved away to Brisbane, where she began another self-destructive relationship with a woman called Donna Staib. Although they lived together, Donna didn't want their affair to be mutually exclusive, a fact that preyed upon Tracey's already deeply troubled mind.

As a reaction, she deliberately sought out sado-masochistic encounters, where she could repeat the traumas of her childhood by being beaten and humiliated. Staib would later testify to the Queensland Mental Health Tribunal that the mood swings she witnessed in Wigginton were all depressive, not violent. Tracey would often curl up in a foetal position and stare into space for hours. She could become so introverted that she would lock herself away for days on end, refusing to talk to anyone, drawing pictures of movie monsters like mummies and vampires acting out gruesome tableaux.

Tracey was in the midst of this relationship when she became involved with Lisa Ptaschinski.

Once she was under arrest, the authorities had to decide whether Tracey Wigginton was clinically insane. She was placed under hypnosis for a series of interviews lasting a total of 26 hours, in which four conflicting personalities emerged. These were 'Big Tracey', a depressed adult, 'Young Tracey', a timid child of eight, 'Bobby', the aggressive murderess and 'The Observer', a cool, detached watcher over the rest of her pack.

It was as Bobby that Tracey revealed that her rage against herself, society and her family had formed her murderous motivation. When she was stabbing Edward Baldock she was stabbing the grandfather who raped her, the grandmother who thrashed her and the mother who left her in their treacherous care.

Myths and mental illness

Dr James Clarke, a clinical psychologist and hypnosis expert, came to the opinion that Wigginton was suffering from a multiple-personality syndrome, and was therefore not legally guilty of murder.

Her arresting officer, Detective Senior Constable Nick Austin, had an entirely different perspective. After interrogating her for six hours, he formed the opinion that Tracey was 'a very calculating woman. She had her story already made up and only admitted things she knew we knew. It didn't worry us, but she could unnerve other people, a typical, psychopathic personality.'

The arguments went back and forth. The sado-masochistic streak that Tracey revealed under hypnosis was considered by some of her evaluators to be at odds with the dominant, forceful personality that had come across in other interviews. That is to misunderstand the underlying behaviour with the sexual etiquette of fetishists. On the S&M scene, it is widely understood that it is the 'bottom', the 'submissive' partner who controls the 'top' or 'dominant'. Being beaten up in a ritualistic way, for someone like Tracey, would be a method of relaxing, of switching off and enjoying the pretence of relinquishing control. A way of turning the pain and subsequent sexual abuse she had suffered as a helpless child into something she could gain pleasure and power over as an adult. It is usually only the very domineering and powerful who seek out their secret sexual kicks this way.

Tracey's mother Rhonda made an impassioned plea on her daughter's behalf. 'All I want to get across to people is that she is not an evil person. She is not a vampire and she did not drink blood.'

Dr Clarke and Dr James Quinn, who performed the interviews with Tracey while she was under hypnosis, did not just rely on what they had heard to form their diagnosis. They pointed out that the abandonment, cruelty and sexual abuse of her childhood had formed her emotional instability.

But the Queensland Supreme Court Judge Mr Justice Ryan, Dr Norman Connell and Dr Gordon Urqhuart also interviewed Wigginton. After they considered all the reports before them, they decided that Tracey did not qualify as legally insane.

In January 1991, Tracey Avril Wigginton pleaded guilty to murder and was given a life sentence, to be served at Brisbane's Women's Jail.

The shadow of the vampire

The only other defendant who would undergo similarly exhaustive psychiatric analysis in this case was Lisa Ptaschinski. Because she had such a lengthy history of self-harm, including patterns of intense, unstable relationships, self-mutilation and recurrent suicide attempts, she fit the criteria of someone suffering from borderline personality disorder. Dr Peter Mulholland, consultant psychiatrist with the Royal Brisbane Hospital, considered she merited this diagnosis.

But another expert disputed this. Dr Francis Vargeese of the Princess Alexandra Hospital disagreed. 'I do not believe that a personality disorder constitutes an abnormality of the mind. It is a variation of the human personality structure,' he told the Queensland Mental Health Tribunal.

Lisa's testimony to her psychiatrists had been full of lurid stories about Wigginton's vampirism, including the blood-drinking rituals. She maintained throughout that she genuinely believed her former girlfriend was a supernatural being possessed of terrifying powers, and had been so afraid of her she was forced to comply with her murderous urges.

This was what the sceptical Dr Vargeese was disputing. Because, although Wigginton didn't deny that she had an interest in the Occult and Satanism, she made no claims whatsoever about vampirism during the entire course of her interviews.

The implication was clear: Lisa was bad, not mad. She was making up tall stories to hide the fact that this was a thrill-kill, plain and simple. Most of the detectives assigned to the case had taken this view, and the team in charge of Ptaschinski's mental health evaluation agreed, finding her competent to stand trial.

And now it was the press and the public who wanted blood.

Live at the witch trials

Strangely, the media scarcely seemed to notice the quiet trial and incarceration of the ringleader of the Brisbane vampire society. All their excitement was saved for the processing of the three who were pleading innocent, the one that promised the equivalent of a modern day witch trial. There was standing room only when the trial of Ptaschinski, Jervis and Waugh opened at the Brisbane Supreme Court on 31st january 1991. The families of the accused, the victim's family and the local lesbian community faced each other across the crowded room.

All of the accused showed stony faces during the trial, rarely speaking or looking at each other. They refused to give evidence in court, and instead their videotaped interviews with the police were presented to the jury by the prosecution.

Lisa Ptaschinski was alone in the room, with no family present. She gave off an aura of defiance, sitting with her arms folded and her face set in a hostile glare. She dressed entirely in black, with the female chromosome symbol that she had tattooed on her forearm in prominent display – as if to imply she was being tried for her sexuality alone.

Jervis, who had been a fragile-looking beauty before this affair, had been clearly worn down by her stay in prison. The dark circles under her eyes were no longer the product of over-enthusiastically applied eyeliner, but of the fifteen months she had spent on remand in custody. She seemed almost unaware of what was taking place around her, and only towards the end of the trial did she show any expression – shy smiles with her former lover Waugh.

Waugh, the only one of the three who had been out on bail for all this time, was accompanied each day to court by her parents. Her unblemished, youthful looks were a stark contrast to those of her fellow accused.

The defence lawyers played the vampire card to the hilt. Julie Dick, representing Ptaschinski, presented Wigginton as a dangerous, manipulative woman who had controlled the others through fear. Lisa, she said, had been under Wigginton's spell, hypnotised by Tracey's 'thrilling and chilling' stories about drinking blood to stay alive. She had been carried away by Wigginton's scheme to murder someone, never for one moment believing it would actually happen.

Dr Peter Mulholland put forward his opinion that Ptaschinski was suffering from borderline personality disorder and that she was incapable of understanding her actions leading up to and during the murder. 'It was obvious that Lisa had a delusion that Tracey Wigginton was a vampire,' he said. She thought the plan to kill someone was all 'a big joke' until Wigginton was standing over her, ordering her to kill Edward Baldock. 'Then she had frozen.'

'She had no protection'

Defending Kim Jervis, Michael Holden took a similar tack. His client, he said, had also thought that Tracey's plan was a fantasy, but was too scared of her to intervene when the victim had been selected and taken to the place where he died. 'I thought it was a bit of a joke, I thought it would be talk – not action,' she said in her taped police interview. 'That was the biggest mistake of my life.'

In the same video, Kim went on to claim that Wigginton had wanted her to watch as she drank the blood from Baldock's corpse, while taunting her with the words, 'I want to scare you, to frighten the living hell out of you. If anyone touches me while I'm doing it I'm liable to rip their arm off.'

Tracey Waugh's defence sounded perhaps the most unbelievable in a 20th century courtroom. In her videotaped evidence, she said that the three women had fallen under Wigginton's spell after a crucifix Jervis was wearing around her neck had broken.

'Once that cross came off, Kim didn't have any protection,' she said, adding that Wigginton was a devil-worshipper who had the ability to turn herself invisible, except for her ever-watchful 'cat's eyes'.

Waugh said she had confronted Wigginton at Club Lewmors that the plan was out of order. 'I told Tracey we didn't want to do it, and she said she had arranged something different and we shouldn't worry. Then Tracey got up to go and put out her hand and I just went with her.'

All the defence lawyers for the three women had agreed to cast the blame for Edward Baldock's murders entirely on Tracey Wigginton. Peter Feeney, for Waugh, went the furthest on his client's behalf. Tracey Waugh, he said, had not tried to stop the murder, or tried to get any help, because she was terrified of the retribution that would come from

Wigginton. He also claimed that, unlike the others, Waugh had played no active role in the planning or the execution of the murder, and even stated to the court that Wigginton had considered Waugh a 'reserve victim' if they had not succeeded in finding a suitable stranger that night. 'All Wigginton wanted was someone who could give her blood.'

'Plain, bloody murder'

The crown prosecutor Adrian Gundelach poured scorn upon the women's pleas. 'What we are dealing with here is plain, bloody murder,' he said. Ptaschinski, Jervis and Waugh were not silly adolescents caught up in some role-playing psuedo-Satanic cult and the jury should not be fooled by how young they looked, he continued. They were fully *compus mentis* adults who had premeditated this murder, sought out a victim and handed him over to his killer barely able to defend himself. Even if they hadn't actually stabbed him themselves, they had as good as murdered him.

He added that none of the three had made any attempt to disguise themselves or to blindfold Baldock when they had him in their clutches, because they knew he would not live to tell on them.

The jury retired after hearing 14 days' worth of evidence and Elaine Baldock was in court to witness the verdict. Lisa Ptaschinski stood motionless as she was found guilty and sentenced to life in prison. Kim Jervis sobbed as she was found guilty of manslaughter and sent down for 18 years. But Tracey Waugh was acquitted, and ran from the court, accompanied by her parents.

In his sentencing of Ptaschinski, Judge Justice MacKenzie said that he had no choice but to impose the mandatory life sentence. 'The abhorrent and cruel nature of events to which you have been party on this night is obvious from the evidence heard during this trial and needs no elaboration,' he surmised.

To Kim Jervis, he said: 'You knew what was likely to happen and you took no pity on Mr Baldock as another human being.'

As the two women were taken down to the cells and the courtroom dispersed, Elaine Baldock stood on the steps of the courtroom, weeping. She had endured not only the loss of her husband, but the mortifying revelations of his final hours in the most heartless and lurid possible detail. She probably spoke for most of Queensland, if not Australia, when she screamed: 'I hope they die. I hope they die in prison.'

Devil woman

She didn't die, but Tracey Wigginton fell into a profound depression when she was admitted to Brisbane's Women's Prison at Boggo Road Jail. Ironically, her incarceration finally brought her closer to the mother who had been so distant when she was a child. Rhonda moved to Brisbane so she could be near her daughter, who eventually found some motivation behind bars and earned herself a Bachelor of Arts degree in anthropology and philosophy in 2002.

The Vampire of Brisbane seemed to fade from the public's memory until September 2003, when Wigginton was moved to a low security Numinbah Correction Centre on the Gold Coast. This act provoked a predictable show of outrage from those who had continued to lobby for her never to be released.

Queensland Victims of Crimes Association's chief executive Chris Murphy claimed that the government had failed in its duty of care.

'Given her history, the violence of the crime, and the court's findings that she was a thrill-killer, I can't understand it,' he said. 'There is a school nearby [Numinbah Valley State School] and with these types of minimum security prisons, if she chooses to abscond she pretty much can. I think the whole community, even the whole of Australia, should be concerned.'

The Leader of the Opposition, Lawrence Springborg, weighed in his opinion that Wigginton personified 'unmitigated evil' and called on Police and Corrective Services Minister Tony McGrady to review the decision.

A spokesman for McGrady replied: 'The prisoner is still in the correction system, she's not been released and she remains under supervision.'

Wigginton has never actually applied for parole, even though she has been eligible for two years now.

Debbie Kilroy, who in December 2004 won Australia's National Human Rights medal for her work with the prisoner support group Sisters Inside, shed some light as to why. 'It's like a witch hunt,' she told *LOTL* magazine at the time of Tracey's move. 'The media went around the community and asked them if they were worried that a vampire lesbian was living near them. It's feeding into a fear that there are actually these types of demon lesbian women running around – it's absolute rubbish. I've known Tracey for 15 years…I can guarantee she's not a vampire.'

Town without pity

The story of Tracey Wigginton and her circle of friends is perhaps the saddest one in this collection. Unlike Berkowitz, Gecht or Ramirez, Wigginton was not a calculating serial killer with a glamorous image of herself as some kind of Satanic messiah. Her frightened co-accused invented that persona for her, knowing precisely how well it would reflect on her in the kind of society they lived in. The media in their turn were delighted to report lurid tales of blood-drinking and vampirism. It only made the accused look more depraved than merely being lesbians – and maybe offered the comforting illusion that all lesbians *were* so depraved.

Though Wigginton, with her threatening, butch physique and smattering of Occult knowledge (gained more from Hollywood flicks than anything like *The Satanic Bible*), may have had a glimmer of the power a psychopath like Gecht had over other people, the stories told by Ptaschinksi, Jervis and particularly Waugh do seem a great deal more opportunistic than the almost demented fear shown by Gecht's disciples, Eddie Spreitzer and the Kokoraleis brothers. Especially as there never was any evidence to back them up.

The fact was, three unfortunate Brisbane Goths got mixed up with someone whose alienation and rage was far deeper and more profound than their own, and then hadn't a clue how to deal with it when Wigginton flipped off the rails. Ironically, if they hadn't so titillated the tabloids with all their vampire shtick, then maybe it might have served them better in the minds of the public. Maybe Ptaschinski could have received the counselling she so desperately needed instead of a life sentence in jail; maybe she and Jervis wouldn't still be locked away 14 years later without any realistic hope of parole.

Nor does this crime appear to be rampantly sexually motivated in the way that Berkowitz's, Gecht's and Ramirez's so clearly were. If there was a sexual element to Wigginton's frenzied stabbing of Edward Baldock, it was perhaps, just as she told her psychiatrists at the time, the symbolic murder of everyone who had ever let her down – represented most strongly of all by her abusive grandfather, another middle-aged family man. And coming at a time when the domineering, patriarchal figure of Bjelke-Petersen had just been ejected from his throne, the crime had a similarly deep resonance within the state of Queensland.

This is not to excuse in any way what Tracey Wigginton did on that fatal October night. Baldock's vile and sudden butchery was a terrible crime that will afford his family no closure, especially when, as it seems sure, the Australian press will never report any story about Wigginton without the attendant tales of the supernatural that will bring back their bad memories all too clearly.

But when the facts are laid bare and the myths put back in their coffin, this story resembles less *Dracula* than *The Crucible*.

Club Lewmors closed its doors soon after the body of Edward Baldock was found, and the building remains empty and shuttered to this day, under a curse, a monument to a crime Tiny Town will never forget. Said the manageress, Bettina Lewis, at the Ptaschinski/Jervis/Waugh trial: 'I can't sleep at night now, knowing that those creeps drank in my club.'

But, in a God-fearing, repressed, intolerant community, Brisbane planted the seeds of its own worst nightmare. Then found a myth of a vampire far easier to deal with than the truths hidden underneath its own, sodden carpet.

Chapter Six

⁓

Count Grishnackh: Burn, baby, burn (1993)

From the land of the ice and snow

The mythology of heavy metal found its most extreme outlet in Norway in the late 1980s and early 1990s. Calling itself 'Black Metal' this new strain was forged from the same furnace that made Led Zeppelin and Black Sabbath – heavy, doom-laden music with lyrics about Satanism and Nordic gods. But Black Metal was much harsher on the ear, in its lyrical content – and in the intentions of its architects.

The first significant Black Metal band was Mayhem, whose lead singer Øystein Aarseth called himself Euronymous and declared to the world: 'I don't want to see people respecting me. I want people to hate and fear.' Aarseth set up his own record label, Deathlike Silence, to propagate not just his music, but his anti-Christian ideals.

Without their black-and-white 'corpse paint', Aarseth and his cohorts might have looked like any other disenfranchised Beavis and Butthead kids with long hair and a snotty attitude. But they were determined to prove their utter seriousness to the world – and they couldn't have chosen a more appropriate name for themselves. Mayhem was exactly what they brought to the bored youth culture of Oslo, and what they eventually would vest upon themselves.

This is a story of two friends who became bitter rivals, of thousand year old stave churches burning to the ground, of suicide and cannibalism and a record shop named Hell opening a portal to brutal bloody murder. It was a time when the spirits of Valhalla were unleashed once more on the Land of the Midnight Sun.

Death comes to Norway

The band Mayhem originally formed in Oslo in 1984, when Aarseth was only 15 years old. They were inspired by a trio of bands that took heavy metal back to its hard blues roots in Sabbath and Zeppelin, dressed it up in black and white face paint and summoned up the spirit of the Dark Lord with deliberately provocative lyrics. These were Newcastle's Venom, Sweden's Bathory (named after the 18th century Hungarian noblewoman Erzebet Bathory, who bathed in the blood of slaughtered virgins) and Switzerland's Hellhammer.

Of the three, the Geordies in Venom who first coined the phrase 'Black Metal' were the least serious about their 'Satanic' stance. They had read *The Satanic Bible* for sure, but just saw themselves as rock'n'roll entertainers provoking a bit of controversy in what at the time was an overcrowded British market. The sterner Swiss Hellhammer were more earnest about their occult leanings, but it was probably the Scandinavian Bathory who would exert the most influence over their Norwegian neighbours.

Bathory were at first influenced by Venom, and mined a similar seam of schlock horror imagery – all upside-down crosses, spikes and Bathomet (goat's head) symbols. But later, they wandered from horror movie Satanism into Nordic folklore for their inspiration. Pictures of the thunder god Thor and his Valkyries adorned their album covers and their lyrics reawakened the old mythologies of their pagan ancestors – something that would become more important to Black Metal as the genre slowly took its form.

Mayhem didn't initially claim to be looking for anything other than having 'a fuckin' good time' and, perhaps as a result of that, didn't manage to release any records until 1987, when they printed up 1,000 copies of the *Deathcrush* mini-album on their own Posercorpse label. Guitarist Øystein Aarseth was always the driving force behind the band. Styling himself as Euronymous (an ancient Greek name that appears in Homer's *Odysseus*), he was joined in his task by drummer Jan Axel Blomberg, who referred to himself as Hellhammer, and singing Swede Per Yngve Ohlin, otherwise known as Dead.

By the time they had reached this line-up, Mayhem stepped up their rhetoric. The band started daubing themselves with black and white 'corpsepaint' and styled themselves as brutal nihilists, who held the world in contempt. They played live with pigs' heads on stakes surrounding them, while the non-too-stable Dead would smash bottles and grind the shattered glass into his body in order to see how the audience reacted. The music itself certainly went with their image – extreme, primitive and brutal, it seemed to be challenging its listeners to see how much pain they could take.

Pain, it seemed, was what the kids wanted. Norway is a predominantly Protestant country, and though few of the population are regular churchgoers, the upright, disciplined and moralistic work ethic pervades the mood of its society, which is also amongst the most tolerant and liberal in Europe. There is very little real poverty in Norway, and perhaps because of the very comfort of their world, there wasn't very much for the kids to protest about or rebel against.

Until Aarseth provided it for them. The idea of rejecting Christianity and worshipping 'evil' instead proved an alluringly anti-authority stance for bored young teens. As the Black Metal scene began to grow around Mayhem, fans from all over the country began to get in touch with Aarseth. They formed a network of fanzines dedicated to the cause, and started up their own bands, keeping in touch, encouraging each other and hanging out as each other's gigs. Bands such as Darkthrone and Immortal grew up around the scene, along with two others who would go on to become as notorious as Mayhem – Emperor and Burzum.

'He hated this world and everything that lives on it'

So far, so teenage, you might think. But Mayhem were about to step their ideals up a notch, and that meant acting out the subjects they espoused. Three years after joining Mayhem, their singer distinguished himself by living up to his stage name. Always a melancholic and depressive character, Ohlin had called himself Dead because death was what he was obsessed by. He used to frequently talk about an out-of-body experience he'd had in Sweden, when he fainted in a hospital and saw himself surrounded by a blue, and then white, light. Since then he had cultivated friends who were morticians and mediums and claimed to have studied snuff movies because, 'I like to research how one reacts when watching real deaths, or preferably real corpses.'

In the end, he involuntarily bequeathed his own body to the furtherance of such research. At the time of his suicide, Aarseth, Dead and Hellhammer were sharing an old house in Oslo where they lived and rehearsed. Hellhammer was over at his parents' house in April 1991, when he had a phonecall from Aarseth to say that their singer had slit his wrists and then blown his brains out with a shotgun. What happened next would go down in the annals of Black Metal depravity.

Upon finding Dead's body, Aarseth went straight out to buy a camera, in order to take pictures of the corpse. He reeled off a film, snapping Dead's death from all angles, then collected parts of his unfortunate singer's shattered skull. He would later nonchalantly hand these fragments out to his friends, telling them to make totemic jewellery with them. He and Hellhammer kept their own parts of Dead's skull strung round their necks, so they could 'remember him better'.

If this wasn't morbid enough, according to Hellhammer, Aarseth finally proceeded to gather pieces of the singer's brain, boiled them up in a stew and ate them. Cannibalism was another taboo he could then boast that he had broken. Only after performing these macabre death rites did he finally call the police to take the body away.

It did occur to friends of the Mayhem circle to ask whether Dead did in fact take his own life or was actually murdered by Aarseth. The latter didn't mind such rumours floating around, on the contrary, it added to his mystique and the frightening image he was doing his best to cultivate. But it seems pretty certain from all his friends and acquaintances that Dead, who frequently cut himself up on stage and talked of his desire to commit suicide, had not been very happy on this earth.

Interviewed by a Black Metal fanzine shortly after the incident, Aarseth put his singer's death down to the fact that no one was taking their music seriously enough.

'We have declared war,' he raged. 'Dead died because trend people have destroyed everything from the old Black Metal/Death Metal scene. Today 'Death' Metal is something normal, accepted and funny (argh!) and we hate it. It used to be spikes, chains, leather and black clothes, and that was the only thing Dead lived for as he hated this world and everything which lives on it.'

Hell on Earth

The next thing Aarseth did was to open a record store in Oslo's Old Town that he proudly called 'Helvete' – the old Norse world for Hell. It quickly became a focal point for the Black Metal scene, and, from behind its counter, Aarseth dispensed extreme music and his own unconventional wisdom to an ever-growing army of acolytes. He began his own label, Deathlike Silence, with which to promote both his own music and that of his followers, starting with a band called Merciless.

Despite his ambitions as a businessman, Aarseth was forced to concede the limits of his market. He may have detested the 'trend' people, as he called them, who he considered diluted the purity of Black Metal, but if he was going to make a living then he had to pander to their needs. 'This will help us earning money so that we can order more evil records for evil people,' he explained.

He dreamed that his evil emporium would look like a 'black church' and that customers would come in bearing flaming torches with which to peruse his wares. But again, Aarseth was forced to be realistic and stick to black and red paint and candles, although he did have an attractive female mannequin dressed in a black cloak.

Still, by mid-1991, he wasn't doing badly. As a specialist record shop he attracted a clientele who were willing to shell out for records that were hard to come by, and, more than that, faithfully collect everything in the Black Metal canon that they could lay their hands on. Aarseth held court dressed all in black, his hair dyed the same midnight shade, with a matching long moustache. Knee-high boots added to this vision of a Roger Corman-esque corrupt nobleman – think Vincent Price in *The Pit and the Pendulum*. Only smaller and less attractive.

Aarseth's vision of 'evil' was partially shaped by a youthful infatuation with Communism. He had been a teenage member of Red Youth, a wing of the Communist Worker's Party, who had long included in their number the Norwegian intelligentsia – prominent writers, journalists and politicians. The idea of strong leaders commanding universal obsequience obviously had its appeal for Aarseth. He had a huge collection of Eastern Bloc memorabilia, including photographs of the Romanian despot Nicolae Ceaucescu, one of his biggest idols.

Satanism was to come into the equation later, when Venom opened the door to the Dark Lord in Aarseth's heart. An interest in Nordic mythology was stirred when he made friends with the singer of a band from Bergen, one Kristian Vikernes. Kristian started his career playing guitar in a Death Metal band called Old Funeral. But he quickly tired of his bandmates and set up his own act in order to maintain full artistic control.

An aficionado of JRR Tolkien, Vikernes called his new venture Burzum, meaning 'darkness' in Tolkein's 'Black Speech'. (The inscription on the One Ring was *agh burzum-ishi krimpatul,* meaning 'and in the darkness bind them'.) He also renamed himself after an orc in *The Lord of the rings* – Count Grishnackh. When Aarseth heard the fruits of the Count's labours he was beside himself with enthusiasm.

Aarseth already had a pretty full roster for his emergent label – Darkthrone, Immortal, Thorns, Enslaved and Emperor. These were the people mean enough to be accepted into Aarseth's Camelot – or the 'Black Circle' as it became known. They wore their corpse-paint with pride, and took a general, though initially undefined, stand against Christianity.

Then into their midst stepped Count Grishnackh.

Lucifer over Europe

During the summer of 1991, Satanism wasn't just confined to the social whirl of Helvte, it was splashed all over the news.

The Satanic Panic that had seized the United States in the early to mid-80s first found its way to Europe via the United Kingdom in 1988, when seven children from a council estate in Nottingham were taken into care. The suspicion was that they were being abused by members of their families and in February 1989 ten men and women were charged with incest, indecent assault and cruelty against a total of 22 children.

While they had been placed in care, the children's foster parents had been asked by the authorities to take written notes of anything they were told about the abuse. This is where the first suggestions of RSA came from. Seemingly ludicrous stories of 'witch parties', infant sacrifice and animal sacrifice were recorded in the foster parent's diaries, for intended use at the forthcoming trial.

The police were not impressed and launched their own separate investigation, which concluded that the notion of RSA had first surfaced in the bi-weekly support meetings between the foster parents and two psychiatrists who had been brought over from the States by Social Services, because they were supposed experts in the field. These sessions had managed to create their own panic, which was passed from the foster carers on to the children.

The police did not want these diaries used as evidence.

However, social workers strongly disagreed. The supposed RSA 'experts' Ray Wyre and Dr Kirk Weir both believed that Satanic abuse was involved. The judge, Mrs Justice Margaret Booth, agreed. An independent enquiry team, headed by police and social workers that had had no previous involvement with the case, was ordered.

They found that none of the places where the Satanic rites had been allegedly performed actually existed and that the children had only begun telling these tales after Ray Wyre had briefed their foster parents on 'Satanic indicators'. The report concluded:

It seemed possible that Satanic abuse only existed in the minds of people who wanted or needed to believe in it. In the USA the result had been a modern day witch-hunt which had ruined the lives of many innocent people.

Furthermore, it recommended that in future the unproven and unsubstantiated notion of RSA should be immediately dropped from all Social Services departments in the UK.

But the report was suppressed by the then Health Secretary Kenneth Clarke, who had initially ordered it to be circulated around all departments of the Social Services Inspectorate.

As a result of this, Ray Wyre went on to spread Satanic Panic to Pembroke in West Wales, resulting in the biggest Mass Offender Mass Victim ritual abuse case in British history. The hoax then spread through other Social Services Departments throughout the UK in the early 1990s, with cases resulting in Rochdale, the Orkney Islands and Ayr. The Government asked Professor Jean La Fontaine to conduct another enquiry into RSA – which again found that no secret underground of Satanic cults had ever existed.

Nevertheless, on 11th June 1991, a long interview with a lieutenant of the Oslo police vice squad appeared in the Norwegian newspaper *Dagbladet* that first introduced the myth of RSA as hot news in Norway. Alongside lurid descriptions of Satanic rituals, the lieutenant introduced the already discredited 'checklists' that had just caused so much havoc in the UK. He alleged that two Satanic rings were operating in Oslo – and the story exploded across the Norwegian press.

One headline in particular, from *Vårt Land* on 19th June 1991, could sum up the feelings that were stirring within the Black Circle.

Satanism is hatred of life.

Over the threshold

Kristian Vikernes was born on 11th February 1973 in the suburbs of Bergen, the second largest Norwegian city, on the east coast of the country. His electronic engineer father Lars moved the family around a lot when Kristian was a child, they even spent a year living in Iraq, which Kristian's mother, Lene Bore, would later pinpoint as the changing point in his life.

'I think it might be here that [his] dislike towards other peoples started,' she considered. 'He experienced a very differential treatment.' Although Bore went on to say that far from being ostracised for being the sole blond European child in a Middle Eastern country, the then 6-year-old Kristian received preferential treatment in the classroom, which he saw as unfair. 'He had a very strongly developed sense of justice. This created a lot of problems, because when he saw students being treated unfairly, he would intervene and try to sort things out.'

But another formative influence was closer to home. Vikernes' father was a strict disciplinarian, who often sought to lay down his authority with his fists. As a child, Kristian witnessed his mother being physically assaulted on numerous occasions. He reacted by defying his father at every turn.

'Their relationship started going bad quite early,' Lene later said. 'Possibly because he had these problems with his father I had a very close relationship with him. I often felt it was appropriate to look after him a bit extra because of all the conflicts between [Kristian] and the school, his father and so on.'

Lene eventually left her husband and settled back in Bergen with 14-year-old Kristian and his older brother. Kristian never settled at school, preferring to retreat into Tolkein's world of orcs, ogres and wizards and developing an interest in the German Nazis of World War II. He became a teenage skinhead, 'socialising with weapons freaks,' he later recalled. 'My hobby was shooting guns, militia training and playing in the woods with a shotgun.'

He also taught himself how to play guitar, joining his first band, Old Funeral, when he was 17. Although Bergen was probably the occult centre of Norway, with several Crowleyist OTO lodges operating on the fringes of the University (groups who would be falsely persecuted for RSA links in the press when the 1991 Satanic Panic hit), Vikernes had not had any contact with any self-professed Satanists.

Until the day in 1989 when he met the older, influential Øystein Aarseth. The two began discussing Death Metal and Satanism. Aarseth told the younger man about his label, and how he only put out music that was 'pure evil'. This was the sort of talk Vikernes had been longing to hear. Inspired by the fact Aarseth had called himself Euronymous in order to sound more malevolent, it was at this time that Vikernes stopped using the name Kristian and became Varg, meaning 'wolf'.

When Old Funeral developed too mainstream tastes for his liking, Vikernes left and began his Burzum project, which led him straight to the core of Aarseth's Black Circle. Here he found a group of people who shared his obsessions with extremity, hatred and the aesthetics of evil. He and Aarseth became close friends and Vikernes moved into the cellar beneath Helvete for a while, along with Samoth, the guitarist of Emperor.

The bands that frequented the shop had fairly interchangeable line-ups at this point. Vikernes played bass for Mayhem on the full-length album *De Mysteriis Dom Sathanas* (*Lord Satan's Secret Rites*).

The musicians would hang in the shop for hours on end, drinking and philosophising. When Aarseth shut up shop for the night they would decant to the Lusa Lotte Pobb, the only Black Metal pub in Oslo.

Aarseth grew closer to Vikernes. Though Vikernes didn't drink beer with the others, he was fascinated by Aarseth's ideas and looked up to him as a leader. More than that, he was a very good guitarist.

Though Vikernes would move back to Bergen when the freezing ante-chamber of Helvete became too much, the two men stayed great friends. Both Vikernes, who worshipped Odin, the Norse God of War, and Aarseth, who was more Satanically inclined, decided to give the 'trend people' a kick up the arse with their ever-more scathing fanzine interviews.

Typical was Aarseth's summation of the then current wave of hardcore punk bands, who eschewed the sex 'n' drugs trappings of traditional heavy metal and called themselves 'straight-edge' – no drinks, no drugs, no meat, no unethical products. 'The hardcore pigs have correctly made themselves guardians of morality,' he sneered, 'but we must kick them in the face and become guardians of anti-morality.'

And they had a cunning plan about just how they were going to achieve that.

In the Houses of the Holy

Unique to Norway, wooden stave churches are fantastical structures, some of them dating back a thousand years. Their ornate gabled roofs arcing up into sharp steeples recall the prows of the Viking longboats, and to make them all the more dramatic they are often darkened with pitch. Their forbidding exteriors are carved with Nordic interlace motifs that further hark back to the pagan gods, and stylised dragons' heads rear from the upper gables. There were once thousands of these churches in Norway, but because of their structural vulnerability, by 1992 there were only 32 originals left.

Fantoft, five miles south of Bergen, had one such example of a 12th century stave church. Originally, it had stood at Fortun, in central Norway, but at the close of the 19th century had been scheduled for demolition to make way for a new burial ground. However, the church was saved, dismantled and taken to Fantoft, where it was resurrected and restored in a suitably Norse setting, on a densely wooded hilltop.

At 6am on the morning of 6th June 1992, this beautiful building was burned to the ground by arsonists. It was the start of a hot, hot summer. As the shock headlines hit the front pages, other churches began to catch the firebug. On 1st August, the Revheim Church in southern Norway was razed; 20 days later the Holmenkollen Chapel in Oslo; on 1st September Ormøya Church and on 13th September Skjold Church.

As summer turned into autumn, the Hauketo Church was torched in October, then the Åsane Church in Bergen and the Saropsborg Church, taking with it the life of a fireman who was trying to fight the blaze.

For a while, the authorities were clueless as to the perpetrators of these deeds. Then, shortly after the destruction of Fantoft, an arson was attempted at a house belonging to Death Metal singer Christopher Jonnsson in Upplands Väsby, near Stockholm in Sweden, on 26th July 1992.

Jonnsson, who had recently argued with Vikernes, was woken by the smoke and the fire was put out before any real harm was done. Shortly afterwards, he received a letter from Norway. It read:

Hello victim! This is Count Grishnackh of Burzum. I have just come home from a journey to Sweden...and I think I lost a match and a signed Burzum LP, ha ha! Perhaps I will make a return trip soon and maybe this time you won't wake up in the middle of the night. I will give you a lesson in fear...

The actual perpetrator of the attack was not Vikernes, but an 18-year-old girl called Suuvi Mariotta Puurunen, who was obsessed by him. When she was arrested by Swedish police, they discovered a diary which accounted for her actions that night.

I did it on a mission for our leader, The Count, she had written. *I love the Count. His fantasies are the best. I want a knife, a fine knife, sharp and cruel...*

Puurunen was sentenced to one year's observation in a mental hospital. But it wouldn't be long before the finger of suspicion for the church burnings once more pointed at Count Grishnackh – mainly because the Bergen berserker couldn't keep his mouth shut.

Twisted firestarter

On 19th January 1993, Vikernes spoke to Finn Bjørn Tønder at the *Bergens Tidende* daily newspaper. The headline on the front cover the next day read: WE LIT THE FIRES over a picture of the Count wearing a suitably menacing grimace. Though Vikernes wasn't mentioned by name, what was reported was pretty damning:

'*"We are behind all the church fires in Norway. It started with Fantoft Stave Church. And we're not stopping now"...The person behind those words is an anonymous man from Bergen, about 20 years of age. By way of two youths that knew him,* [Bergens Tidende] *was able to meet him,*' the story went. The 'youth' went on to explain his actions: '*"Call us what you want. We worship the Devil, but prefer not to use the word Satan. That name has been made ridiculous by foolish groups of poseurs. Morons who think they are tough."'*

Vikernes went on to tell the reporter tantalising details of what he had been up to, which were duly checked out. Some of the details even surprised the police. He claimed they had captured and sacrificed a rabbit on the steps of Fantoft Church before setting fire to the building. Investigator Associate Professor Inge Morild from the Gades Institute confirmed that a headless carcass had been found, adding that, 'I don't even think the police knew it.'

He further boasted that only one man had been responsible for setting the fire, on the symbolic date of 6th June (the sixth month), at 6am: *'The intention was that our contacts all over Norway should do the same with other churches at exactly the same time. But the others chickened out. They let it remain just talk. Luckily, their cowardice led to us gaining more power over them.'*

Vikernes then went on to describe the activities at Åsane Church, which was destroyed on 23rd December, *'because the word "peaceful" was said on TV. We got so irately mad at all the righteousness of society.'* Again, Vikernes' story checked out with police information.

An arch-revisionist of his own history, Vikernes would later laugh off this interview as 'absurd', but it seems obvious his desire to brag about his achievements was stronger than any sense of self-preservation. The *Bergens Tiende* article would bring an intense wave of media and police scrutiny on the Black Metal scene, seeming, as it did, to bear out the previous summer's allegations that Satanic sects were operating in Norway.

Once the story had made the front pages, the police came knocking on Vikernes' door. They had already found some flyers promoting Burzum's mini-album *Aske*, which carried a picture of the smouldering ruins of Fantoft Church. Vikernes had kindly put his own address as a contact on them.

Mayhem and murder

It wasn't just the arsons that the police were interested in either. Vikernes had also been telling fanzines about a 'murder' that he knew about of a homosexual man in Lillehammer, and now he had made himself a suspect, along with his Black Circle associates Samoth and Bård Eithun of Emperor. It was in fact Eithun who had committed this crime, as well as lending Vikernes and Euronymous a helping hand with their church-burnings. But for now, all denied everything and, because there was no physical evidence, were released without charge following their interviews.

Far from learning a lesson about the perils of publicity, however, both Vikernes and Aarseth next distinguished themselves by giving a cover story to the biggest heavy metal magazine in the world, the British weekly *Kerrang!* Under the banner '*Arson...Death...Satanic ritual...The ugly truth about Black Metal*' the story appeared in March 1993, only two months after Vikernes' narrow squeak with the police. If anything, his defiance and megalomania seemed to be running out of control.

Both he and Aarseth claimed that they were the 'Satanic terrorists' behind the recent Norwegian crimewave, and referred to their 'inner circle' of core members who they directed to carry out the action. Helvete, said Aarseth, was the 'economic basis' for their acts, although he denied any involvement in the actual crimes, because if he were to be arrested then their organisation would fall apart.

This article was also the first to point out a further sinister slant to the Black Circle's ideology. After quoting Cronos of Venom reiterating that the Satanism in the band's lyrics was not supposed to be taken literally, it reported the UK doom metallers Paradise Lost referring to an experience they had in Norway when youthful Black Metallers set upon them for not being really evil. 'They're fucking nuts!' said singer Nick Holmes. 'It's a Manson cult-type thing. It's like the fucking Nazis in East Germany...the same sort of power game.' Vikernes replied that he supported all dictatorships, and that he would soon become 'the dictator of Scandinavia'.

Vikernes was working himself up for a dramatic final act, but even the insiders of the Black Metal scene had no idea quite how dramatic that would actually be.

Over the course of the next few months, Vikernes and Aarseth had an epic falling-out, mainly over who was the real leader of the scene. Aarseth was forced to close his record shop because of all the attention swirling around him – his parents had helped him finance the venture and now they demanded that he shut up shop and distance himself from the heat of the accusations. Helvete and Deathlike Silence both went out of business, the record company owing royalties to several bands on its roster, including Burzum. Vikernes, sensing that the old leader had fallen, primed himself to take his place. He began bad-mouthing the one-time Prince of Darkness, deriding him as a Communist and a homosexual, mocking his business acumen and reticence to take part in any criminal activities.

Within a matter of months, the protégée was consumed by hatred for his former leader, and everybody on the scene knew about it.

Then, on 10th August 1993, the body of Black Metal's founding father, Øystein Aarseth, aka Euronymous, was found in the stairwell of his Oslo apartment block. He had been brutally stabbed to ribbons and most of the wounds were in his back. He was 25 years old.

Malice aforethought

It took the Oslo police only four days of interviews with insiders on the Black Metal scene before they came knocking once again at Varg Vikernes' door. Aarseth's girlfriend Ilsa, a 16-year-old Swedish girl, would not name the Count for fear it would lead to her own death, but she gave the detectives enough clues to go on. Then they interviewed a recent edition to Mayhem's ranks, guitarist Snorre Westvold Ruch, who had actually been with Vikernes on the fateful night. Ruch was also very afraid of Grishnackh, and it didn't take long for his version of events to come tumbling out.

It appeared that the Count had put a lot of thought into the murder of his one-time best friend. He had attempted to cover his tracks with the help of two accomplices, Ruch and Andreas Nagelsett, who stayed back in Vikernes' Bergen apartment as part of their alibi.

Firstly, the trio rented out a video, which Nagelsett was to play loudly in the apartment after Vikernes and Ruch had left for Oslo, while continuing to batter away at a typewriter – typical noise that their neighbours would recognise. The film was one that all three had seen before, so they could give details of the plot if they were ever questioned. Vikernes also left his cashpoint card with Nagelsett in Bergen, with orders to make a withdrawal later that night, which would supposedly prove Vikernes had still been in town. Only in his hurry, Vikernes left the wrong card, and the withdrawal couldn't be made – another killer undone by a piece of plastic.

Vikernes took with him a contract, drawn up and actually signed by Euronymous on behalf of Deathlike Silence, to release further Burzum records on the label. Despite the friction between the two men, Aarseth was still serious about promoting Vikernes' music, and maybe thought this would solve the disputes between them. Vikernes signed and dated his contracts on 9th October, something he later admitted had been a mistake. But the idea at the time was that these documents would prove that he had only seen Aarseth for a friendly business meeting.

Wary of being recognised, Vikernes spent the journey to Oslo in the back of his mother's Volkswagen Golf car, lying under a pile of T-shirts while Ruch took the wheel. They drove straight to Aarseth's apartment and Vikernes demanded to be let in. Disturbed from his sleep, his former friend answered the door dressed only in his underwear. Vikernes went inside the apartment for long enough to leave his contracts before he started shouting and wielded his knife on the prone Aarseth.

The fight that happened next spilled out of Aarseth's flat and over the stairwell, as Aarseth desperately tried to escape his attacker. Vikernes ran after him, stabbing his former friend over and over, until he eventually got him on the floor of the first floor landing and pounded his head into the concrete.

Ruch, who had been unwillingly loitering in the stairwell waiting for Vikernes, saw it all. He later said: 'When I stood outside Øystein's door I heard a noise inside and Øystein came out, with the Count on his heels, covered in blood, rushing down the stairway. I realised this was going to hell. We had intended this to happen in the apartment and fast – no big dramatic thing with a hundred knife-stabs or something.'

Ruch ran past them out of the door and towards the parked car. Vikernes was right behind him. They got back in the car and drove back to Bergen, not knowing whether they had left Aarseth dead or alive.

Out for the Count

Soon enough, the murder of Aarseth was flashing all over Norwegian TV screens. And people were starting to talk – about Vikernes and his big mouth and about Bård Eithun too. The murder of Magne Andreassen in Lillehammer on 21st August 1992 had been unsolved, with no leads, until the Black Metal fraternity was thrown into chaos and police stations with the death of Aarseth. Now fingers were pointing. Vikernes had told a number of people that he knew Eithun was responsible for the murder, which he approved of, because the victim was a homosexual and gays were another group of people who the Count despised. Eithun had been less than taciturn with people too. He was brought in at the same time as Vikernes, and immediately confessed.

Eithun claimed he had been out for a drink in Lillehammer on the night in question, but the bars were too crowded for his liking, so he had begun to walk home when he was approached by a man who was 'obviously a drunk and obviously a faggot'. Despite this realisation, when Magne Andreassen suggested to Eithun that they take a stroll in the woods, Bård did not indignantly proclaim his heterosexuality and tell the man where to go, but instead accepted the invitation. 'I had decided that I wanted to kill him, which was very weird because I'm not like this – I don't go around and kill people.'

Nevertheless, Eithun found within himself the power to stab the defenceless Andreassen repeatedly once they had reached the woodland, and then kick him in the head with his steel-toe boots to make sure he had killed him. When he returned home to his mother's house, she was asleep, so Eithun managed to make good his escape without anyone seeing him. Only the next day, he called up Vikernes to tell him what had happened. And now his chickens had come home to roost.

Vikernes described the ensuing chaos of his own and Eithun's arrest with typical magnanimity:

'So they started to arrest others, because this one stupid bitch from Romania...confessed that Bård had killed a guy, exactly what he told her. Of course they didn't have any proof at all, but he admitted everything... Then it went on to the next guy, and on to the next guy, until everything was revealed. It's typical, these unimportant people could be important this way, by ratting each other off. So they did. Of course, I was the big bad guy.'

Explosive evidence

When the police came for Vikernes in Bergen on 20th August, they found 150 kilogrammes of dynamite and glynite in his home, which they claimed had been stored with the intent of blowing up the Nidarsodomen Church in Trondheim, an 11th century national monument which houses the Norwegian crown jewels.

Vikernes denied this, just as he denied the other charges laid before him when he finally came to court nine months later.

In custody, he complained that prison in Norway wasn't brutal enough, and expressed a wish that he could be thrown into a dungeon and that the police would use 'real violence' on him. 'It's too nice in here,' he said. 'It's not hell at all.' When a doctor wanted to take a blood sample with a needle, he refused, saying that as a Viking he should only be pricked with a real dagger.

As well as the murder of Øystein Aarseth, Varg Vikernes was charged with possession of the dynamite and arson on three churches. He said he was innocent of everything and claimed that he had killed Aarseth in self-defence, having been tipped off by a friend that Aarseth was intending to murder the Count. In one version of this story, it was claimed that Aarseth had seen a psychic who warned him of his own impending death at the hands of the Count, so was planning to thwart destiny by killing Vikernes instead. In another, Vikernes claimed that Aarseth had intended to torture him to death, filming the proceedings for a snuff video which he could then show to his opponents.

He also insisted that Aarseth had come for him first with a knife, despite the fact that Euronymous had opened the door in his underpants.

Perhaps in view of the line his client took for his defence, Vikernes' voluble lawyer Tor Erling Staff tried to get him to plead insanity. Norway's most controversial and outspoken legal eagle was the best defence Lene Bore could buy and Erling Staff wanted to convince the court that Vikernes was not aware of his actions at the time of the murder. But when the Count was evaluated by two separate psychiatrists, they both found to the contrary, that Varg knew exactly what he was doing.

Vikernes would never have made an insanity plea anyway – it would have been insulting to his proud, Viking beliefs. If he went to prison for Norway's maximum sentence, 21 years, he would remain a defiant hero to his followers, who had stood by all his maxims of brutality and evil. If, on the other hand, he were reduced to the status of a mental patient, he would have been just as 'weak' as the 'Communist faggot' he had just put to death.

Grishnackh certainly didn't try and win the sympathy vote with the jury.

'You christened Norway with swords, we will make it heathen again with flames and machineguns,' was one of his defence statements. In another, when asked how he would feel to be found guilty, he simply replied: 'It will be a positive experience for the Black Metal community and the music.'

Vikernes refused to answer any questions about the murder of Aarseth being premeditated, sticking to his line that he was provoked. According to the coroner's report (which Vikernes disputes to this day) Aarseth had received 23 knife wounds, 16 of which were in the back, which didn't make his case look all that strong to the jury. But the Count did explain some of the reasons he had fallen out with his former mentor in the first place.

'He was a Communist who wanted a race-blended kingdom,' whereas Vikernes wanted to keep things pure and white in Norway. In one of his most dramatic pieces of trial theatre, he said smilingly to the court: 'While you people have Jewish morals and want to live in peace, I myself have a Germanic psyche and wish to die in war.'

When, eventually, Vikernes was found guilty of Aarseth's murder and three church arsons, the sentence reflected the judge's displeasure not only at the crimes he had committed, but at the sort of neo-Nazism that he continually espoused in his answers to the court. Norway had been occupied by Nazi Germany during World War II and the collaborator-ruler Vidkun Quisling had sent hundreds of Jews to the gas chambers. Vikernes boasted he was related to Quisling.

'This sentence convicted a type of ideology and the faith in it,' claimed Erling Staff.

But, as Judge Ivar Haug laid down a 21-year maximum sentence, Vikernes merely smiled. To his mind, and to his legion of 'neo-pagan' followers, Count Grishnackh was now a superstar. To prove his point, the following night two more churches were burned to the ground.

Soft cell

Well might Vikernes have mocked the liberal jail system in Norway. It allowed him not only to continue communicating with his fanbase, but to write three books, release a number of Burzum records and distribute them along with his books on his own Cymophane label, make continual statements through the burzum.org website and establish a platform for his political views, the Norsk Hedensk Front (NHF) 'dedicated to saving the Germanic peoples from the clutches of Judeo-Christianity'.

His ideas continued to ferment around the network of fanzines and websites that now connected pagans, neo-Nazis and Black Metal fans around Europe, especially in the former Eastern Bloc countries. It wasn't long before the Count's fans attempted to come to his aid.

In 1997, a plot to slaughter many prominent liberal politicians and religious leaders was unravelled by Norwegian police. Five members of the self-styled Einsatzgruppen neo-Nazi terrorist organisation (named after WWII murder squads) were arrested on Saturday 12th April, in possession of sawn-off shotguns, bulletproof vests, dynamite and a war chest containing about 100,000 Norwegian Kroner (about £8,300), allegedly supplied by Lene Bore. The police claimed the money and firearms were to be used to bust Vikernes out of prison so he could lead his followers to their bloody Valhalla.

But in the end, it would prove easier for the Count to simply follow the rules and escape from prison. On 25th October 2003, Vikernes failed to return to the low security prison in Vestfold where he was serving his sentence, after being granted 17 hours' leave. His lawyer John Christian Elden refused to disclose to the press whether his client had been in contact, but offered an explanation for his actions:

'I believe it stems from frustrations that have been built up. [Vikernes] has been serving his sentence in an exemplary fashion, he's put the sins of his youth behind him, and he's held hopes of re-entering society in a relatively normal manner. Then a couple of weeks ago, he saw a newspaper article in the local press where the media once again focused on the fact that a 'dangerous' person was being held [in the locality].' This, claimed Elden, sent the ever-sensitive Count off the rails.

So Vikernes hijacked a family's car, in the Numdel valley in Buskerud County, on the afternoon of Sunday 27th. The victims said they had been flagged down by a pedestrian, who had then threatened them at gunpoint to hand over the car keys.

Police eventually found Vikernes on the morning of October 28th, after receiving information that the fugitive was travelling in the car on the E6 road to Oslo, where he was apprehended mid-flight. Later it would be claimed that the Count was 'carrying enough arms and military equipment at the time of his arrest to pass for a Commando', but at the time of his arrest, police spokesman Knut Svalheim told wire service NTB that they had found only a knife in the vehicle. There was to be no Valhalla this time, either.

By the time he was apprehended, Vikernes was only set to serve another two years of his original sentence. But as ever, Lene Bore had a rationalisation for her son's behaviour. The law had recently changed and Varg thought he would have to serve another four years behind bars.

'I do wish he'd chosen another way out,' she said. 'He's spent his entire adult life incarcerated and is a good boy.'

Bore also claimed that her son had no more contact with neo-Nazi groups, including the NHF – something that the most cursory click over the current Burzum website might find rather hard to substantiate.

Vikernes was back in court again, and though the charges of hijacking a car with a lethal weapon were dropped because of insufficient evidence, he received an additional 14 months for this latest escapade.

A blaze in the Northern sky

Lene Bore's 'good boy', ignored by his father, indulged by his mother, still sits in Trondheim prison, writing great tracts on Nordic folklore and literary criticism. Everything that has ever been written about Vikernes – including the vastly sympathetic book *Lords of Chaos* by Michael Moynihan and Didrik Søderlind, with whom he co-operated – is, according to him, a lie. So he spends his time putting things right, weaving new mythologies around himself as he spouts the only constant theme in his life – his hatred of other races and his belief in Ayrian/Nordic superiority.

There are still plenty of people who want to listen to him. The Burzum website is fiercely, if not threateningly, protective of the Count. As their biography so romantically puts it, '*Varg Vikernes is so far still the only musician to have crossed the border from fantasy to reality and put into practice his beliefs in a bid to forge his own destiny...for a short time at least he led a musical movement like none before it. A blaze in the Northern sky, no less.*'

Vikernes claims that upon release he will retreat to the mountains to live a healthy, outdoorsman's life. In that case, Norwegian police might fear that a survivalist compound training up soldiers for a new Viking Reich would soon be active. For it seems very unlikely indeed that a man who has spent his entire life seeking the maximum attention possible would ever willingly fade into the background.

The fatal influence his ideas have already had over other disturbed teenagers will be explored further in the next chapter. For even while incarcerated, Varg Vikernes remains a dangerous young man.

Chapter Seven

~~~~~

Hendrik Möbus: An Absurd Inferno (1993-2001)

The fugitive

On 29th August 2000, agents from the US Marshall's service swooped on a 24-year-old German man who had been on the run from his country for the past two months, outside a family restaurant in Lewisburg, West Virginia.

The fugitive, Hendrik Albert Viktor Möbus, was a convicted murderer who had broken his parole in Germany, where he was notorious not only as a teenage killer but as a member of Varg Vikernes' Norsk Hedensk Front (NHF), active in recording and distributing music by white supremacist bands. The reason German police had issued a warrant for his arrest was that he had been distributing records bearing Nazi insignia – illegal in Germany since the end of World War II.

But thanks to the enthusiastic network that had sprung up around the Norwegian Black Metal scene in the early Nineties, ties had forged between the underground music scene in Europe and the States – and there were vast, unregulated fortunes to be made from it. As a result, Möbus had been able to enter America, be wined and dined by the moneyed neo-Nazi elite as he travelled up and down the country, and even have lawyers provided for him when, after his arrest, he attempted to claim asylum.

It was a pretty incredible trajectory for a man who had first hit the headlines at the age of 17, when he and a group of schoolfriends from the former East Germany had brutally and nonchalantly killed a younger boy for a crime no greater than being a social irritant.

Hendrik Möbus came from a place that was between worlds old and new, state-controlled and free market: a former Eastern Bloc town that had been run by the Communist dictatorship of Moscow and the feared Stasi secret police until his teenage years, close in miles but far removed from the decadent West of Europe. Then came the fall of the Berlin Wall. A lot changed, and quickly. When the barriers came down in 1989 and the ideas of the consumer society poured in, there was a whole generation there who were ripe for rebellion. Having grown up under dour Party rule all their lives, how could they not look eagerly to the products of the bright, free West to alleviate their boredom and relative poverty?

However, what Möbus and his friends found was something very different. Something that Germany had desperately hoped to purge from its society forever.

Over the Wall

Sondershausen lies amid the picturesque mountains of Kyffhäusern, in the Northern Thuringia region of the former East Germany. Before World War II, this area of the country had been a celebrated centre of Central European culture and learning. Sondershausen itself had been the capital of the principality of Schwarzberg-Sondershausen from the late 16th century right up until 1918.

During the long years of post-war Communism, the town had been heavily industrialised, manufacturing textiles, clothing and paper; its mineral-rich surrounding countryside used as a potash-mining centre. But despite the ravages of war and totalitarianism, Sondershausen still retains many of its historic treasures. Its old market place is surrounded by beautiful townhouses and watched over by the commanding 16th century castle, the largest in the region, and the elegant former Prince's Palace.

But up until 1989, time had stood still in Sondershausen, the clock stopped at around 1940. Youth culture had never existed here, and children were supposed to be good Party members, finish their schooling, go to work in the factories and start a family of their own. So when the first steady trickle began to flow in, the videos and records that portrayed the past 50 years of teenage rebellion on the other side of the Berlin Wall – and still more dazzlingly, the other side of the Atlantic Ocean – the effect was overwhelming. It must have provided for these thrill-starved kids the equivalent moment of when Dorothy and Toto went from black-and-white Kansas to Technicolour Oz.

Social workers, teachers, psychiatrists and priests have since pinpointed this overflow of indiscriminate information as the starting point for a violent change in the psyche of East German youth, who never had any context of reality to put it all in. 'Our teenagers are as helpless in the face of the barrage of violence that comes from the

United States as South American Indians are to influenza infection,' as one psychiatrist put it. 'Their immune system is simply kaput.'

In Sondershausen there was certainly trouble brewing, and the older High School students in the town led the way.

Slasher flicks and teenage kicks

A group of teenage boys in particular stood out – Hendrik Möbus, Sebastian Schauscheill and Andreas K, whose obsessions with the dark side had been budding even under Communist rule. They seemed to be the first kids in town who could get their hands on all this new bounty from the West, and their favourite pastime was watching slasher movies on video. They were particularly enamoured of the cult horror movie *Evil Dead*.

Sam Raimi's 1981 *grande guignol* is about five students who take a holiday in the woods and unwittingly raise ancient demons that transform them into monsters. With its lurid and none-too-convincing special effects, it's universally recognised as more of a comic than a horror classic, which was intentional on Raimi's part. But to the Sondershausen kids, even primitive special effects and outrageous storylines looked impressive, and it's likely the amusement understood by Western teenagers with years of B-movie history to draw upon could have been lost in translation. Not that Möbus and his mates have ever come across as particularly humorous types.

However, the film's creepy, mountainous woodland setting was not so far removed from the place where they lived. Sondershausen is surrounded by acres of wild woods, pitted with quarries and shafts, the scars of potash mining. Möbus' father had even built a cottage in the middle of them.

Möbus was always slightly more culturally sophisticated than his peers; like Øystein Aarseth he was a scene-maker, a leader of the pack. Together with his older brother Ronald, he had done his best to defy the Party line and listen in to rebellion on the airwaves, tuning his radio to catch broadcasts of British and German punk and metal and occasionally getting his hands on Polish or Hungarian bootlegs. When the Wall fell, he eagerly embraced Thrash, Death and Doom metal acts like Slayer, Destruction, Morbid Angel and Possessed.

It wasn't just the urgency of the music he appreciated. It was the philosophy behind it that really appealed to him.

So, when he heard the Norwegian Black Metallers Darkthrone's prophetic 1991 album *A Blaze in the Northern Sky*, the earth moved for

Möbus. It was then, at the age of 16, that he decided to form his own Black Metal band with Schauscheill and Andreas, which he named Absurd, because, as he later explained: 'as we understand it, absurdus equals diablus, i.e., a maelstrom that's sending out ravaging, entangling, wrecking, decaying influence; an expression of Chaos.'

The fledgling Absurd, all dressed in black and covered with Pentagram symbols, were not taken straight to the bosom of their hometown contemporaries. They were mocked by both left-wing punks and right-wing skinheads for being earnest and humourless poseurs. But crucially, as any budding Manson knows, the little girls understood. Möbus, with his square-framed glasses and slight cleft palate was not a likely heartthrob, neither was the weedy Andreas. But Sebastian Schauscheill was dashing enough to stoke up some girl trouble.

Fanning the flames

Möbus later claimed to have been 'wholly electrified' when he first heard about the Fantoft church burning in 1992. With their posse of schoolgirl admirers, Absurd began to form a small circle of Black Metal adherents in the suitably rugged surroundings of the local rock quarry – another location that chimes with the setting of *Evil Dead*. Here they would perform Satanic 'baptism' sessions, which supposedly involved a 'leader', dressed in black and praising Lucifier, cutting the arm of each initiate with a knife and drinking his blood.

When not in school, Absurd spent their time between the quarry, the woods and the local Youth Centre, where they rehearsed their material, much to the disgust of the members of the Christian Young People's Club, which also held their meetings there. Into this hormonal melée stepped a 14-year-old boy called Sandro Beyer, who became increasingly enamoured of Absurd's music and rhetoric and started passing them letters stating his admiration.

At the time, letter-writing was a strange form of secret communication between the youths of Sondershausen, who, devoid of home computers, the Internet or mobile phones, preferred to express their opinions by swapping notes. This was done with real urgency, the missives passing between people who only lived a few doors away from each other, their secretive nature more alluring than open conversation.

Beyer started dressing like Möbus' clique and attempted to hold his own in opinions with the older crowd. It worried his parents, who got hold of one of his Pentagram T-shirts and burned it, forbidding Sandro to have anything to do with the local heathens. But a two-year age gap is a yawning chasm to an older teenager, and Absurd were not impressed with his attentions anyway. Irritated by his hanging around like a lost puppy, they began to publicly mock and scorn him.

Humiliated, Sandro ripped down all the Satanic accoutrements he had collected in his bedroom and promised his mother Cornelia, 'I won't hang around with these people any more, they're too brutal to me.'

But Sandro's wounds still smarted. He plotted a crude revenge. Somehow he found out that Sebastian Schauscheill had been having an affair with a married woman who was now pregnant with his child, and he threatened to reveal the adultery to the rest of the town. Catching wind of this intrigue, Schauscheill responded by sending Sandro a written challenge: *Primitive violence is not our thing. Sorcery is more effective.* Möbus weighed in with further, more overtly violent threats, in badly-spelt English: *The hell will come to your home. You will die. Sathan awaits! Stay away from us you whimp and poser! Sathan be my guard.*

The fact was, Schauscheill's illicit relationship had already caused tensions between himself and the rest of Absurd. His married mistress was a Christian who had coerced him into joining in with her enthusiasms for animal rights and environmentalism. He divided his time between Satanic band rehearsals and earnest letter-writing about Green issues to the national newspapers. Perhaps because of this schism in their midst, the partying that went on with Absurd and their followers became more violent and out of control. One night, after getting thoroughly drunk and singing Luciferian hymns, they broke into a deserted house and destroyed most of its contents in an inebriated frenzy.

They needed a focus for all this rage. And that focus became Sandro Beyer.

Invitation to a murder

Like Varg Vikernes before him, Möbus decided that the best way to deride his enemies was to get as big an audience as possible and speak to the press. In this case it was only his High School magazine, but it was a start. At the beginning of 1993, he gave an interview in which he took pains to point out his displeasure with the young upstart. 'Sandro B', as he referred to him, was the very epitome of everything Absurd reviled.

'It was only lately Sandro had got on our nerves with his appearance,'

Schauschiell would later tell the police. 'Because we were slightly fixated upon him, this caused an idea to form.'

Absurd had by now stopped rehearsing at the Youth Centre and had moved their equipment to the little cottage Möbus' father had built in the woods. Here they plotted to raise some ancient demons of their own, and take their revenge on the hapless Beyer. They went about it a very calculating way.

Using a mutual female friend as a messenger, they sent a trick message to lure Sandro out. The messenger, 'Juliana', claimed that she shared Beyer's hatred of Absurd and asked him to meet her on a specified evening at the round tower in town so that they could discuss how they could combine to bring the band's reputation down.

Sandro fell for it, hook, line and sinker. At 8pm on the evening of 29th April, he arrived at the designated spot. The girl who had written the letter wasn't there. The members of Absurd were instead.

Deep in the woods

Acting as if it was mere coincidence that they should meet, the band spoke kindly to Sandro for the first time, and flattered by this unexpected turn of events, he agreed to accompany them to the cottage in the woods where they could lay their animosities to rest.

Once inside, they maintained their convivial air and offered Beyer a seat. But by then, far away from the safety of the town centre, he was wary of their real intentions and tried to make his excuses to leave.

Too late.

Andreas K grabbed an electrical cord and wrapped it round the boy's neck. Sandro tried to fight his way free and then, realising he was overpowered, to scream for help. Möbus pulled a knife and started slashing at his victim, while the others tied his hands behind his back.

Desperate now, Sandro begged to be released, promising he would never reveal what had just happened and even offering his tormentors his life savings of 500 Deutsche Marks (about £130). For a moment, the three attackers considered this idea, wondering if they should just let him loose in the woods. But Beyer had been so free with his accusations before they decided that he would never stick to his promise, and in fact, would probably make straight for the police. Sandro had already seen too much.

So instead, they set upon the screaming, crying, terrified boy. Möbus grabbed his legs. Andreas K and Schauscheill got the electrical cord around his neck and tightened it from both sides. They held on until the last shudders had left Sandro's body and they were sure he had taken his last breath.

'Oh shit,' said Andreas as the realisation of their madness slowly dawned. 'Now I've completely ruined my life.'

But his friends had no time for such reflections. They knew now that they had to get rid of the body, in order to get away with the crime. The three of them hauled Beyer's body about a hundred yards away from the cottage, where there was a dilapidated shed by a stream. Exhausted, they went home for the night.

Meanwhile, Sandro's parents, beside themselves with worry when their son hadn't arrived home by 10pm, had already made one futile search for him. Returning home to an empty house, they called out the police.

Satanskinder

The next day, Möbus, Schauscheill and Andreas K returned to the scene of the crime. They wrapped the corpse in a blanket and carried it to a nearby excavation pit, where they quickly and none-too-thoroughly buried him.

With police dogs and volunteers scouring the woods, it only took six days before the body was found, and the very public feud between Beyer and the Absurd members led the police straight to the killers. Möbus later expressed his annoyance that the cops had moved too quickly for them to work out any alibis, confident he could have worked out a scenario to save them. But his friends were never as together as he was.

All three attempted to deny the charges at first, but none of them took long to cave in. Schauscheill didn't offer much by way of defence. 'It had to happen,' he told investigators. 'It was simply inside of us, like a compulsion.' He also admitted the murder had been premeditated, the scheme hatched at least a week before. 'The guy had to go.'

Was the imagery they had absorbed from Black Metal a motivation? Schauscheill shrugged. It may have been, he conceded, but he was reluctant to lay the blame on music alone. He instead spun a strange story about voices in his head telling him to kill Beyer about six months before he did so.

However, the press had other ideas. The German news weekly *Der Spiegel* reported the story under the headline *Infernus and Sacrifical Blood*, next to Nazi imagery taken from the Satanic fanzine alluded to in the title, *Infernus*. The article went on to describe the black magic ceremonies that had taken place in the old quarry in Sondershausen, and how the sinister craze sweeping the town had eventually led to Sandro Beyer's untimely death. They dubbed the Absurd trio *Santanskinder* – Satan's Children.

Two journalists from Berlin, Lianne von Billerbeck and Frank Nordhausen, took the name and weighed in with a book about the case, which was published in 1994. Subtitled *The Murder Case of Sandro B, Satanskinder* attempted to unravel what had gone on in that unremarkable little town that could have evoked such terror. They couldn't get the co-operation of the killers themselves, so most of the testimonies came from friends and hangers-on who were now disgusted with what Möbus and company had done. A picture emerged of a group of youths who lived in a fantasy world.

But this couldn't have been further from the interview Möbus later gave to the authors of *Lords of Chaos*, in which he demonstrated no leanings towards the fantastical at all. Indeed, his answers are all cool, clear and to the point.

Möbus had grown up under a totalitarian regime. 'People raised in the "Free World" will never wholly understand the way of dictatorship,' he said, unconsciously echoing what his opponents would also say about where he went wrong. His way of rebelling was to find something else equally as extreme – paganism, Black Metal, ultimately Nazism. He left very little doubt that this was his actual conviction, even though he dressed it up in quasi-mystical terms like 'blood and soil cosmology' stating his aim was to reclaim the beliefs of the Germanic tribes of the last millennium. 'We are proud to be of pure German descent, because we view the Germans as the *crème de la crème* of the White Race,' he stated.

Möbus scorned the press' black magic angle as 'B-movie trash', preferring, in B-movie terms, to compare himself and his comrades to John Milius' 1982 Arnold Schwarzenegger vehicle *Conan the Barbarian*: 'it's splendid to see the "might" of a Semetic demigod perish in front of the steely will of a firm, determined "barbarian".'

In fact, the German press probably did their public a disservice in portraying Möbus as a deranged Satan-worshipper. It might be comfortable to separate off reality into a fairytale world of good folk and 'monsters' that appear in the night. But Möbus is no monster. He is instead an extremely clever, calculating young man with a chilly disregard for other people's feelings and a conviction that he alone is right.

And that's a lot more scary than the bogey man.

Will to power

Möbus was still only 17 years old when he was tried at the Muehlausen regional court in February 1994, and as such received the maximum sentence for youth punishment in Germany – eight years. Schauscheill received the same treatment, but Andreas, who was perceived more as a hanger-on than a ringleader, had his sentence set at six years and his identity protected – his real surname was not allowed to be published. In the end, he served only three years.

Using Vikernes as a role model, Möbus put his time behind bars to good use. With the publication of *Satanskinder*, his notoriety had spread, and there were others out there more than willing to bring his music, and more importantly, beliefs, to a wider audience. The Polish National Socialist Black Metal (NSBM) band Graveland released Absurd's demo tape *Thuringian Pagan Madness* in the summer of 1995. Its tasteful front cover depicted Sandro Beyer's grave and the line: *He was murdered by Absurd on 29 April 93*. The tape contained the song 'Into The Forest', a proud depiction of what had happened that night: *'In the forest no one hears the victim's cry/The gruesome act is done/The dead one's last words were: God stand by me!/And the full moon shines into the pitch black night.'*

The authors of *Lords of Chaos* also interviewed Möbus from his prison cell in 1997, and he was able to expound at length on his theories of 'esoteric racialist mysticism' to a global audience for the first time.

'National Socialism is the most perfect synthesis of the Luciferian will-to-power, and neo-heathen principles and symbolism,' Möbus enthused, adding some more of his fanciful terms for Nazism. 'If "Aryan" stands for the noble, the illuminated creative power of the White, then "Jewish" means just the opposite.'

Möbus also declined to offer any remorse about the death of Sandro Beyer, or as he referred to him: 'that Leftist faggot'. 'Every passing second a human dies, so there's no need for such a big fuss about this one kill,' he opined. This comment would land him in trouble again once the book was published, but as with Vikernes, Möbus seems to be more attracted to self-publicity than self-preservation. When e-zine *Mourning the Ancient* asked him a similar question, he turned it around so that Beyer's death was 'a beneficial act for mankind'.

Spirit of Resistance

In America, where *Lords of Chaos* was first published, another sect of White Supremacists took note, among them the most public neo-Nazi of them all. William Pierce had a long career in bigotry. He began associating with George Lincoln Rockwell, the founder of the American Nazi party, in 1966, and after Rockwell's assassination in August 1967, Pierce went on join the National Youth Alliance, a far-Right group with Nazi leanings begun by Willis Carto in 1968. The Alliance's aim was to recruit students to smash liberal causes on campus. But, riven by feuding, the group splintered in 1974, and Pierce's wing became known simply as the National Alliance (NA).

The former physics teacher still continued to focus his efforts on recruiting young people, and by the Nineties he was fully exploiting the advantages of the World Wide Web to this end. He wanted to extend the tentacles of race hatred to as many other countries as he could.

Pierce was most infamous in America for his 1978 pulp racist novel *The Turner Diaries*, written under the pseudonym Andrew Macdonald, which described an Ayran world takeover and is considered by the US Anti-Deflamation League to be 'the bible of the far-right terrorist movement in America'. This book was believed to have inspired Timothy McVeigh and Terry Nichols, the Oklahoma Bombers, whose strategies in blowing up the Oklahoma City Federal Building perfectly imitated the bombing of a government building as outlined in the book. McVeigh had picked up his copy at a gun show. Pierce was selling copies through the NA's website translated into Swedish, French, German, Portuguese and Russian.

In April 1999, Pierce bought the white power music label Resistance Records, which put out rock, Oi! and heavy metal music, together with its in-house magazine *Resistance*. Pierce was such a connoisseur of youth culture that he knew that the current *Resistance* roster was already sounding a bit old hat. He knew where the sort of disaffected kids that would make good foot soldiers were getting their thrills from these days – Scandinavia and Eastern Europe. He made it clear from the beginning that he wanted to use Resistance as a means to move into the distribution of NSBM records. In his August 1999 National Alliance website bulletin he wrote:

'*The resurrected company will handle a much broader spectrum of white resistance music, including genres such as Gothic and Black Metal.*' In every subsequent issue of the magazine, he hyped up the Black Metal references.

Meanwhile, in prison, two pen-pals from nearer climes had begun corresponding. For Pierce's future plans, this couldn't have been more exciting – or more helpful.

A meeting of minds

Möbus first mentioned he had been in touch with Vikernes in a 1998 interview with *Mourning the Ancient*. 'It's amazing to see that we share almost all the same ideas and ideals,' he enthused. 'Varg is a superior man and a supreme personality. If there is any way to get him out of jail, then I wouldn't hesitate to participate in such a project.'

But, while both were forced to languish in detention, they began a steady stream of correspondence with a view to cementing a future business partnership.

Because he kept his head down within the prison population, Möbus only served five years of his sentence and was paroled in August 1998. Shortly after his release, he appointed himself as head of the German branch of Vikernes' NHF, which now has chapters in seven countries – Norway, Sweden, Finland, Germany, Russia, Holland and the United States.

Part of their agenda was to release records and books by Vikernes and like-minded NSBM bands, and to that end, Möbus and his brother Ronald took over a Back Metal label, Darker Than Black, and incorporated Vikernes' Cymophane releases into his schedule.

Möbus also hooked up with the Saxonian Hammerskins, a chapter of the ultra-violent international skinhead/football hooligan group Hammerskin Nation. This allowed him to up the ante and the pennies started rolling in when Darker Than Black made a distribution deal with Germany's Hate Records, one of the biggest distributors of white power music in Europe. Next, Möbus started to look towards the United States.

Extremist links between the USA and the former East Germany had already been long established, with the Americans taking little heed of the difference in laws between the two countries. Nebraska-based publisher Gary Lauck was jailed in Germany for four years in 1995 for selling race-hate literature in the country, and as a youth movement based around Satanism and Nazism flourished via the World Wide Web, the authorities were ever vigilant.

It only took two months before the police became aware of the comments Möbus had made to the authors of *Lords of Chaos* and the high profile he was forging for himself on the international NSBM scene. At the instigation of the then Thuringian Minister for Justice Kretschmer, two lawsuits were launched against Hendrik Möbus – one for reviling the deceased, the other for the use of anti-constitutional symbols. The Tiergarten district court sentenced him to eighteen months and the district court at Eisenacht levied a further eight months. Möbus lodged an appeal and disappeared from sight.

On the lam

For he was now part of a well-organised network, with its adherents spread across the globe. To try and draw away some heat, Möbus publicly announced his departure from Darker Than Black, although he continued to run the label from hiding, while officially his parole was revoked.

On 6th October 1999, the authorities raided a series of locations in Germany in an attempt to locate the miscreant and get their hands on as many illegal recording operations as possible. Although Möbus still wasn't captured, Darker Than Black, No Colours Records and Burznzag Productions, amongst others, were all charged with distributing Nazi propaganda. Darker Than Black was shut down and Möbus' new sentence upped another 18 months accordingly. Now faced with a possible five-year jail term, the brave Sondershausen soldier decided his only option was to run – and he knew exactly where he was going to be welcomed with open arms.

Möbus had not been slow to lay down his plans for a bold new American venture. According to information published in the British anti-Fascist magazine *Searchlight,* the would-be entrepreneur had worked out a deal to distribute Darker Than Black products through Bestial Offerings, a small distributor in Midland, Texas, who agreed to become DTB Vinland, a mail-order outlet for their products. He also came to an arrangement with another Texan firm who dealt in NSBM products, Ancestral Research Records. He had plenty of other people to see and options to discuss Stateside. Among them, William Pierce.

So, in December 1999, Hendrik Möbus got on a plane and flew to Seattle. He had a 90-day visa waiver stamped in his passport, and no one stopped him on his way.

Coming to America

The man who apparently paid Möbus' airfare was Nathan Pett, a leading figure in the White Order of Thule (WOT), a small, esoteric neo-Nazi group that bases its philosophy on a ragbag of ideas that range from Fredrick Nietzsche to George Lincoln Rockwell. They describe themselves as 'a Brotherhood, a loose alignment of Aryan minds, hearts and souls, together only for the philosophy, fraternity, and spirituality, respectively, which will further all work for the Cause'. To that end, they self-publish an irregular journal called *Crossing the Abyss*.

The WOT teaches its members various programmes that chime with the ideas of both The Church of Satan and Vikernes' and Möbus' Nazi folk-fairytales – everything from 'Practical Occultism', 'Jungian psychology' and 'Archetypal Pathworking', to 'Folkish Hygiene' and 'Hermetic Philosophy'. They recommend the reading of such diverse studies of extremism as Ryszard Kapuscinski's *Imperium*, Adolf Hitler's *Mein Kampf*, Oswald Spengler's *The Decline of the West*, Ragnar Redbeard's *Might is Right*, Julius Evola's *Revolt Against the Modern World* and Nietzsche's *Twilight of the Idols*.

The WOT provided Möbus with a network of helpers that got him across the United States, starting in Pett's hometown of Elk, Washington to his eventual destination, Richmond, Virginia. Pett himself was the editor and publisher of another magazine with a NSBM flavour – *Fenris Wolf*, strapline: *The Revolutionary Voice of the Pagan Liberation League*. According to *Searchlight*, *Fenris Wolf* was also affiliated with NHF.

But whatever their esoteric links might have, Möbus and Pett didn't keep their minds, hearts and souls together for long. Soon after arriving in the northwest of America, Möbus fell out with his host, and rapidly made his way across the States to the Richmond chapter of the WOT, staying with sympathetic white power activists along the way.

Already a warrant was out for his arrest. The German authorities had discovered Möbus' destination, and asked the Americans for help in March 2000. The warrant was applied for on 7th July, by which time the US authorities knew where he was.

Hammer time

However covert it may have seemed, Möbus' passage to Richmond was not without incident. The German impresario had already made himself some nasty enemies. According to postings on various Internet discussion groups, Möbus was attacked when he reached Virginia, in most accounts, by Pett and an accomplice. In a grim echo of his pitiless treatment of Sandro Beyer, Möbus was reportedly handcuffed and methodically beaten with a hammer all over his body. By the time his attackers left him, he was seriously injured.

Of course, with Möbus' status as a fugitive, no complaint could ever have been made nor charges brought for this injury, but immediately afterwards, Pett came under attack from various white power organisations. Alex Curtis, the editor of the *Nationalist Observer* e-zine, declared that Pett and his group 'cannot be trusted and should be shunned as rats and detriments to Ayran honour'.

It seemed like no matter where he was, trouble and Möbus just couldn't leave each other alone. What he needed was a bigger, better, more powerful sugar daddy. Möbus headed for William Pierce's National Alliance headquarters in West Virginia. He arrived in June 2000 and stayed for almost three months.

Despite the fact that there was an international arrest order out for Möbus at the time he was staying with him, Pierce and his laywer Victor Gerhard claimed to be unaware of their guest's fugitive status. Which was rather at odds with the article about him they had just run in the Spring edition of *Resistance* magazine, which explained Möbus' plight in great detail, concluding that he faced five-plus years in a German jail if caught. Investigators later found out Möbus had written the article himself.

The truth was, Pierce needed Möbus and his contacts in the NSBM scene in Europe if he was to realise his record distribution dream. He had already paid out $250,000 for the Resistance brand – and now he was looking to turn his investment into some seriously filthy lucre.

Black Metal, white cash

So far, Pierce's inroads into Europe had consisted of his acquisition of the Swedish racist label, Nordland. But he had his eye on a greater prize – Varg Vikernes' Cymophane – and Möbus was the conduit to these riches. With an eye to the main chance, Pierce later explained: 'I invited him to stay as my guest and help me establish new outlets in Europe for my records. And that's what he did for 10 weeks. He stayed as my guest, and we talked about the role of music in our overall effort.'

It obviously didn't take them long to cut a deal – on 30th June, Pierce registered Cymophane as a listed company, with himself as organiser and manager. Möbus had clearly handed over at least part of Cymophane and now Pierce had the US rights to both Vikernes' and Möbus' music, and access to some of the most popular white power bands in the world.

Which might seem an obscure and dubious method of raising finance to an outsider's eye. But these record labels are not run as others. Interpol reported in 1999 that neo-Nazi music had become a £2 million-a-year criminal enterprise. Because CDs are bootlegged by criminals, no taxes, royalties or record company mark-ups are deducted from profits. Taking into consideration the fact that the CDs themselves cost bootleggers about £1 a copy to produce, Interpol estimates that the profit margins are better than for selling hashish.

As with any such racket, the price of controlling such profitable ventures is the constant threat of violence from rivals. Which could explain why Möbus received such a beating when he decided to take his labels away from Pett and deliver them to Pierce.

The acquisition was highly important. *Searchlight* calculated that it was likely to lift his profits to as much as $1 million in a very short time. Not only that, it would help broaden Pierce's influence as much as his trash paperback did in the Seventies, as more young people tuned into the sounds of race hate. Pierce was out to assemble his own global version of Hitler Youth.

The law closes in

However, on 29th August 2000, Möbus' little sojourn in America came to an abrupt end when agents pounced on him near Pierce's house in Lewisburg. Pierce made a public show of outrage, accusing the police of breaking Möbus' arm when they took him in, an injury that was much more likely sustained during the hammer attack in July.

But it was proof of how much the 'quiet, skinny, non-violent intellectual', as Pierce put it, meant to the National Alliance leader that he immediately threw his weight and cash behind Möbus' attempts to stay in America. With Pierce's assistance, Möbus filed paperwork with the US Immigration and Naturalization Services (INS) requesting political asylum.

On 9th September, in an unprecedented move in the Alliance's history, Pierce put out a plea to his members to raise funds to hire a lawyer for his young German friend to fight extradition. It stands as a measure of his power that he quickly raised $9,000. The lawyer that Pierce hired to defend his business partner? Mark O'Connor, who had defended John Demjanjuk – the so-called 'Ivan the Terrible' – who was charged with brutally torturing and murdering Jews at the Treblinka concentration camp in World War II.

Then Pierce began a campaign on Möbus' behalf, placing banner headlines on *Resistance's* website and around the network of far-Right sympathisers in the US. Reading *Free Hendrik Möbus!* if you clicked on the banner (some of which were still operational at time of writing), you'd get more information: *Hendrik Möbus of the Black Metal band Absurd sits in jail with no way to speak to the outside world. He served his sentence for murder, but now his right to free speech makes him an international criminal.*

Pierce's argument was that the things that Möbus had said and the imagery he'd used would all have been legal in the United States, which was to form the basis of his asylum plea. As usual, he was using popular phrases like 'free speech' and 'censorship' to try and attract more young people to supporting his cause. Needless to say, the INS were not impressed and started action to deport the fugitive as soon as he'd applied for asylum.

'Stupidity, lies and ignorance'

From his holding tank in Batavia in New York – where he was placed in solitary confinement for his own protection from the mainly black and Hispanic population – Möbus immediately penned a self-righteous missive which Pierce, obligingly, posted on the Net for him. Alluding to the subtitle of Hitler's *Mein Kampf*, Möbus vented an icy rage at the 'seven years of stupidity, lies and ignorance' he had suffered at the hands of the German, and now the international, media.

With his carefully moderated prose, he intended to prove that he was nothing like the raging madman of popular image, pointing out that two prison psychiatrists had assessed that he was not insane, and that he would never have got early parole otherwise. What he really took exception to was being portrayed as a psychopath – a 'cold-blooded, remorseless killer', but in his familiar defence of his attitude towards Sandro Beyer it is hard to conclude otherwise.

'I really grow tired of listening to all the many voices who demand a public display of remorse,' he wrote. *'Let me tell you, nothing I did caused the concrete death of the victim. I didn't strangle him or break his windpipe. I abetted the killing, though, and was thus punished as severely as the others. What I've done is nothing I'm proud of, but it is nothing to regret either. My mind doesn't work the way others would like it to work. My ethics are anarchic and in no way compatible to Judeo-Christian morality. If I were to weep, cry and beg for forgiveness, I would be a hypocrite.'*

Möbus then went on to pour scorn upon the 'Satanist' label he'd been lumbered with in his homeland.

'*Talk to anyone who is seriously dedicated to Satanism and you will find that he will just sneer at me. For the true initiate, I'm as "Satanic" as the Pope: not at all. This doesn't bother the journalists, of course. They have even dreamed up another name for me: "Nazi-Satanist"...Frankly it is beyond my humble imagination how you can lump together Satanism and National Socialism.*'

However, he did conclude that this was an effective way of stigmatising him '*with a mark of evil*'. Then, without any irony, Möbus ended his essay by comparing himself to Hitler.

'*Adolf Hitler's struggle against stupidity , lies and ignorance was not victorious for most of his life. And compared to what is said about him, I may have actually been treated rather well by the media! But there are a few people, including myself, who understand the truth about him...Hence I am hopeful of finding people who are able to grasp the truth about me also. It is to these people that I am addressing this essay.*'

Germany must have been really pleased to have him back.

Back in black

On 5th March 2001, the INS turned down Möbus' asylum request on the grounds that he was being pursued in Germany not for his original crime but for crimes committed since his release, in knowing breach of his parole. Pierce's subsequent appeal against deportation failed, and Möbus was handed back to German authorities on 28th July 2001 and made to serve the rest of his original sentence for the murder of Sandro Beyer.

In the former East Germany he returned to, Satanism was still shocking news. On 31st August 2001, three teenagers who had been part of a Satanist webring jumped to their deaths from the 78-metre high Goeltzaschtal Bridge, near Reichenbach in Saxony. Aged between 14 and 18, they were all boys who had been dabbling in Internet chat on various Satanic forums, including one identified as Blue Rose. Neither drugs nor alcohol had been involved, and the boys left a suicide note saying that they were so deeply unhappy with their lives that they couldn't go on.

Worried officials ordered an inquest into the morbid craze that had so fascinated teenagers in East Germany since reunification. It was estimated that there were a hardcore of between 3,000 and 8,000

Satanic followers that had built up in the years since 1989, when the promised dreams of freedom and riches had significantly failed to come true in the impoverished East of Germany. The dissatisfied adherents of the Dark Lord were not just defying the adult world, but bonding in their mutual disappointment of very uncertain futures. They took part in 'death chats' on the Internet, where they exchanged unpleasantries on their grim outlook on life. The German Protestant church feared this was creating a wave of virtual death cults. More and more of these kids were not just using symbols like Pentagrams as statements either. They had taken up Möbus' preferred Nazi insignia.

Since the 2001 incident, there have been 15 other occult-related teenage suicides in Saxony. Four other youths survived suicide attempts. Teachers in the area told police and youth authorities that there was a 'depressed atmosphere' hanging over their classrooms. 'It is very troubling what is happening to our youth,' commented one unnamed headmaster, while vicar Andreas Breit added: 'The occult scene is thriving in this region. They have black masses in the ruins of buildings and in the open. They have rituals and swear oaths.'

'Glorifies brutality, disdains human dignity'

Worse was to come. Möbus' home county of Thuringia had been awash with church burnings and grave desecrations since the first time he'd been put in prison. Now the youth had gone wild to the extent that the first USA-style classroom massacre took place in the capital Erfurt in 26th April 2002. A 19-year-old former student, Robert Steinhauser, of the celebrated Johann Gutenberg Gymnasium, one of Germany's finest schools, went on a berserk rampage of his alma mater with a pump-action shotgun, mowing down 12 teachers, two female students, a policeman who tried to stop him, and, finally, himself. Steinhauser had been expelled for bad behaviour earlier in the year, and the motive could have been revenge – he carried out the shootings as his former classmates sat for their leaving exams. But leading clergymen thought there had been a far more pernicious influence on the generations that had grown up since the fall of the Wall.

'I am certainly not advocating censorship,' said the Rev Johannes Richter, the former bishop of nearby Leipzig, 'however, somehow we have to get a handle on what comes across the Atlantic via television and the Internet.

'Especially here in the East, young people are very vulnerable to the violence that comes gushing out in news reports and in Hollywood films. Remember, we have lost the ground under our feet. The Nazis and the Communists have had 56 years to destroy our social structures, which had taken millennia to develop. The traditional family is largely gone. Congregational life too, has vanished for most.

'The only reality many young people know is the virtual reality they experience electronically. It's a reality without values, a reality where parental neglect had become acceptable, a reality that glorifies brutality, waffles about human rights but disdains human dignity.'

Fellow clergyman, the Reverend Wilhelm Togerson, Provost of the Independent Evangelical-Lutheran Church of Berlin, added a further dimension. Most of the teenagers involved in Satanic cults, he said 'tend to come from broken families without any religion. They were raised in soulless, Soviet-style housing estates, whose tenants no longer have even a faint memory of Christianity.'

East Germany, it seemed, was in crisis.

Into the Abyss

Meanwhile, Hendrik Möbus still had more crimes to pay for. As his original sentence came to an end, he was tried again on 23rd April 2003 for his activities with Darker Than Black, including Holocaust denial and calling for a 'fight against the Jews', his continued badmouthing of Sandro Beyer and his absconding to the States. Ten years after his first trip to jail, on 15th May, he was sent back to Suhi-Goldlauter prison, condemned by a regional court in Erfurt to serve another four years locked up.

In his 1997 interview with the authors of *Lords of Chaos*, Möbus had considered that the four to six years he was likely to serve for the murder of Beyer was a 'rather good deal' for 'experiencing the death of your foe'. He also, to his cost, boasted how being in prison had never stopped him from being active in music or politics, and that 'bad publicity is the most useful promotion'.

He will be 31 years old by the time his current sentence ends, and it seems unlikely Möbus will be considered for early parole this time. The price of his personal freedom has certainly gone up, from four years to almost half his young life. Unlike Varg Vikernes, Möbus does not have a high Internet profile at the current time of writing, let alone his own fan site. No one talks very much about Absurd any more.

William Pierce was never to get the Black Metal empire he dreamed of either. He died suddenly from cancer on 23rd July 2002, at the age of 68. Up until the last moment, Pierce had been trying to infiltrate popular youth movements to further his cause – including the hugely popular anti-globalisation movement. The US Anti-Defamation League consider that Pierce's death will have widespread ramifications for the National Alliance, whom, without such an insidiously intelligent leader, may easily splinter. 'Pierce played a crucial role in its operations and his absence may prove fatal,' they predicted at the time of his death.

But one person who has been forgotten in this whole sad, shocking story is Cornelia Beyer. Sandro's mother still lives in Sondershausen, tending to the grave of her son that is routinely defiled by fans of Möbus, who come to smear their excrement on Sandro's headstone. Interviewed on German TV in 1993, she had taken early retirement due to the stress caused by her son's murder and the constant publicity surrounding his killer. 'Each new newspaper article about Hendrik Möbus tears the old wounds open again,' she said. 'I wished they would have kept him in the USA, far away from Thuringia and Sondershausen. I wish I could finally come to some kind of peace of mind over this. But I can't.'

Chapter Eight

Nico Claux: Murder in the Rue Morgue (1994)

Interview with the Vampire

In late 2001, an incredible story began circulating in the British press, with the publication in *Bizarre* magazine of an interview with 29-year-old Frenchman Nicolas Claux. Under the headline *Interview With A Vampire*, the magazine presented a Q&A with Claux, who was at the time incarcerated in Maison Centrale Poissy, a prison about 15 miles northwest of Paris which houses long-term offenders. It was the first time British readers had heard about this case, and the story boggled the mind for two reasons.

One was that Nico Claux was a self-confessed necrophile, grave robber, cannibal and murderer, dubbed the 'Vampire of Paris', who had broken into mausoleums, stolen blood and bodies from mortuaries and shot a man dead in his first foray into murder. 'I had a grave robbery kit at home, but I only carried it in my backpack when I wanted to rob a grave,' Claux blithely informed readers. 'I only carried my gun when I was out hunting humans. If I had not been jailed, I would have continued. Then I would have moved to another country if things started to get real hot.'

Two, despite the disturbing nature of his crimes and the fact he had been deemed insane at his trial, he was due for release in only a year's time. 'Most people who know me wish I were dead, they're scared shitless,' were his thoughts on that. 'Fuck them and their pathetic lives.'

In the meantime, thanks to the liberal regime of the Maison Centrale prisons, a string of ten such penitentiaries who have put a lot of effort into the rehabilitation of their prisoners through various educational and art therapy programmes, Nico was bringing to life his Satanic interior world in oil paintings. *Bizarre* printed one of his portraits of Anton La Vey, another of Christopher Lee in his classic 1960s Hammer studios *Dracula* role. Readers could buy prints and canvasses of his work if they so desired, they might even prove profitable investments –

by 2001, 'art' works by the now dead serial killers John Wayne Gacy and Ottis Toole were certainly worth hundreds of pounds. Rock stars like Korn's Jonathan Davis and the cult filmmaker John Waters were among many avid celebrity collectors of such 'Murderobilia'.

Claux also provided the magazine with some handy recipe cards, including instructions on how to 'choose', 'carve' and cook your meat. 'Which is worse,' he asked *Bizarre* readers, 'being God's worst enemy or being nothing?'

Significantly, this interview had been conducted with Warren Schofield, the co-editor of the Black Metal magazine *Amon*, who had approached *Bizarre* with the story. Was the Black Metal underground offering up a new anti-hero here? If they were, they had targeted the right magazine. The only 'alternative' culture monthly to get serious shelf-space in the UK, *Bizarre* at that time had a circulation in excess of 100,000 a month.

One thought lingered long after the article had been put down – would the French capital be safe once the blood-hungry Nico was back on the streets?

If this was a very 21st century freak show, it was going to get freakier still once Claux gained his release on 22nd March 2002. Right now, you can go to his website – *http://nicoclaux.free.fr* – buy his artwork and take a look at his online journal. It's an endless round of parties, gigs and book launches around the capital cities of Europe, with a curious (particularly the British) press enthusiastically following his movements. In the ever-expanding interface between outsider art, fetish, Goth and vampire cultures, Nico has become something of a celebrity. But how, exactly, did he manage to get there – and what were the real crimes of the Vampire of Paris?

Gay slayings

In the autumn of 1994, there had been a frightening spate of gay murders in the French capital of Paris. Seven men had been killed in the space of a couple of weeks, all of them felled by slugs from a .22 calibre gun. Detectives from the Brigade Criminelle suspected there was a serial killer at large in the city. Then, at the beginning of October, they had a tip-off. A young man had been caught trying to buy a top-of-the-range camcorder at an expensive store with a cheque in the name of Thierry Bissonnier – a gay man who had recently been found with a .22 bullet in his head.

The shopkeeper was unaware of this fact, but he had noticed that the signature on the cheque the young man signed in front of him was different from that on the required ID to back it up – in this case, a driving licence, also in Bissonnier's name. When the shopkeeper looked closer, he noticed the photograph on the license had been tampered with – the original picture removed and another one crudely inserted over the top. Realising he was about to be rumbled, the customer took fright and ran, leaving the tell-tale documents behind him.

It took less than a month for the police to find the man whose photograph had been left in the forged driving license. They arrested 22-year-old Nico Claux outside the famous Moulin Rogue cabaret club, in the notorious Pigalle red light district, on 15th November. At the time of his arrest, Claux was harassing a young woman in the middle of the street. The police mugshot of him taken at the time of his arrest shows him wearing a hooded top and a fancy, trimmed beard and moustache, with closely cropped hair and an expression of haughty disdain. What you couldn't see were the occult tattoos spread all over his body, the words *Serial Killer* spelled out in English down both of his arms.

While the suspect was taken in for questioning, crime scene investigators were dispatched to Claux's flat on 9 rue Coustou, in the heart of Pigalle. There they found a .22 calibre handgun hidden under his bed, which they immediately sent off for ballistics tests. They also found piles and piles of video cassettes, comprised of slasher films and hardcore S&M, and a stash of similar pornographic magazines. The walls were covered with posters for such notorious banned movies as *Cannibal Holocaust, The Texas Chainsaw Massacre* and *Ilsa, She Wolf of the SS*.

And, according to Nico: 'Throughout my apartment, bone fragments and human teeth were scattered around like loose change, vertebras and leg bones hung from the ceiling like morbid mobiles…On one wall hung a bullet-riddled target, while across the room sat a TV set with jars of human ashes resting on top of it…In addition to my tastes and choice of décor, investigators also discovered several stolen blood bags inside my refrigerator.'

Well, you've got to hand it to Nico. He was certainly a lot more erudite – literary, even – than Möbus or Vikernes.

House of horror

The ballistics tests came back positive – the bullets in Claux's handgun matched the ones left in Thierry Bissonnier's head and body. Confronted with this irrefutable evidence, Claux admitted the murder.

But what about the body parts, the multitude of bones and bagged-up blood in the fridge? The four other gay men who had been victims of the recent crime spree had been killed in the same way as Bissionnier and with exactly the same type of weapon. But Claux says he explained away his grisly trophies not as the remains of other murders, but as the tokens of his many night visits to Paris' vast Gothic graveyards. The blood bags, he said, were taken from his day job, working at the mortuary of St Joseph's Hospital, Paris. The contents were what he liked for a tipple.

'Working as a mortuary assistant from ten months, I had been using my position as a means to fulfil a lifelong fantasy of mine, revolving around cannibalism,' Claux later told the Crime Library website. He went on to describe how he had cut strips of flesh away from corpses and taken them home to cook and eat. For maximum shock value, he claimed that his first meal had been taken from an 11-year-old girl.

Had anyone been aware of how he had been living? As he told *Bizarre*: 'I had some friends but they hardly ever went to my place. When they came, I cleaned the place up. I wasn't leading a double life. Everybody who knew me knew that I was a psycho but I never talked about my crimes. I'm a solitary guy. I don't like people.'

Only one man claimed to have remained friends with Claux before and after his conviction. Igor Mortiis (possibly not his real name) told American author Sondra London what he knew about Nico for her book *True Vampires*. It would have made interesting reading for someone like Robert Ressler, revealing as it did how Claux had long been fixated and amused by severe S&M videos and how he liked to torture animals. Igor claimed that Nico once put a dog into a blender and blew up cats in a microwave oven. One thing that can be substantiated is a video Claux made of himself torturing a mouse to death with a scalpel – he circulated this film via the Net and it doesn't take much searching to find a site offering to sell you a copy.

How long had he been behaving like this? According to Nico, for quite some years.

Lonely only child

Nico Claux's version of his past is as exotic as his later testimonies about his crimes. He was born on 22nd March 1972 in the African country Cameroon, the son of a banker who was often posted to foreign climes for long periods of time. He says he has no recollection of his early childhood, remembering only that his family moved to

London when he was five, then to the south of Paris when he was seven, where they stayed until he was 12.

As a result of an itinerant upbringing without the ballast of any siblings for company, young Nico recalls being a withdrawn and lonely child, who wasn't shown much demonstrative affection from his parents. 'They never hugged me or kissed me, they just let me be in my own most of the time.'

Like that other lonely only child, David Berkowitz, Claux's reaction was to withdraw into a fantasy world, unwilling and perhaps unable to form any real relationships with people. The fact that he never seemed to show any emotion towards his mother and father has often been remarked upon. It seemed he preferred to create his own reality.

'This was when I discovered the occult,' he remembered, and spent long hours reading everything he could lay his hands on about werewolves and vampires. 'A photo of the Sumerian demon Pazuzu especially fascinated me...it symbolised something extremely ancient and powerful...A few years later, I saw the same statue in the movie *The Exorcist* and my interest in the occult grew stronger.'

He pinpoints a major trauma in his life as the death of his maternal grandfather when he was ten years old. Apparently, the two of them were arguing when the old man was stricken with a cerebral embolism and dropped dead in front of young Nico. He says that after that point, believing himself responsible, he became obsessed with death.

Igor also believed this was the turning point for his friend: '...he asked his grandpa to play tennis, but he declined saying he was too tired. But Nico insisted again and again... Finally, the old man told him he would play. As soon as they began the game, the grandpa...died right there in front of him.'

Igor also noted the effect this had on Claux's mother. As he told Sondra London: '...his mother became paranoid, saying it was Nico who killed his grandfather'. Apparently she became convinced her son had killed her father through 'supernatural powers' and remains afraid of her prodigy to this day. 'And so,' said Igor, 'a demon was born.'

Reign in Hell

At the age of 12, the Claux family moved once again, to the Portuguese capital of Lisbon, an ideal place, you might have thought, for a morbid child to let his imagination run wild. It is a once-grand city fallen on harder times, an air of faded grandeur surrounds its elegantly decaying buildings, while on the streets, African refugees can often be seen begging in doorways, bearing the hideous disfigurements of tropical disease, and the poor clamour around tiny hostelries dispensing hallucinogenically-alcoholic cherry brandy shots, waiting for their next fix. Lisbon is also a place that does most of its living by night. Yet Nico was unable to adapt to life there: there was a language barrier that left him ostracised at school and without a confidante at home. His feelings hardened here, he says, into deep misanthropy.

When he was 16, the Claux family moved back to Paris, and Nico says he finally found some measure of inner peace exploring the city's graveyards. 'My favourite things were mausoleums. The most impressive ones can be found at Pere-Lachaise, Monmatre and Passy.' It was not long before he wanted to get a much closer view than just a peer through the windows would allow.

Nico claims to have spent his teenage years working out just how he could gain access to these tombs, picking locks or using a crowbar, studying each tomb 'like a botanist studies plants and flowers'. He would hide himself away in the graveyards during the daylight hours and wait until nightfall, when the gates would be locked, to carry out his investigations into waking the dead. 'I felt like an emperor, reigning in Hell,' he later reflected. He claimed that as his curiosity evolved, he would steal away trophies from the tombs, prise the lids off coffins and mutilate the corpses within. For this he put together the tool kit he told *Bizarre* about: a wrench, a flashlight and a sharpened screwdriver.

Of course, Nico wasn't the only person who had another use for cemeteries after dark. Monmartre and Pere-Lachaise are also notorious cruising grounds for homosexuals – a fact that would later be brought up at Claux's trial.

The increasingly disturbed and isolated Claux once more echoed Berkowitz's trajectory and enrolled into the army at the age of 20. Like Son of Sam, his major fascination was with firearms and he trained as a gunsmith with the 23rd Artillery Corps at Haguenau, cleaning and repairing weapons. But he didn't last long in the demanding world of the military. He was out of the army after only a year.

Eating human flesh

In 1993, Claux says that he made a major career change, one that allowed his obsessions to bloom. He began working at the St Vincent-de-Paul hospital in Paris as a morgue attendant. But he didn't spend long working there either. By December of that year, he had a position as a morgue attendant and stretcher-bearer at St Joseph's Hospital, also in the city. This is where, he claims, he was first able to develop a taste for human flesh.

'It tasted like tartar steak or carpaccio,' he considered. 'People often ask me what went through my mind the first time I indulged my cannibalistic fantasy. Well to be honest, I said to myself: 'Wow! I'm a cannibal! Cool!'

Paris had been rocked by a highly disturbing case of cannibalism in recent memory, one that had also had a most unexpected outcome. In 1981, Issei Sagawa, the son of a wealthy Japanese industrialist, had been studying in the French capital at the prestigious Sorbonne University. He became obsessed with a fellow student, a very beautiful Dutch girl called Renee Hartevelt, whom he invited back to his apartment to discuss the literature that was part of their coursework. Hartevelt had already made it clear to Sagawa she was not interested in him as more than anything than a friend, so Issei laid a series of traps for her in order to get his way.

Once she arrived at his apartment, Sagawa plied Hartevelt with whisky-spiked drinks until she became drowsy. Then, he shot her in the back of the neck with a .22 calibre rifle, had sex with her corpse and began to eat her nose and part of a breast. Over the course of the next two days, he dismantled her bit by bit, keeping back the parts of her he most favoured, and chopping the rest up. He packed the discarded body parts into suitcases, which he then abandoned in the Boise de Boulogne, a landscaped forest park on the west side of Paris. Not long after that, the police came knocking.

Issei Sagawa was happy to confess his crime and describe everything he had done in minute detail. He was so clearly and utterly insane that the judge found him incompetent to stand trail and instead ordered that he be detained indefinitely in the Paul Guiraud asylum in Paris.

But Sagawa's family were not happy about that. Because he was so rich and influential, Akira Sagawa was able to have his cannibal son transferred from Paris to the Matsuzawa psychiatric hospital in Toyko in 1984. Then, after only 15 months' treatment, Akira Sagawa decided Issei was now fully cured and managed to have him released, much against the wishes of the superintendent of the hospital.

Whereafter, this ghoulish-looking young man became a national celebrity. First he wrote his memoir *In the Fog*, in which he described the sensation of eating human flesh. 'It had no smell, no taste, and it melted in my mouth like raw tuna. Finally, I was eating a beautiful white woman and nothing was so delicious!'

The book sold 2,000,000 copies. Sagawa appeared in food magazines chewing on barbecued ribs and made the front cover of one Japanese gourmet periodical. He even had his Parisian affair parodied in the song 'Too Much Blood' by the Rolling Stones.

Nico Claux is a big fan of Issei Sagawa's. He told Sondra London, 'In terms of a post-prison career, Issei Sagawa is who I'd like to equal. He's a food critic, a TV star and a porn movie director.' Claux entered into correspondence with Sagawa and had photographs of Sagawa's arrest and even Hartevelt's autopsy posted on previous website, *vampireofparis.com*. This site has since been taken down, but these photos are still circulating the web, with Claux's name as a credit. Obviously, the (im)moral of Sagawa's flesh-eating fame had been as keenly digested as a tartar steak or a nice piece of raw tuna.

Hunting humans

One of the few parts of Nico Claux's various testimonies to the press that can be absolutely verified is that on the morning of 4th October 1994, he woke up with only one thing in mind – to hunt down and kill a human being. He had no luck searching the streets for likely prey, so he turned instead to the Minitel, France's embryonic version of the Internet, which he knew was the system gay men increasingly favoured to meet, chat and set up assignations. 'It was quick and easy for them,' he later said. 'I found out that it was an easy way for me to kill them without any witnesses, plus I had the guarantee of remaining anonymous, since there was no possibility of tracing back the discussions on Minitel.'

Claux soon became engaged in conversation with a man named Thierry, who was interested in bondage and sado-masochistic sex. Though he claims his choice of victim was solely engineered by the fact that 'survivors never report to the police when they're shot during what they thought would be a gay encounter', Claux was a skilled enough conversationalist to convince his victim he was genuinely interested in some no-strings sex. Thierry Bissonnier gave Nico his address and told him to call round at about noon.

Claux loaded up his .22 handgun, hid it underneath his jacket and made his way to Bissonnier's apartment. Thierry opened the door on the last face he would ever see, invited his Minitel pal in, and shut the door behind him. When he turned around, he found himself staring down the barrel of a gun. Claux squeezed the trigger and the bullet shot through Bissonnier's right eye, lodging itself in his skill. The victim fell to the ground and was shot four more times – once in the chest and three more times in the head.

In his utterly dispassionate accounts of the killing, Claux says that Bissonnier did not die right away, but held on for 15 minutes with five bullets inside him before Claux finally caved his head in with a concrete plant pot. In the meantime, the intruder made himself at home, casing the joint for likely things to steal and helping himself to some cookies, which he ate while calmly regarding Bissonnier's agonising death throes. Once it was over, Claux lifted Bissonnier's wallet with his credit cards in it, his chequebook, his driving licence, an alarm clock and an answering machine. He wiped down the flat for fingerprints and left.

Strangely, he didn't perform any of his beloved necromancy on the corpse. He would later explain this away with the statement: 'I don't like gay men and I didn't want to get AIDS'. Bissonnier was merely 'target practise' to see how efficient Claux's weaponry was, a trial run for killing women whom Nico 'would not just have shot'.

Or, could it have been more simple than that? Could it have been that, in fact, Claux had no vampiric or cannibalistic leanings at all?

Fact and fiction

Thierry Bissonnier's body lay on the floor of his apartment for the next three days, until his increasingly distraught parents, used to hearing from him on a regular basis, went in and discovered the hideous scene.

From the moment Claux was captured and charged, the real details of his subsequent trial are difficult to discern, thanks to a media black-out placed over the courtroom proceedings. This was imposed by the judge, to protect the victim's family, who didn't want the minutiae of Bissonnier's life to be exposed to public scrutiny. All that can really be gleaned about Thierry was that he was 34, a restaurateur and a part-time classical musician who had been involved in a steady relationship with another man at the time of his death.

This is also the time when Claux's subsequent testimonies about his capture, interrogation, trial and charges diverge significantly from the court documents that officially list what crimes he was charged with and found guilty of committing.

On 15th November 1994, Nicolas Jean Paul Claux was charged with first-degree murder, armed robbery, attempted fraud, use of forged documentation and use of a stolen cheque. When he finally came to trial he was found guilty of all these charges by the court on 12th May 1997.

No grave robbing and no cannibalism charges were ever made against him. The blood bags and the bones of corpses supposedly found in his flat were not referred to in any of the official documents, which is surprising as these were all supposedly stolen too.

Between the time the charges were made and the time of his eventual sentencing, Claux was detained in Fleury-Merogis remand centre for extensive psychiatric evaluation, to deem if he were capable of standing trial. Here was where Claux began to give his long and detailed accounts of his lunar activities in Pere-Lachaise and other cemeteries.

The chief investigator in Claux's case was the celebrated detective Gilbert Thiel. Such was Thiel's stature that he was promoted to head up Paris' anti-terrorist squad midway through his primary investigation into Claux. But Thiel obviously had strong feelings about the Bissonnier murder. He carried on working on the case as well as fulfilling the demands of his new role. It wasn't just Bissonnier he was worried about. It was the other dead gay men with .22 bullets in their heads.

Claux's initial claim that he had merely killed Bissonnier as part of a botched robbery did not stand up for long. The fact that he had not forced entry into the apartment and the careful way in which he had wiped down the murder scene saw to that. There didn't appear to be a clear sexual motive, so why had Claux targeted a homosexual?

The accused told his interrogator that he had had an argument with a gay man in the Pere-Lachaise cemetery on the morning of the killing. This had provoked him to single out a homosexual to kill in revenge, using the Minitel to stalk his prey as calculatingly as he had dispatched him. In view of the fact that so many of the other unsolved gay murders had been carried out this way, it must have seemed to the police that they had their serial killer.

But, despite the fact that Claux fitted the profile, and that witnesses claimed to have seen him hanging round gay bars that the other victims frequented, there was never enough physical evidence to charge with Claux these murders. Not that it stopped him making insinuations when he gave interviews: the 'hunting humans' line he fed *Bizarre*; the sly angle he pursued with Sondra London: 'The shootings took place in a one-month period, ending 3rd October 1994. All shootings involved queers shot inside their apartments, house ransacked, no fingerprints, same MO (people shot standing next to the main door), and all were contacted via Minitel. The files were apparently closed on these cases. The year is mentioned in *The Guinness Book of World Records* as being the year when there were the most unsolved cases of this nature in Paris.'

Strangely, Claux gets the date of Bissonnier's murder wrong by one day – if that was the significance of 3rd October he was alluding to.

Psychotic reactions

Claux's defence for the Bissonnier murder was that he was clinically insane. It was therefore important for him to prove this. Dozens of psychological tests were made over the 23 months Claux was kept in Fleury-Merogis. These are the confessions that form the basis for all the subsequent press profiles of Claux, and are presented in such a way that the reader will assume these were used as part of the evidence used in court – not as part of his mental evaluation process. But then, the authors of all these pieces were provided with this documentation not by the French courts but by Claux himself. One such example is used both on the Crime Library website and in *True Vampires*.

'I woke up one day feeling this sinister urge to dig up a corpse and mutilate it. I gathered a small crowbar, a pair of pliers, a screwdriver, black candles and surgical gloves in a backpack. Then I took the subway until the Trocadero station. It was nearly noon. The gates of the Passy Cemetary were wide open, but nobody was inside. The undertakers were out for lunch. Passy is a small Gothic graveyard with plenty of huge mausoleums, which were built during the 19th century. It is located right between two large avenues, so it is impossible to climb in at night. But anyway, nobody could ever imagine there was someone robbing graves at noon.

'I had this special grave in mind. It was a small mausoleum, the burial site of a family of Russian immigrants from the 1917 revolution. I had already pried open the iron door a few days before, and I had closed it afterwards so it would seem that nobody had ever touched it. All I had to do was kick it open…At this point, my mind was in total chaos. I had flashes of death in my head. I took a deep breath and I climbed down the steps leading to the crypt. It was rather a small one, with damp walls, buried deep inside the cemetery ground. There was no other source of light than the candles I had brought. To begin, for more than an hour, I removed one of the heavy coffins from its stone casing. It was especially hard not to let the coffin fall all of a sudden to the ground but somehow I managed to slowly lay it down without making too much noise. However, one edge of the coffin scratched my lower leg when it touched the ground. But that didn't stop me at all.

'I examined the casket for a while. It was solid oak and sealed with big screws. It looked like brand new, so I expected to find a recently *deceased corpse. First, I unscrewed the coffin, which took less than ten minutes. Then I pried it open with the crowbar. Once opened, a horrible stench of putrefaction came out of the box. It smelled like Thanatyl, the product embalmers use on a corpse in order to delay the process of decay. Then I saw the body inside. It was a half-rotten old woman, shrouded in a white sheet, covered with brown stains. Her face seemed to be smeared with oil, but it was simply the death fluids oozing from her skin. The stench was so intense that I nearly fainted. I tried to lift one side of the sheet, but it was glued to her petrified skin. The teeth were protruding from the mouth, but her eyes were gone. I stared into the empty eye sockets, and all of a sudden something broke into my mind. I felt like I was falling into a whirlwind. That's when I picked up the screwdriver. The corpse inside the coffin started to move slightly, like if it had guessed what would happen next. So I began to stab the belly, the rib area and the shoulders. I stabbed her at least 50 times. I really can't remember. All I can remember is that when I woke up, my forearms were covered with corpse slime.'*

With testimonies like these, Claux was hoping that his examiners would find him the violent schizophrenic that he later said that they did. In fact, after multiple experts had seen him, he was diagnosed with a borderline psychotic personality disorder. The psychiatrists did not, however, find any evidence of any neuro-psychic disorders that would have interfered with his discernment or control of his actions. Therefore, he was fit to stand trial.

Malice in chains

Claux's trial eventually began on 9th May 1997, at the Cour d'Assises de Paris, and was presided over by Judge W Wechter, who had already selected his jury. Claux's defence lawyer, Irène Terrel, went ahead and entered a plea of not guilty by reason of insanity. The prosecution began by showing the jury photographs of the scene of the murder and of the piles of violent videos and posters they had found at the accused's flat.

They then stated that Claux had voluntarily admitted to the premeditated murder of Bissonnier and to taking the items from the deceased's apartment that he later used to try and buy goods with. The cheque he had forged to try and buy the camcorder and the tampered-with driving licence were offered up for jury inspection.

There was never any doubt that Claux was guilty of everything he had been charged with. The main arguments raged over exactly how insane he was, with the defence attempting to prove he was schizophrenic and therefore incapable of controlling his actions. After all the arguments had been heard, the jury deliberated for just three hours before finding him resoundingly guilty. He was sentenced to 12 years in prison and given a civil fine of 25,000 Francs.

Claux was sent back to Fleury-Merogis, where he remained for four years, until he was transferred to the more liberal Maison Centrale Poissy in 1999. Here, he was able to study computer programming, work out at the gym, and discover his talent for artistic recreations. And it was from here that his exploits reached the ears of the American publishing company Feral House, who were also responsible for the *Lords of Chaos* book, from its author, Michael Moynihan. In the 2000 anthology *Apocalypse Culture II*, edited by the imprint's founder Adam Parfrey, Nico Claux said good morning to America with an essay entitled *The Vampire Manifesto*.

The contents of this essay suggest that Claux had been devouring the same reading list offered up to adherents of the White Order of Thule. Echoes of Social Darwinist tracts like *Might Is Right* and *Revolt Against the Modern World* pepper the world-view expressed by the prisoner in Poissy. As does a scant knowledge of history, archaeology and science. But the self-righteous, boastful tone of the tract brings to mind immediately the crowings of Messrs Möbus and Vikernes.

In it, Claux claims to be part of a master race of 'superpredators' who possess the same DNA as the long extinct Neanderthal race. Neanderthals, he explains, were the human race's natural predator, superior in every way, including brainpower, to their weedy *Homo sapien* counterparts – which is certainly news to science. Sadly, these cannibal kings of yesteryear were all wiped out in the ice age – but their DNA lives on and has manifested itself in the form of our most celebrated serial killers.

Ignoring the reams of such murderous types noted in history – including the two perennial vampire faves, Erzebet Bathory and France's infamous Gilles de Rais, the nobleman friend of Joan of Arc who supposedly raped and murdered hundreds of young boys as offerings to Satan – Claux considered that it was the Industrial Revolution that awoke the Neanderthals, in the form of Jack the Ripper. Their mission was to save the planet from the parasitic humans, round them up like cattle and gorge on their flesh. Most serial killers, he claimed, were full of the urge to drink blood and eat human flesh – even if they didn't actually get around to doing it.

Claux, of course, was part of this heritage, a superpredator, hotwired to kill. He couldn't be rehabilitated because he wasn't part of the human race.

Making friends and influencing people

The line-up of contributors to *Apocalypse Culture II* reads like a *Who's Who* of a particular brand of American counter-culture. The cover is by Joe Coleman, outsider art's ultimate practitioner, whose minutely-detailed paintings of the decline of Western Civilization offer up iconic imagery of virtually everything that has informed the way we live now. Coleman's art knowingly draws the line through rock'n'roll culture to the cult of the serial killer, from Hank Williams to Charles Manson, cataloguing the fragmentation of society along the way and ultimately presenting the world as one big freakshow spiralling towards Armageddon. As a chronicler of American society, Coleman is hard to beat.

Then there are the writers, spawned from a nucleus of Parfrey, Michael Moynihan and the avant garde musician and fully-paid-up Grand Priest of the Church of Satan, Boyd Rice. The story of this trio goes back decades and pulls together virtually every killer and cult icon mentioned in this book so far.

In 1989, Bostonian Moynihan joined San Franciscan Rice in a side project out of the Church of Satan Rice had begun in 1984, the Abraxas Foundation. Abraxas is a Gnostic diety that combined within itself the forces of light and darkness, good and evil. Rice hoped that his foundation would create 'a new demographic of people who are into the occult, Fascism and Social Darwinism. It is out there as an alternative for kids who are growing up and need that information.'

Moynihan was only too happy to further Rice's cause, only, interestingly enough, he dubbed his particular wing of the organisation Axis Sanguinaries (Blood Axis) because:

'Blood can be seen as LIFE and at the same time it can be equated with DEATH. It is essential to violence in almost all instances. It has powerful sexual connotations. It is the key fluid of history.'

Moynihan is reputed to be a blood-drinker himself. He was also suspected of setting fire to a manger scene in the Cambridge Commons, across the road from Harvard University in 1987. A note left at the scene of the Boxing Day attack read: *'How many more fires before you realize your gods are dead? DEAD!'*

Both Moynihan and Rice were pioneers in the early industrial music scene. Rice, who goes under the musical moniker NON, released his first 'noise music' epic *The Black Album* in the late 1970s, producing music from tape reels of found sounds and cut-ups of teenie-pop music from the 1960s. Moynihan founded his own 'power electronics' group Coup de Grace in 1984. In 1989, the two toured together in Japan, and at around the same time, Moynihan renamed his project Blood Axis.

Moynihan, Rice and Parfrey were first brought together in the early 1980s. Parfrey had begun his publishing career with a southern California-based journal about punk culture called *IDEA*. He then moved to New York, where he met the graphic designer George Petros and Joe Coleman, who was then playing performance art gigs where he would bring his freakshow ideas to violent life by 'geeking' (biting the heads off chickens) and blowing himself up on stage.

In 1984, Parfery and Petros created *Exit*, a New York-based journal, which covered, amongst other things, filmmaker Richard Kern's Cinema of Transgression, the surrounding industrial music scene and arts world. Through *Exit*, Rice joined fellow industrial music contributors Genesis P-Orridge of Throbbing Gristle and Clint Ruin, aka Foetus. The artists displaying their wares in these pages included not just Coleman but Richard Ramirez, John Wayne Gacy, Charles Manson and John Lennon's assassin, Mark David Chapman.

At first a *success de scandale*, the magazine floundered after Parfrey left on issue three. *Exit* limped on another three issues, all the while becoming increasingly obsessed with Fascism. The final issue included contributions from Moynihan and James Mason, an American neo-Nazi whose book *Siege* was later published by Moynihan.

Enter the Dark Lord

Moynihan and Rice were now working closely with Anton La Vey, who gave a detailed interview to Moynihan in 1984. The resulting essay, *The Faustian Spirit of Fascism* was printed in the New York-based music magazine *Seconds* and the Church of Satan's own journal, *The Black Flame*. La Vey also contributed an introduction to the new edition of *Might is Right*, which was enthusiastically promoted by Rice on his 1995 album *Might!* The editor of the new edition of Ragnar Redbeard's Social Darwinist treatise is named as Katja Lane. She is the wife of David Lane, the leader of a far-Right paramilitary group called the Order, who is now serving a life sentence for conspiring to murder a Denver radio DJ, Alan Berg. Joining La Vey in this effort, the afterword was penned by George Hawthorne – none other than the original founder of Resistance Records.

More and more familiar faces now join the fray.

Parfrey's next venture after *Exit* was the formation of Amok Press, with Ken Swezey of the Amok catalogue, which published an intermittent directory of alternative press, record companies and other counter-culture enterprises. Their first release, *Michael*, was an English translation of Nazi Propaganda Minister Joseph Goebbels' novel. The first *Apocalypse Culture* compendium followed in 1988, along with *The Manson File*, a collection of correspondence with Charlie co-edited by Nikolas Shrek (boyfriend of Zeena La Vey) and Rice. Rice was at the time a regular visitor to Manson, and even campaigned to get him released from jail through an Abraxas sideline called the Friends of Justice. However, thanks to their far Right connections, the Abraxas crew became so unpopular in liberal San Francisco that Rice moved to Denver, Colorado. It was here, in 1991, that he and roommate Moynihan were visited by Secret Service agents who accused a stunned Moynihan of plotting with Manson followers to assassinate the then-President George HW Bush on a forthcoming visit to the city.

Parfrey, meanwhile, was also moving around the country – from New York to Los Angeles, then, following the LA riots, to Portland, Oregon. He began to publish under the Feral House imprint and hired one Keith Stimely to write his press releases. The late Stimely was previously the editor of the journal of the Institute of Historical Review, the world's leading Holocaust Denial outfit.

Back in Denver, Moynihan set up his own Storm Press, and in 1992 published *Siege*, an anthology of the writings of James Mason, a former member of the American Nazi Party and head of the National Socialist Liberation Front who was also a friend of Charles Manson. Editing the book under the alias Michael M Jenkins, Moynihan thanked both Anton La Vey and Parfrey in his acknowledgements. Mason's book chimed with the thinking of the Black Metal elite in Europe – he praised both his former ANP colleague, killer Joseph Franklin, who tried to start a race war by shooting inter-racial couples in 1980; and James Huberty, who massacred the largely Hispanic clientele of a McDonald's in San Francisco in 1984 – as expressing 'Viking berserker rage'.

One year after *Siege*'s publication, Varg Vikernes killed Øystein Aarseth, and to Moynihan this was irresistible – he had found a Norwegian Charles Manson. '*Both have become media bogeymen in their respective countries, and both knowingly contribute to their own mythicization,'* he wrote. *'Both understand well the inherent archetypal power of symbols and names – especially those they adopt for themselves.'*

But while Moynihan was making new friends in Norway and East Germany, he was falling out with his old mucker Rice. He moved to Portland to work full time for Feral House, stating that Blood Axis 'will not ever work with Boyd Rice again, due to personal differences'. The difference being that Rice considered himself a Fascist only in aesthetics and not in politics, which to Moynihan was a cop-out. He told *Momentum* magazine: 'If you're going to espouse "Fascist" ideals, then I believe you have to accept some of the responsibility for their application in the real world.'

Moynihan also has his connections in France. He contributes to a Right-leaning publication called *Filosofem* (named after a Burzum LP), which is published by another group called Blood Axis, who have their headquarters in Metz. From the same address, 5 Rue Gabriel Price, have originated a series of Vikernes' Cymphane publications.

And it was since Moynihan began working for Feral House full time that the imprint also published Sondra London's *True Vampires*.

Making Murderobilia

From his cell in Poissy, Claux became very busy indeed. As his network of press contacts grew, he was able to stoke the legend of the Vampire of Paris, while at the same time working on his new career as an artist.

Well aware of the market for Murderobilia, Claux chose to depict the most famous names in the modern canon of killers – Charles Manson, Ted Bundy, John Wayne Gacy, Richard Ramirez. Echoing his 'Neanderthal' philosophy, he told London, 'I don't consider myself a member of mankind, I belong to a worldwide brotherhood of people who decided to make a career in mass destruction.' He hinted that the 'unsolved' Paris killings gave him legitimate entry into the club – to be considered a serial killer by Robert Ressler's definition, you have to have killed five people. To further his loving bonds, Claux began corresponding with his favourite killers, among them Issei Sagawa and Richard Ramirez, both of whom seem to form the basis of his reconstructed image: the cannibal killer as Satanic rock'n'roll star, with an army of groupies to go with it.

Rock stars in their turn began courting Claux. From obscure Black Metal acts to Marilyn Manson's original bassist Gidget Gein, they all wanted a piece of art from the brush of the Vampire of Paris. And with the arrival of the eBay website in the mid-1990s, collecting Claux and his spiritual comrades' works became all the easier.

This was despite the 'Son of Sam law', passed by the New York Assembly in 1977 after David Berkowitz was reportedly offered a huge sum of money for his story, to prevent criminals from profiting from their crimes. The law was struck down by the Supreme Court in 1991, and it was left to individual states to decide how they defined 'profit from crime', which mainly covered book, film and interview rights. No one seemed to anticipate the Murderobilia art wave until 2001, when California State Senator Adam Schiff pushed for further amendments to the legislations in his state to cover the sale of killer art, a move soon copied by several others. This barely dented the market, however – the killers all got themselves art dealers, to act as legitimate agents.

Nico Claux may be many things, but stupid isn't one of them. He came out of jail having made a name for himself in all the right places, and continues his flourishing artistic career apace. In recent interviews, he has begun to namedrop Joe Coleman as his main influence, which is stylistically impossible to discern in his actual canvasses – Claux's straightforward reproductions of photographs of killers and autopsy scenes are worlds away from Coleman's intricate, dementedly brilliant narrative tableaux. The only thing they really share in common is a circle of acquaintances. Claux has recently become involved in another Boyd Rice project, the Unpop movement, which expounds Rice's original NON ethos – using cut up tapes of 1960s girl groups to create atonal noise music – into the realms of figurative art, movie-making and literature. Other members of this little clique include the ubiquitous Parfrey, Feral House author Jim Goad, Seattle artist Charles Krafft (a member of the Slovenian arts collective NSK, originally founded by the comedy-industrial band Laibach), original Murderobilia collector Anton La Vey, musical collaborator and documentary maker Nick Bougas, and the aforementioned Gidget Gein, who lists himself on the website *www.unpopart.org* as 'the original baSSist' in Marilyn Manson. Parfrey, typically in tune with the mood of a nation, describes this familiar collective's ideals as 'aesthetic terrorism'.

Claux now says that his immersion in art has staved off his killer impulses, giving him another outlet for his inner demons – a creative rather than a destructive cycle. On his website he talks about the price he has paid, not only of being incarcerated for eight years, but on a spiritual level too. He feels that he has been damned for all eternity – perhaps to join his friend Richard Ramirez and all their favourite killers in Hell. He is not quite talking up the same storm as he did when he was behind prison walls, but now he really doesn't need to. Just as in Anne Rice's original *Interview with the Vampire*, Paris now has its own Theatre des Vampires sideshow, and its ringmaster is Nico Claux.

Chapter Nine

⌒⌐

Kentucky Vampire Clan: The Sign of V (1996)

Children of the night

At night he walked in cemeteries performing blood rites. By day, he told his classmates in Murray, Kentucky that he was a 500-year-old vampire named Vesago. At the age of 16, Rod Ferell had suffered such a traumatic childhood – allegedly abused by his grandfather, ignored by his occult-dabbling mother, shuffled around between Florida, Michigan and Kentucky – that he had created a whole new personality for himself, helped along the way by a role-playing game called *Vampire: The Masquerade* and a love of Anne Rice's Vampire Lestat novels that blurred the line between wish-fulfilment and harsh reality.

With his tall, gaunt figure and long black hair, Rod became a magnet for other disenfranchised teens – his girlfriend Charity Lyn Keesee and his friends Howard Scott Anderson and Dana Cooper. Together they distanced themselves from the rest of their crowd, dressed like outsiders, lived by their own rules. Then, in the last few months of 1996, a series of troubling events in Ferrell's personal life tipped him over the edge of his fantasy world.

Before 25th November of that year, Murray, Kentucky was perhaps best known for being the home of the American Boy Scout Museum. But ever afterwards it would be known not for the wholesome side of childhood, but for youth gone wild. For it was from Murray that the Kentucky Vampire Clan set out on their killer rampage, travelling down to Florida with murder on their minds.

A respectable, self-made family man would be found bludgeoned to death at the hands of teen maniacs that day, alongside his common law wife, who had been so frenziedly assaulted that her brains were bashed out of her skull. It didn't take long for police to catch up with the miscreants, who included in their number the 15-year-old daughter of the murdered couple. They were, after all, driving the victims' jeep, headed for New Orleans where the Queen of the Vampires lives.

The five teenagers that comprised the Kentucky Vampire clan, and most of all, their leader, Rod Ferrell, would tap into every one of Middle America's worst nightmares. With youth violence already spiralling out of control on school campuses throughout the land, Ferrell and his fangtastic friends were just the type of teenagers to frame wanton aggression in the kind of language the moral majority would understand – vampires, role players, devil worshippers. The climate of fear that was already abroad now virtually demanded it – it was time for another Satanic Panic.

Child of God

Roderick Justin Ferrell was born on 28th March 1980 to 17-year-old Sondra Gibson and 20-year-old Rick Ferrell. The couple married nine days after Rod was born, but separated only weeks later, Rick filing for divorce and joining up with the military. From the very beginning, this kid was in for a rough ride through life.

Sondra had long had her own problems. Her strict, Pentecostal parents had attempted to keep her grounded throughout her short life, forbidding her to go out with kids her own age, let alone dates and dancehalls. Floundering with her young son to look after, she would often leave Rod with his maternal grandparents in Murray while she worked minimum wage jobs to try and support them – flipping burgers, working as a dancer, or trying to get by on benefits alone. Needless to say, this did not impress her mother and especially her domineering father Harold, who accused her of being a bad mother. Sondra's reaction was to escape into drink and drugs, and begin dating a series of unsuitable men.

Stuck in the middle of all this, Rod grew up with the conflicting attitudes of his grandparents and a mother who wanted him to see her more as a friend than a forbidding parent. He was made to strictly adhere to biblical scriptures by the elder Gibsons, while his mother, the party animal, would tell him not to pay them any attention. Meanwhile, his father's sporadic attempts to have contact with Rod would often be turned into unpleasant scenes by Sondra. Rod was only five years old when he first claimed to have been raped by Harold Gibson, who Rod would claim was involved in a religious cult called The Black Mask that used him in one of their Satanic ceremonies.

On top of this, his childhood was peripatetic – he was either moving around with his mother from boyfriend to boyfriend, or with his grandfather, a travelling salesman.

It was his father Rick who introduced Rod to the role-playing fantasy game *Dungeons and Dragons*. Rod quickly developed a taste for this strategic sword and sorcery epic, and was extremely imaginative and creative over it. Needless to say, when he attempted to play the game around his grandparents, it was decreed the work of the Devil.

They made him pray and read the Bible. Meanwhile, his mother taught him how to read the Tarot cards. Rod Ferrell had no choice about growing up strange.

Mark of the Vampire

By the time he reached his teens, Rod's secret way of expressing himself was by cutting himself. He had marks on his arms self-inflicted by a razor, and when he got really angry, he would throw himself against walls, trying to knock himself out. Clearly depressed, he often spoke about suicide.

While he was 15, Rod and Sondra had been living Eustis, Florida when Sondra met a man called Darren Brevin and re-married. Her new husband wanted her to move to Michigan with him immediately, so she took Rod back to the scene of his childhood misery and left him back in Murray with his grandparents. She was fully intending for Rod to join them when they were settled in, but someone, allegedly the new husband, told the boy that his mother never wanted to see him again. When Sondra heard this, she was horrified and moved back to Murray, filing for divorce. But by now, Rod was already slipping deep into delinquency. And when he set up home again with his mother, her attentions towards him and his friends were of all the wrong kind.

Fed up with his tumultuous home-life, Rod started to reinvent himself. With plenty of biblical retribution, mystical mumbo jumbo and *Dungeons and Dragons* imagery to draw upon, he started to become a creature of the night. Encouraged by a teenage accomplice called Stephen Murphy, he swapped his childhood favourite game for a new craze that was sweeping youthful America, *Vampire: The Masquerade*.

His grandparents would have shuddered to read the games' press release: '*In addition to vampire skills and powers, gamers will be able to call upon a devastating arsenal of weapons, including stake guns, shotguns, flame-throwers, sub-machineguns and sniper rifles, to name a few. Once players arm themselves to the teeth they will be able to tackle the host of human vampire hunters, ghouls, werewolves and enemy vampires that inhabit the City of Angels after nightfall.*'

Murphy, who went by the names of 'Jayden' and 'King of the

Vampires' introduced Ferrell to this fantasy vampire world, 'crossing him over' and giving him the name 'Vesago'. Rod enjoyed this new identity. He started telling people he was a 500-year-old vampire, who had lived for most of his life in Paris – just like the lead character in Anne Rice's *Vampire Lestat* stories. He held court in cemeteries late at night, cutting himself now for others to drink his blood. Rod had matured quickly into a formidable physical presence: almost six feet tall and reed thin, with a long mane of hair that he dyed jet black. This, and his pallid complexion, meant he certainly looked the part.

With Sondra as a mother, he was able to live the part too. She allowed him to stay out at night and sleep all day, didn't worry when he got in trouble at school: skipping lessons, smoking on campus and generally defying the officials. Rod had by now started smoking, taking drugs and living off junk food. He had also had more success with girls than many of his contemporaries. To the teenage misfits of Murray, Rod was indeed a cool renegade.

Troubled teens

Ferrell's gang – the ones who would eventually be dubbed the Kentucky Vampire Clan – were a loose-knit group of kids who shared Rod's interest in vampires and role-playing. The three he was closest to in Murray were all from similarly troubled backgrounds.

His best friend was 16-year-old Howard Scott Anderson, who he'd known since his childhood sojourns in the town. Anderson had also spent his early years being shuttled from pillar to post – at one time he'd been taken into the care of foster parents, but in 1996 was back living with his biological parents. He was thin and weedy looking, with thick glasses to match, and saw the more outgoing Rod as a veritable god.

Sixteen-year-old Charity Keesee, who he referred to as Che or Shea, was Rod's girlfriend, and she held him in similar esteem. The product of another broken home, Charity lived in Murray with her father, but kept in touch with her mother, who now lived in South Dakota. Ferrell would later tell police that there was a special bond between them because Charity had been raped at the age of 12 and they both used to cut themselves as a way of releasing the pain these memories engendered. She loved Rod, but feared the darkness that could well up inside him in an instant – he could break furniture apart when he was angry, and moreover, he kept inventing tests for her to prove her love for him. He'd provoke fights to gauge her reaction, criticise her if he thought she had said the wrong thing. Desperate to please him, Charity was simply not worldly-wise enough to see these games for the power-play they were and have nothing more to do with him. Instead, her devotion and fear increased as the relationship progressed.

Charity's friend Dana Cooper was a shy, overweight 19-year-old who suffered from low self-esteem and was grateful for any kind of company she could get. Because she had her own flat, the group started hanging out there, as well as the crumbling pavilion in the woods that they daubed in paint with the words: *The Vampire Hotel*. Here they carried out their blood rituals, and listened spellbound to Rod's tales of Vesago and the vampires.

Rod's other friend was a girl he had known before the others, when he had lived with Sondra in Florida. Fifteen-year-old Heather Wendorf came from a vastly more affluent background than Ferrell. Her father, Richard, was a self-made man who had been able to provide his common law wife Naoma Ruth Queen, and daughters Heather and 17-year-old Jennifer, with a beautiful house and a good standard of living. But, considering herself different to all the other girls in school, Heather had been drawn to Rod, and had confided in him her secrets. Consequently, in the spring of 1996 when Heather was not a happy girl, she started to call Rod long distance. She told him that her parents were hurting her and that she wanted him to come and take her away.

Like Rod, Heather used to cut herself when she was unhappy. She also suffered from migraines and insomnia. When she had first started to hang around with Rod, she had been inspired to dye her hair purple and begin dressing in the gothic manner he favoured. She told her friends she had taken part in blood-drinking rituals with Ferrell, and had changed her name to Zoey, a 'demon name'. But as far as most people could make out, Heather was hardly a wild child. Her parents were quite strict, and liked her and her sister to stay in at night with them, watching TV. At the time she began calling Rod, rows had been brewing over her sister Jennifer's attempts to stay out late with her new boyfriend. Heather was sick of the atmosphere at home and told Rod that he had to save her – even if that meant killing her parents in the process.

Mommy dearest

But Rod was having his own troubles, mainly stemming from Mommy dearest. Sondra was still an attractive 35-year-old, and she often flirted with his friends. They liked being able to hang out at Rod's house, where his mother would allow them to behave any way they pleased, but Rod himself was deeply embarrassed by her and always on the lookout for a new place to stay. Once, his friends got a glimpse of Sondra's darker side when, in the midst of an argument, she began to smash up her son's room and then drag him out of the house by his hair.

To make matters much, much worse for Rod, Sondra developed a crush on Josh, the 14-year-old brother of Stephen Murphy, Rod's vampire mentor. She wrote the child a letter expressing how she dreamed of being 'French kissed and fucked' by him, then followed this up with an invitation for him to move in with her. She was envious of her son being 'crossed over' into the vampire cult, and desired that Stephen Murphy could do the same for her. 'I longed to be near you...to become a Vampire, a part of the family immortal and truly yours forever,' her second letter went on. When the Murphys' mother saw these love notes, the reaction was catastrophic for both Sondra and her son. Stephen turned on Ferrell, beating him up severely, although he would refuse treatment for his injuries when he was taken to hospital. Sondra was charged with 'soliciting rape and sodomy' from a minor. She would subsequently be sent to jail for six months.

Rod's rage at this humiliation knew no bounds. He told his friends he would kill his mother, and his grandfather Harold, who he described as a 'sick bastard'. He also offered to kill another friend's parents. He'd already been in trouble with the police of late, for breaking into a local animal shelter with a bunch of other kids and mutilating two puppies. Another friend would later claim he'd seen Rod kill a kitten by slamming it against a tree.

The familiar pattern was taking its twisted shape. Rod was on course for collision.

He was also taking so many drugs that his girlfriend Charity was really scared of him and his constant threats to kill people. Yet from where Rod was standing, he was being picked on for looking strange and not conforming to society's wishes. He decided it would be better for him and all his friends if they were to just run away, and he talked Howard, Charity and Dana into making a fatal road trip with him. He had just the destination in mind – New Orleans, where his vampire alter ego Vesago would introduce them to the real bloodsucker underground. But they had just one stop to make on the way – Heather Wendorf's Florida home.

The road to Hell

Late on the night of 22nd November 1996, each of them packed some clothes and set off on their road trip in Howard's old Buick. Rod was pleased when, on the same day, Charity told him she was pregnant with his child. However, he had a feeling her father wouldn't share their joy.

Howard's old car just about made it to Eustis, where the gang arrived on 25th November. Shortly after their arrival, the Buick blew a tyre and they were pulled over by police officers about the condition of the vehicle. They ran a check on Howard's license, suspecting something was not quite right with this bunch of scruffy teens. But everything came through as Howard said it would, and they had to let the kids carry on their way.

Still, Rod realised that if they were going to make it to New Orleans, they were going to need a better mode of conveyance. It was convenient, then, that his chosen port of call had a sports utility jeep parked in the drive.

The first person that the gang of four met with in Eustis was one of Rod's old girlfriends, Jeanine LeClaire, who was also best friends with Heather. They drove to her house, where she and Rod discussed their need for a new car, as well as Heather's problems with her folks. Rod decided that after he had liberated Heather from her parents, he would take their Ford Explorer to use for the rest of the trip. He didn't tell anyone else his plan, just explained to the other girls he was going to pick up someone else who'd be joining them on the trip. Ferrell called Heather to let her know he was in town, and went to meet her, just down the road from where she lived, under cover of darkness at about 7pm.

Then he sent the three girls, Heather, Charity and Dana, off to visit Heather's boyfriend and pick up Jeanine on their way. He made Howard stay behind, filled him in on what he was intending to do. Then, armed with clubs, Howard and Rod set off towards the Wendorf home.

Because he had never actually been invited over to the place while he'd lived in Eustis, Rod had to rely on Jeanine's description to know which house he was going to. He almost went wrong straight away, walking up to a neighbour's house first. But when he looked inside and saw little children playing, he realised this wasn't the right residence. Luckily, no one had noticed him and the wary Howard, and they made it unseen into the Wendorf's unlocked garage next door.

Here they searched around for some better weapons. Rod finally settled on a crowbar, and tried the adjoining door that led into the house. It was open, and led straight into the kitchen. Rod helped himself to a drink from the fridge before getting his bearings. He could hear a shower running somewhere else in the house. Sprawled out on the couch in the front room, 49-year-old Richard Wendorf was sleeping, as he so often did after a long day at work. Howard followed nervously behind his friend as they walked into the room. Rod showed no such hesitation.

Battered to death

Rod went up to the sleeping man, raising his crowbar. He thought of all the times that Heather had cried down the phone to him about her parents' cruelty, a subject he knew about only too well. He brought down his weapon hard on the head of the prone man.

The first few blows would probably have been enough, but Rod kept on going, reigning the blows down so that blood and brain matter flew across the room. He delivered more than a dozen hits to Wendorf's skull, until his face was unrecognisable. Then he stopped to light a cigarette.

Bending down, Rod lifted up the dead man's shirt and used the burning cigarette to sign a macabre signature onto the chest of his victim: a letter V, the sign of Vesago. Then he flipped him over and removed his wallet from his back pocket. It had his credit cards inside it.

Faced with the horrendous reality of what he was seeing, Howard just froze, unable to move or utter a sound for the duration of the battery. Which, according to Rod's later statement to his arresting officer, took, 'about twenty fucking minutes...I swear, I thought he was immortal or something.'

Until that moment, Howard had been romanced by the vampire stories, the blood rituals they had performed at The Vampire Hotel. This was something different, something nothing had prepared him for.

While Howard stood there, Rod walked into the hall, on the lookout for some more cash to steal. At that moment, 54-year-old Naoma Queen appeared fresh from her shower, holding a cup of coffee. Startled at this long-haired apparition in her house, she asked him what he thought he was doing. Rod said nothing, just raised the crowbar he had in his hands. The blood on the end of it registered with Naoma and instantly she threw her hot coffee at him. A fight ensued, with Rod flailing the crowbar and Naoma fighting back any way she could, clawing at him with her nails. But the enraged Ferrell soon had the better of her, smashing at her head with his weapon over and over again. 'I just continually beat her until I saw her brains falling on the floor,' Rod later told the police. 'She...pissed me off. So I made sure she was dead.'

After which, Rod moved through the house, pulling the phones off the walls as he did so, until he found the keys to the Explorer jeep. He knew that Jennifer would be home soon, and wondered if he should wait behind to kill Heather's sister too. In the end, as he later recalled, he decided, 'Nah, why bother. Let her come home, have a mental breakdown, call the police.'

Instead, he rounded up the bewildered Howard, got him into the jeep, and made him drive back to Jeanine's house, where they swapped plates with the Buick.

Once Heather saw her parents' car, she had a fair idea of what had just happened. But it didn't stop her from getting in. Rod dropped a couple of hints before finally admitting to her that he had killed them both. As Howard drove away with Rod, Heather, Charity and Dana in the jeep, she started to scream and cry, or as Rod later put it, 'she flipped for about a hundred miles or so'. According to Heather, she then decided she'd better calm down or she may be next.

Howard was still speechless from what he'd seen. Charity and Dana had had no idea that this was what they were in for either. Now they were in a stolen car, its owners battered to death by the leader of their group, and the owners' daughter, who they'd only just met, utterly distraught.

Suddenly, that exciting road trip to New Orleans didn't seem like such a great idea after all.

The Big Uneasy

Why had New Orleans seemed such a mecca for these teenage misfits? Because it was for every black-clad child of Nineties America, and many more around the world too. New Orleans is, after all, the home of Voodoo, the city where the dead cannot sleep in their tombs, the place of Mardi Gras and magic. Anne Rice knew why New Orleans was perfect when she chose to set *Interview with the Vampire* in that particular city. It is the one settlement in America that is so much *other* than the rest of the country, the one place where the rules of the majority can be completely ignored.

New Orleans, so the legend goes, was settled on an ancient Indian burial ground. The natives warned the immigrant French not to build a city there in the haunted bayou. The French ignored this warning and their city promptly burned to the ground. New Orleans has been destroyed several times since, by fire, hurricanes, pestilence and war. The horrific impact of Hurricane Katrina in August 2005 would seem to prove the longevity of the curse – and the city's own innate desire for resurrection.

The slaves that were bought here in the early 1800s to work on the plantations brought with them their voodoo religion, which terrified their masters, who tried to outlaw it. The transplanted Africans responded by adapting the names of their deities to fit in with the French's Catholic counterparts.

But it wasn't until the 1830s that the strange religion really came to prominence, in the formidable form of Madame Marie Laveau, a free black woman who worked as a hairdresser and listened very carefully to the gossip and scandal her aristocratic white customers traded. She used these nuggets to set herself up as a medium, giving readings that terrified her sitters with their accuracy. As her fame increased, Laveau paid slaves to spy on their masters, using their information to fuel her dark arts. Before long she had every politician and policeman in her pocket, charged fortunes to cast spells and is said to have literally voodooed her rivals to death.

Voodoo is now big business in New Orleans – and continues to be practised there beyond the shop fronts selling tarot cards and bags of *gris gris*. In one memorable recent case that still remains unsolved, an Italian tourist called Ylenia Carrisi disappeared on 12th Night (6th January) 1993 after spending time with a feared local Voodoo priest called Alexander Masakela – a name that means 'evil' in creole. Carrisi was the daughter of two Italian celebrities and the granddaughter of Tyrone Power, and had been the host of the Italian version of *Wheel of Fortune*. After her vanishing, planeloads of Italian journalists descended on New Orleans in search of both her and Masakela. No trace of either was ever found.

In New Orleans, the cemeteries are called the Cities of the Dead. Because the city is built on a bayou below sea level, before there was proper drainage in place, corpses just wouldn't stay buried and would float back up out of the ground. So it was necessary to construct these vast, overground networks of mausoleums, decorated with gothic iron railings and hidden behind high walls. Nowadays you can peruse these labyrinthine monuments on 'Haunted', 'Voodoo' and 'Vampire' tours.

Marie Laveau is buried there. The Vampire Lestat came out of hiding in Anne Rice's novel from within such a tomb.

He found the city that Ferrell was headed for, the place where Marilyn Manson boasted of smoking human bones to get high, the place where they hold the annual Vampire Ball at the City That Time Forgot, where you can dance the night away in the city's first mortuary, now a Goth hangout called the Babylon Club. He could even have attended the annual Vampire Lestat Fan Club Party without anyone realising. Even *National Geographic* has called New Orleans 'the most vampirically active city in the country'.

It is easy to see why so many could fall under Lestat's spell. Rice's tale is beguiling. An aristocratic loner is destined to walk the earth under the shadow of night for all eternity, a handsome, misunderstood artist. What teenager wouldn't fall in love with that image? Yet Lestat is not Satanic in the slightest. Richard Ramirez would probably loathe him. His 'family' of fellow vampires help each other to survive within their own community in a caring, almost Christian way. They are even at pains to keep their damage to the human race to the bare minimum. When the ancient entity Akasha comes back to life to the tune of Lestat's music in *The Queen of The Damned* and offers our hero the opportunity to reign with her forever and massacre the population of the Earth in the process, Lestat is horrified. He bands together with his family to destroy her once and for all.

In the end, what is seductive about Rice's tales is not just the Byronic romance of their hero, but the comforting familiarity of his actual values. He is a gentleman, not a psychopath. And his creator has gone on the record as saying: 'I don't believe in vampires at all and I don't believe in blood-drinking.'

Something which may well have been going through the minds of most of the occupants of Richard Wendorf's Explorer jeep as they sped on through the longest, darkest night of their lives.

The Kentucky Vampire Clan never made it to their mythic New Orleans.

Nowhere to run to, nowhere to hide

Howard was driving west along Interstate 10, through Tallahassee. He and his companions had very little money, nothing to eat, and only the vaguest of notions of where they were going and what they were going to do when they got there. They also proved what amateur criminals they were when, at their first stop for petrol, in Crestview, Florida, they used Richard Wendorf's Discovery credit card to buy gas and a knife. For by this point, Jennifer Wendorf had of course returned home to find her world ripped apart. The police had been summoned and now there was an APB out on the vehicle.

At some point, it dawned on Rod that the jeep was a liability, that it wouldn't have taken the cops long to find the switched plates on the dumped Buick. He suggested driving it deep into the woods somewhere off the beaten track and living off wild animals he could catch in the forest while they continued on their way on foot. The pregnant Charity really didn't think much of this idea.

After four days of drifting uncertainly around the Interstate between Florida and Louisiana, she made them stop for the night, in Baton Rouge, Louisiana, where they parked in a motel forecourt. Rod argued that this was foolishness, but by then, no one was in a mind to listen to him any more. From the motel's payphone, in a state of high anxiety, Charity made a distress call to her mother in South Dakota. It didn't take long for the cops to trace the call and move in on the hapless teenagers, who by now were in a state of total disarray. They were arrested at the scene, by the Explorer, where the Baton Rouge police also discovered a bloody bedsheet, two books about vampires, a paperback book giving spells for conjuring demons and a dismembered toy doll. All the paraphernalia the hungry press would need to fuel their stories the minute this came out.

The Baton Rouge police took the teenagers down to the station and questioned them individually. A weary Ferrell admitted to the murders straight away. He told the chief interrogator Sergeant Ogden and two Detectives, Moran and Dewey, that he alone was responsible for killing Heather's parents, that Howard had done nothing to assist him at the scene of the crime and that the others had been totally unaware that this was what he was up to until Heather saw her parents' car. What little he offered by way of defence for himself was that his granddad had raped him at the age of five and destroyed his world, and that his mother's second husband was a drug dealer who should be arrested. 'I don't have any concern for life any more,' he said. 'My own, especially.'

However, he was at pains to spare Charity any suffering by association. When asked if the murders had been premeditated he denied it, but did say that he, Heather and Janine had been planning to take off for New Orleans for over a year. But by that time, he had got Charity pregnant and, he said: 'Che had no choice. I told her, either she agreed or I'd hogtie her, take her with me. Dana came with Che because she was worried about Che.'

Ferrell told the police officers that he had told them his true story because they were the first cops he'd ever met who hadn't 'beaten me upside the head'. He added that if the Florida police treated him differently, he might not tell them anything at all. 'I didn't speak once for two years,' he said, 'so that won't be a problem.'

Rod may have thought he'd done all he could to save his friends by offering himself up this way. But by the time the Baton Rouge cops handed him over to the Lake County Sheriff's office in Florida, Ferrell really didn't have any friends left.

They walk among us

In the week between their extradition from Baton Rouge to the regional juvenile detention facility in Ocala, Florida, the press had plenty of time to paint a lurid picture of the Wendorf murder gang. First, they had gone down to Murray, where locals whispered stories about vampires meeting out in the woods, mutilating animals and drinking each other's blood. The stories about Sondra Gibson and her underage love-letters also came out, along with the passages about her longing to be turned into a vampire. The prosecutor in the case, David Harrington, told the press that the youths in custody had been involved in a role-playing game, but that Ferrell had begun to take a more sinister lead in this, citing the incident with the puppies and the animal shelter as reason to believe that Rod had started 'going beyond game-playing'. Just so as the public were in no doubt about what kind of monster they were dealing with here, the press filled in a few lurid gaps about what happened to those puppies: one was 'stomped to death' and the other 'had its legs pulled off'.

The police had, of course, questioned Rod's old girlfriend, Jeanine LeClaire, as well. Jeanine was supposed to have gone with the gang, but at the last moment had decided it was too much hassle to sneak out on her parents. Now she told the cops that the other teenagers had drunk each other's blood at her home minutes before they left for the Wendorfs, saying they were off to kill Heather's parents. She'd also filled them in about Rod's Vesago alias and Heather's Zoey *non-de-plume* – and all these details went into the press reports too.

One person in Murray seemed more distraught than anyone else, but for entirely different reasons. Rod's despised grandfather Harold wept as he told AP: 'They're saying Rod is a monster. A monster! He's not a monster, he's not.' The old man clearly feared the small town mob mentality too, saying: 'What if they come after me?' Prosecutor Harrington tried to speak sensibly and rationally when he said: 'I think you had a group of kids that just wanted to be a part of something, wanted to belong to a group. And it went too far. Hopefully, it's over.'

Far from it.

When the youths arrived in Lake County, Rod stuck his tongue out at the ranks of massed reporters and kissed a jail window as news crews filmed. It was a different story the next day, Saturday 7th December. When the Marion County Judge Frances S King found there was enough probable cause to hold all of the teens in custody and gave them each a court-appointed lawyer, Heather Wendorf looked more upset than anyone else. She bit her lip and gazed at the floor as she stood there shaking while the Judge spoke. The intricacies of the case were not discussed at this preliminary hearing, but Assistant Public Defender Bill Stone was appointed to represent Ferrell, while private attorneys were appointed for all the others, to avoid a conflict of interests – the Public Defender's office usually handles the most serious case.

On 17th December, Ferrell, Anderson, Keesee and Cooper were all indicted as adults in Lake County. Prosecutor Brad King said that he wouldn't seek the death penalty against Charity and Dana but he would seek it against Rod and Howard. Separate trials for all four were agreed and scheduled for February 1998. Heather Wendorf, however, was a separate matter. A Grand Jury would convene to hear her case and decide if any charges should be brought against her.

Never for Heather

On 28th January 1997 Heather testified to the Grand Jury for two hours about whether or not she had plotted with Ferrell to kill her parents. She denied malice aforethought, painting a picture of herself as another of Rod's victims, drawn to him through her own unhappiness and then dominated by him after he had 'crossed her over' into his vampire world. Although she agreed that she had been planning to run away with him for some months, she denied that she had asked Ferrell to kill her parents as part of the deal.

Heather's sister Jennifer didn't quite see it that way. She had already told the police that Heather and Rod had been in constant touch since his move to Murray and that, in the month before the murders, Heather had asked Jennifer if she had ever thought about killing their parents. When Jennifer said no, Heather went on to tell her sister that she had decided Rod Ferrell would be a good person to ask if you ever wanted someone killed.

Several of her schoolmates also testified that she had told them she wanted her parents dead, though one later recanted.

Heather denied all of this, reiterating that she had no idea Ferrell would do what he had, only that she had planned to run away with him because she was under the complete mind control of a psychopath. She was only 15 years old, and now both her parents were dead. Unlike the other four Clan members, Heather was attractive and came from a 'good family'. Perhaps because of these factors, the Grand Jury decided to take a merciful attitude towards Heather that was at marked odds with the treatment of the equally unaware Keesee and Cooper. They decided she was completely innocent of all murder charges and would not have to face a trial.

Meanwhile, whether the Florida cops treated him worse than the Louisiana ones can not be discerned, but Rod Ferrell had changed his story, blaming a rival gang for the killings. It was not a story he was likely to get away with, given his previous confession and the DNA evidence against him – he still had particles of Naoma Queen's skin under his fingernails when he was arrested. But as far as fantasies go, it was at least on a par with what some of his old friends had been telling investigators about him.

On 21st March 1997, before the first pre-trial hearings, an investigative report was released to the press that was supposed to shed light upon the activities of Ferrell and friends. This report contained the testimony of John Goodman, a self-confessed member of the Vampire Clan from Murray who had declined to join the fateful road trip. According to this teenage source, Ferrell 'had become obsessed with opening the Gates of Hell, which meant he would have to kill a large number of people in order to consume their souls. By doing this, Ferrell believed that he would obtain super powers.'

Goodman also explained the sign of 'V' that had been made on Richard Wendorf's body as his vampire calling card. He added that the numbers of individual burns made on the 'V' indicated the number of adherents to Ferrell's cult.

In the same document, Heather Wendorf described how Ferrell wielded those powers over her as her vampire 'sire' who had 'crossed her over' by making her drink his blood. 'The person that gets crossed over is like subject to whatever the sire wants...Like the sire is boss basically. They have authority over you.'

Just to add to this picture, there was a psychological profile of Sondra Gibson, who had been evaluated by the court after pleading guilty but mentally ill to the charge of enticing a minor in November 1996. She told the psychologist that Rod's vampire group were running rampant in her home and she couldn't control any of them. Not only were they verbally abusive to her, she said, but she had also been repeatedly raped during vampire ritual sessions.

Courtroom shocker

Ferrell stuck to his new story right up until the time of his trial. Then on 12th February 1998, he shocked the Florida court and his own defender, William Lackey, by stopping the openings of the trial proceedings to change his plea. He now admitted guilt to all the charges brought against him – armed burglary, armed robbery and two counts of first-degree murder. Now the jury had only one job – to decide whether Rod should get the death sentence.

Lackey's team now presented the facts they knew about Ferrell's life. They told the jury about his miserable, itinerant childhood, and Sondra's dubious parenting skills. The psychologist that had assessed her at her trial had also stated she had the emotional maturity of a 12-year-old and was sometimes delusional, a fact the press hadn't let get in the way of a good story.

Rod testified about the abuse he had suffered as a very young child, but as he was also claiming to be a 500-year-old vampire, no one put much stock by these comments. However, Sondra did testify that after her father had taken him out one day fishing he had come back traumatised and vomiting. He later drew pictures of demons and others that suggested oral and anal abuse. Sondra's sister Lyzetta also told the court that her father had kissed her and fondled her when she was a child too, the reason why she had left home at the age of 14. No charges were ever brought against Harold Gibson, and he strongly refuted them as an upright, Christian member of the community.

Rod had told his psychiatric assessors that as a result of being sexualised at such an early age he had become a nymphomaniac and had numerous lovers. He was evaluated as having an emotional age of only three, as a result of such extreme emotional and mental disturbance.

But he did diverge from his original statement in other ways too: this time it appeared that he was trying to spread the blame around. Instead of agreeing that Howard had 'frozen' when he saw Rod start to bludgeon Richard Wendorf, he now said that his companion smiled while he watched and seemed 'high' when they left the scene of the crime. He also suggested that Heather had masterminded the murders, something that Sondra planned to back him up on by saying she had heard them plotting on the phone. But she failed a lie-detector test on the subject so she wasn't allowed to testify on it.

In the end, the jury didn't consider that any of this consisted of mitigating circumstances. On 23rd February, they voted unanimously to give Ferrell the death sentence. After hearing additional testimonies from both sides, Judge Jerry Lockett accepted the jury recommendation four days later, and sentenced Rod to the electric chair. He was the youngest person ever to go to the Florida Death Row.

After the sentencing, Judge Lockett also urged prosecutors to charge Heather Wendorf, pointing to unanswered questions about her parents' death and saying: 'There is genuine evil in this world.' Sondra Gibson fully agreed with him. 'There's one person walking around who's just as guilty as he is,' she said.

However, a second Grand Jury hearing, prompted by the insurance company who were due to pay both Heather and Jennifer $250,000 from their parents' life insurance, found Heather not guilty. She was able to move away from the area and go back to school, helped by a court-appointed guardian.

The rest of the Kentucky Vampire Clan faced a very different future.

We are the Damned

Howard Scott Anderson was the next to face the music. From what he had told the Baton Rouge cops in his original statement, his prospects weren't good. He said he had planned to kill Naoma Queen while Rod dispatched Richard Wendorf, but when he saw Ferrell land the first blow, he knew he couldn't go through with it. He also said they had told Charity and Dana that they were going to commit the murders minutes before they left to do the deed, but that Heather was unaware of this. However, he couldn't explain why he had even agreed to this plan in the first place, or why he had been unable to stop Rod from going ahead with it when he knew what he was doing was so badly wrong.

Poor old Howard was never the sharpest card in the pack. He was charged with being a principal accessory to murder, which meant that he also faced the death penalty. His lawyers made a plea-bargain so that he didn't have to face a jury. On 30th March 1998, he agreed to plead guilty in return for two life sentences with no possibility of parole – his life effectively ended at the age of 18.

Charity, who lost the baby she was carrying in the weeks following her arrest, and Dana, both charged with being principal accessories to murder, refused to accept a similar plea that would have sent them to jail for 40 years. Instead, Charity was sentenced to 10 years, but it is likely she will be freed before her due release date of 16th June 2007.

Because she was older, Dana, who had only come on the road trip in the first place out of concern for her pregnant friend, received a sentence of 17 years and six months.

The distinction of being an 'adult' at the time of the crimes as opposed to a 'juvenile' was not only applied to Dana's case; both Rod and Scott were tried as adults and faced adult penalties. It took two appeals by Ferrell's lawyers to have his sentence commuted to life imprisonment without possibility of parole. Finally, after Florida's high court ruled that the state could not execute killers who committed their crime before they reached the age of 17, in November 2000 Ferrell was taken off Death Row. The Supreme Court ruled that to allow such a rare punishment would be cruel and unusual and therefore unconstitutional.

Just two weeks after Ferrell's original sentence had been handed down, on 10th March 1998, it was announced to the press that Heather Wendorf had accepted $1,000 from the journalist Aphrodite Jones to tell her side of the story in a book about the case. She had, of course, been inundated with offers like this, and many of them much more lucrative, but had rejected them all because she didn't want to make money out of her parents' deaths. This one was different, said her attorney Lou Tally, because, 'Aphrodite already planned to write a book. We were concerned if we stonewalled her and didn't have anything to do with it, the one enduring piece of work out of this story would be without her.'

Jones' account, *The Embrace: A True Vampire Story*, duly vindicated Heather, but not without provoking the ire of her relatives. 'She didn't need to sell her story,' Heather's aunt, Gloria Wendorf, told reporters. 'This indicates to us exactly what Heather Wendorf is.'

Our dark places

What the tale of the Kentucky Vampire Clan most clearly reflects is American society's unwillingness to look into its own dark places and desire to evoke superstition to instead explain away the actions of its miscreants. Two loving parents who had done everything they thought right to give their daughters the best start in life had been bludgeoned to death by a young man who had been screaming out for such stability all his life. In the rush to attribute blame and demonise the killer, no one was willing to take on board what had made Rod Ferrell the way he was.

The lessons to be learned from this case were all about the biggest demon loose in our cosy world – child abuse. With a family and upbringing like his, Ferrell had hardly been given the chance to become a model citizen. Similarly, Anderson, Keesee and Cooper had all been at best neglected, and at worst violently abused, throughout their short lives. The fact that they bonded together to try and form some protective shell against a world that had already shown them how much it really cared shouldn't surprise anyone.

But the mythological word 'vampire' seemingly let the nation's conscience off the hook. These young people and all their problems were reduced to ciphers, branded as irredeemably evil and treated as harshly as possible in the actual courts and those of public opinion. Howard, Charity and Dana were effectively punished for being gullible children who didn't have any stability in their lives, or the necessary sophistication to realise that Rod Ferrell was far from being a vampire god, but instead a deeply disturbed young man. They were only really under one spell, and that was the fear of seeming inadequate, something even the most well brought up young person will suffer from throughout their teenage years. But the hopelessness of their own lives had made them particularly vulnerable. They ended up being carried away by a train of events they could never possibly have foreseen.

As for their leader, Rod Ferrell had one moment of clarity when he faced his sentence. 'If I was a god,' he said, as if it had only just occurred to him, 'I wouldn't be here, would I?'

When asked by the *Orlando Sentinel* in August 1998 why she had found Rod Ferrell and his fantasy world so attractive, Heather Wendorf replied: 'It was like a fairytale. So much more interesting than getting up, going to school, going home and going to bed.'

America was going to continue listening to those fairytales, spinning them into witch hunts.

Chapter Ten

Natasha Cornett: Hell is for Children (1997)

Killers on the road

They say lightning doesn't strike the same place twice. But in April 1997, just five months after Rod Ferrell struck out on the road to damnation and death, another carload of juvenile delinquents blasted a hole in Kentucky's heart. This time there were six of them, three boys and three girls. Youngsters with bad reputations, Gothic freaks who cut themselves up and pledged allegiance to Satan, fans of Marilyn Manson and Oliver Stone's *Natural Born Killers*.

In Oliver Stone's cinematic critique of juvenile delinquency and the media, Mickey and Mallory Knox are two victims of traumatised childhoods who get married, kill her parents and hit the road on a nationwide killing spree. Hard at their heels, slavering press-hound Wayne Gayle turns the Knoxes into celebrities. Stone's frenetic, multi-layered movie, based on a Quentin Tarantino script and released in 1994, was just crying out for vilification. It got it in cartloads, not just from an outraged media (the film was banned in the UK for six months, thanks to a campaign waged in the ever-vigilant trenches of the *Daily Mail*) but from the within the film industry itself. Peruvian novelist Mario Vargas Llosa publicly cursed the film when it premiered at the Venice Film Festival and David Puttnam, who had previously worked with Stone on *Midnight Express*, called it 'loathsome'.

But that was not the only fallout that was to land the director's way. In March 1996, teen lovers Sarah Edmonson and Ben Darras dropped some acid, watched *NBK* then left their Oklahoma home and went on a shooting spree, killing a businessman and paralysing a waitress before they were apprehended. The waitress, Pasty Byers, sued the film's distributors Time Warner for 'distributing a film they knew, or should have known, would cause and inspire people to commit crimes' in a campaign supported by the writer John Grisham. The case was thrown out, but the film's reputation was forever sealed; Stone's attempts to expose evil misread as promotion of violence, the irresponsible press he sought to condemn triumphant in turning the director into the bad guy.

Maybe Oliver Stone was just being too clever in his presentation of inflammatory material. But his film struck a chord with a generation of kids who started out just like Mickey and Mallory – being beaten and raped by their own families. The sort of kids who might not get the irony, just the adrenalin rush of the pair of renegades shooting their way into infamy. Kids like 21-year-old Joseph Risner, 18-year-old Crystal Sturgill, 20-year-old Edward Dean Mullins, 17-year-old Karen Howell, 14-year-old Jason Blake Bryant and, most notoriously of all, 19-year-old Natasha Wallen Cornett.

On the night of 6th April 1997, these six kids took a ride out of Pikeville, Kentucky along a desolate stretch of highway known as Route 23. Here they encountered a family of Jehovah's Witnesses on their way home from a convention, a Norwegian immigrant couple called Vidar and Delfina Lillelid, with their children Tabitha, 6, and Peter, 2. The family had recently moved to the area from New York, because they were afraid their children might grow up in too violent an environment.

But the Lillelids couldn't read between the signs that line Route 23, the stretches of road named after country singers who warned of the darkness couched in the hills between Kentucky and Knoxville. Instead, in a truckstop on the side of the road, they were friendly towards the gang of weirdly-dressed, multi-pierced teenagers they encountered. In return, in a grim echo of an old murder ballad penned around such a lost highway, the gang of six picked up a gun and sent the devoutly religious Lillelids all the way to Hell.

Born bad

In the furore that erupted around this most polarising of cases, all attention focused on one member of this gang. All six of them offered different versions of the chain of events that led up to the murder of Vidar, Delfina and Tabitha, and the shooting of Peter that left him a paralysed orphan with only one eye. Only Jason Bryant had been in trouble with the police before; he was on probation for stealing cars and his own father had called the cops when he took off this time. The one detail agreed in all the separate statements of the other five was that it was Bryant who raised the gun and pulled the trigger, something he continues to deny. But it isn't Jason Bryant who became the personification of evil in this case. The real-life Mallory Knox was instead Natasha Cornett.

Natasha was a witch, the stories went. She got married in a black dress on her 17th birthday. She cut herself and drank her own blood. She signed her name backwards: *Ah-Satan*. The last three stories were at least true. But on the advice of her first lawyer, Eric Conn, who thought she could cop an insanity plea and was later dismissed, Natasha also gave jailhouse interviews claiming she was Satan's daughter and she had been speaking to demons since she was two years old. In smalltown, God-fearing, Pikeville, Natasha already had a bad reputation. Now she had just voiced what every right-minded Christian had already been thinking. She was born into trouble, and trouble followed her around, like the dog that was her wedding present, who she called Evil.

Natasha's home was a trailer in a depressed hillside suburb of Pikeville called Betsy Layne – the sort of place no amount of hokey, homespun names can turn into *The Waltons*. The result of an extra-marital affair with a local policeman, she was born on 26th January 1979 to Madonna Wallen, a woman who'd already endured a lifetime of bad luck.

When Madonna was four or five years old, she was molested by a pastor at her local church. It being the Forties, the crime was hushed-up, but Madonna's mother did send her to a doctor to deal with the resulting physical injuries. Her second daughter, Natasha, was also around this age when she first considered suicide. 'I was in a crib and I tried to suffocate myself with a blanket,' she later recalled. 'I remember that my mom was like yelling at me for something. She was just like, like I couldn't do anything right to her, or for her, no matter how hard I tried. It's like I couldn't make her love me. And one night it just kind of all hit me.'

Madonna was 17 when she married her first husband, an abusive, alcoholic Pepsi Cola salesman called Don Atkins. She had her first daughter, Velina, in 1960, but six years later the marriage came to a disastrous end. Madonna was granted a divorce after firing a shotgun at her husband as he advanced on their home, threatening to kill her. His wounds weren't fatal and she wasn't charged, on grounds of self-defence.

On her 17th birthday, Natasha married Steve Cornett, a local boy she had made friends with. It lasted about six months before, driven mad by her possessive behaviour, he fled Kentucky. Natasha went after him with a friend, taking a road trip to Lexington and then New Orleans, where they spent a month hanging out with 'gutter punks', sleeping in abandoned houses and experimenting with heroin. Natasha had already started taking soft drugs, smoking her first joint at the age of 15, but as soon as she had married Steve, she cut out all such substances, including alcohol, in order to try and get pregnant. But her methods were not met with approval by her husband: 'I just went crazy, period,' she later admitted. She demanded sex constantly, even tried to stop Steve from going to work some mornings, threatening to kill herself if he left her. The reason she was so desperate to conceive is revealing: 'I've always wanted a baby. I don't know if this will make sense or not, but I thought that having a baby and treating it good, doing it right, would heal my pain.'

Hole in the heart

Madonna's second husband, Ed Wallen, continued the cycle of abuse. Velina said that she was abused by him for years; Madonna took refuge in an affair with local cop Roger Burgess. When she got pregnant in 1978, she knew the baby wasn't her husband's. Natasha Cornett was born with a hole in her heart. At the age of 16 months she went back to hospital for an operation to heal this defect and she says that her first memory is of being alone in that hospital room, feeling the itch of her surgical scar.

It was an itch she seemingly never could scratch hard enough. At the age of five, when her mother was working in an army surplus store, Natasha's greatest delight was to dress up in camouflage outfits, complete with little boots. She also loved the knives Madonna brought home – not just Swiss Army knives but hunting blades too. It seemed that her mother couldn't keep her away from them.

But then, at the age of five, Natasha was also being abused. By the man she thought was her father.

As Natasha grew older, her behaviour became increasingly depressive. Her mother remembers children at school laughing at Natasha's surgery scar, revealed by what was up until then her favourite dress. But there were more scars forming than this physical one. One morning when she was in the fifth grade, she woke up of her own accord, instead of to the usual shouts of her mother. There wasn't a sound in the trailer, and this was unusual. Filled with fear, Natasha wondered if Madonna had carried out one of her many threats to up and leave her. She walked nervously out of her bedroom and tentatively opened her mother's bedroom door. She found Madonna sprawled out naked on the bed, an empty bottle of pills lying on the floor beside her.

The 13-year-old girl had the presence of mind not to go to pieces completely but to call her mother's former boyfriend, who came and got Madonna to hospital in time to save her life. Trying to be good, Natasha didn't accompany them, but instead went to school, where she burst into tears in front of her teacher on arrival. The teacher was at a loss about what to do. By the time she got home, her mother had been discharged and was sleeping. Natasha spent the night sleeping on the floor outside Madonna's door.

At the age of 15, Natasha stopped eating. First she'd go without meals for a day, then a week, then finally she attempted to starve herself for an entire month. When her weight plummeted by 30lbs, Madonna had her hospitalised in nearby Lexington. There, Natasha was psychiatrically evaluated. Doctors in the Charter Ridge Behavioural Health system pronounced her not only an anorexic but also a severe manic depressive. When she was discharged they told Madonna that her daughter would need a lot more help, but unfortunately they couldn't provide it for her – the state's health insurance would only pay up for 11 days of treatment.

Madonna's methods of treating and disciplining her wayward daughter all came out at the trial. 'I never hit her with my fists,' she later said. 'I don't know, maybe she thought I did, but I hit her always with my hand open. I've hit her with a plastic bat, a hollow plastic ball bat, maybe thrown a few books at her…I've whipped her hard. I really have. I have whipped her too hard, I know, at times. Because she'd lose it and I'd lose it too.'

Suffer little children

Natasha first started cutting herself on her ankles, then moved up to her arms. By the time she was arrested she had slash marks running from her wrists up past her elbows. She encouraged others to join in the ritual of self-harm – and she found plenty of willing participants in Pikeville.

The members of the gang caught by the police on 6th April had all been brought up hard. Crystal Sturgis never knew who her real father was, but he couldn't have been any worse than the stepfather she grew up with. In December 1996, Crystal filed charges against Gene Blackburn, accusing him of rape. The detective who investigated said that Blackburn admitted having sex with his 17-year-old stepdaughter 'about ten times'. After had made her report to the police, Crystal was completely disowned by her family, who all took Blackburn's side. She ended up staying in Natasha's trailer.

Karen Howell suffered similar trauma. She says she was molested for five years of her childhood by both an uncle and a cousin. After her parents split up, as a result of her father's drinking, her mother had a nervous breakdown. Like Natasha, Karen found cutting herself up offered a weird form of catharsis.

The boys hardly fared better. Joe Risner also never met his real father; Jason Bryant's dad was an alcoholic and his mother abandoned the family when he was young. Ed Mullins, who was close to both of his parents and his sister, still came from a divorced family.

Apart from fractured and often violent upbringings, the other thing these six had in common was that all were brought up in homes where the Bible was wielded like a weapon. The peace and love part of the message was only for public occasions, like going to church. At home it was all hellfire and damnation, an Old Testament view from a society inclined to take a medieval stance on good and evil. This attitude extended into the schoolroom too. Natasha continued to be bullied at school. When she tried to get help from her teachers, she was told she had brought the abuse upon herself by looking the way she did – like a 'freak'.

Like the Kentucky Vampire clan, it's easy to see why these alienated adolescents would shun the straight society that so disdained them and try and create their own rules for living. Easy to see why the soundtrack for their angst would be the music of Nine Inch Nails, White Zombie and Marilyn Manson – music that articulated the pain and rage they felt inside, that taught them to embrace their differences. After all, as Marilyn Manson responded to Michael Moore in his essential documentary about murder in the schoolyard *Bowling for Columbine*, when asked what he would have to say to the teenage killers: 'I wouldn't say anything. I would listen. And that's what nobody did.'

When Natasha Cornett was 13, she and her friends used to congregate under the concrete drainage tunnels in the scrubland on the outskirts of Pikeville. They adorned the walls of these tunnels with graffiti, Natasha leaving her mark in letters two feet high, the title of a song by Pat Benetar: *Hell is for Children*. She signed it *Natasha Ah-Satan*.

Reading Weird Tales

Christianity, the way it was preached to them, had seemingly failed Natasha and her friends. Like any adolescents, they looked around for other options, ones that didn't seem quite so hypocritical. There were plenty of them, and Natasha soon discovered many of the popular pastimes of her peergroup: the parallel universe of the occult, the role-playing *Vampire: The Dark Ages* game and the imaginary world of another suicidal depressive from 70 years earlier, the horror writer HP Lovecraft.

She began to study *The Necromonicon*, a mythical occult bible first conjured up by Lovecraft in his 1920s stories for *Weird Tales* magazine. A story within a story, this grimoire was said to be a translation of ancient Arabic chants, spells and curses written down by the mad Arab Abdul Alhazred. Lovecraft conjured it up so powerfully that fellow horror writers in the early 20th century began to incorporate it into their tales too, adding their own fragments of the book.

In the Seventies, someone calling himself 'Simon' published what he claimed was the actual *Necromonicon*, which grafted spurious Lovecraft links to what experts consider to be a fairly decent version of Sumerian magical systems. This inspired George Hay's *Necromonicon*, a compendium of writing by such diverse voices as magic realist Angela Carter and true crime supremo Colin Wilson.

The Necromonicon is also often mentioned as another influence on Rod Ferrell when these two cases are linked, as if it were an actual, ancient black magic bible that they both drew upon to cast spells with. It is not often pointed out that it was a sheer figment of Lovecraft's fertile imagination. Most of this hugely influential author's work was inspired by his own nightmares.

But by blending her own nightmares around works of fiction, vampires and her personal blood-letting, Natasha managed to become the central figure in her own little group. So wise in the ways of alienation herself, she knew instinctively how to attract and engage others who felt the way she did. Unlike Lovecraft, or other depressives in history who have channelled their emotions into literature, music or film, Natasha was about to commit all her energies into self-destruction.

None of them had parents who were prepared to put a lid on their behaviour. Madonna Wallen, in an echo of Sondra Gibson, said that she preferred it if Natasha brought her friends round to the trailer to dabble in drugs and the dark arts because: 'It was better than her running around the town doing it.'

But by 1997, Natasha and her friends didn't want to hang around a dead-end town like Pikeville any more.

Raising Hell

Their road trip was planned in advance. Joe had a Chevrolet Citation they were going to use, although it was too small and too old to get them to the destination they dreamed of – New Orleans. But that didn't matter. Natasha had been watching *Natural Born Killers*, her friend John Salyer would later tell the court. She was planning on a cross-country murder spree, and like Mickey and Mallory, she'd just pick up new vehicles as they went along. 'Natasha said she would like to kill people,' he added.

Two days before they left, the six members of the clan hired a room at the Colley Motel in Pikeville to perform a black magic ritual, part of which involved arranging black candles into triangles on the floor and attempting to summon up demons from within them. Blood-letting was also a big part of the ceremony, and as well as opening up her own veins, Natasha carved an upside-down cross into Jason's forearm.

The motel manager, Jim Cochran, later told a reporter: 'There was blood in there and there was a place in the carpet burned that formed the number six. Looked like they tried to burn 666 in the carpet,' he surmised. 'And yes, there was a lot of blood. More than you would get if you were shaving.'

Karen Howell would later testify that she and Natasha had planned to bleed to death that night, but that the bond between them as 'soul mates' prevented them from going through with it. Just like Rod Ferrell and Charity Keesee, opening up their veins together had given them momentary relief. Karen and Natasha both denied their bond extended to a sexual relationship, although friends of the two would later tell reporters that they were indeed girlfriends, and that Natasha had been active as a lesbian with other girls too. Whatever the reality of their relationship, the impression of homosexuality worked in a religious and repressed society exactly the same results that being openly gay had done for Tracey Wigginton in late Eighties Brisbane – it made them appear even more evil.

Bonded by their bad blood, they then concentrated on the practicalities of leaving town. Natasha thought there were two essential things they'd need for their trip, both of which Karen stole from her father Joe – $500 in cash and a gun from his cabinet. They also acquired another weapon from a friend. When the gang left they were equipped with a .9mm and a .25mm pistol.

They met up in a McDonald's restaurant to discuss their plans. Top of their agenda was the need to find a better vehicle to make the trip.

'Joe said we could stick somebody up for their car in a mall parking lot,' Natasha recalled in court. 'I said, what do you mean a mall? Like a K-Mart? He said, no, a big mall like they have in Lexington.' They decided to look for a mall in Tennessee, as it was on the way to New Orleans. Then, locked and loaded, they hit the road.

Innocents abroad

A native of Norway, Vidar Lillelid first settled in Miami when he emigrated to the United States. There he met the former Delfina Zelaya, who was born in New Jersey to Honduran parents. The couple were married in 1989 and settled in New York, but after the birth of their daughter Tabitha in 1991, they grew concerned about the effects of inner-city crime and determined to find a safer haven in which to raise their children.

After taking a holiday that included a visit to the Great Smoky Mountains, they fell in love with the area and moved to Knoxville in 1992, where Vidar got a job as a hotel bellman while Delfina raised and schooled Tabitha at home. Active in the church, one of the first friends they made was John McLaughlin, a congregation elder at West Knoxville Jehovah's Witness Kingdom Hall. They met him one afternoon as they walked from their apartment on Walker Springs Road to the Kingdom Hall on Andes Road, Vidar carrying little Tabitha on his back.

McLaughlin was taken with the couple, who were devoutly religious and eager to get involved with the local congregation. He welcomed them into the community, and celebrated the birth of their son Peter with them in 1995. The Lillelids continued to take an active role in the church. On the fateful day of Sunday, 6th April, the family had attended a day-long religious convention in Johnson City.

They were in high spirits. There was only a month to go before Vidar was going to take the family on their first ever trip together to Norway, where he could finally let Tabitha and Peter meet their paternal grandparents and extended family. Because their savings were stretched by the approaching holiday, the Lillelids hadn't had enough money to join their fellow worshippers for a meal at the end of the day, but they didn't let that affect their good cheer. They started out on their 100-mile trip home in their cream-coloured Dodge van, singing as they drove.

To break up the journey, Vidar pulled over at the mile marker thirty-six rest area on Route 23, at the borders between Pike and Floyd counties, so they could use the washrooms and eat the picnic they'd taken with them and stretch their legs before the next stage of their journey.

If only they had been driving a smaller vehicle, maybe things would have been different.

If only they hadn't been so religious, maybe things would have been different.

The inhabitants of the Chevy Citation parked in the same rest stop had been eyeing up the Lillelid's van. It was perfect for their purposes.

Candy kisses

Vidar Lillelid approached the group of strange-looking teenagers outside the public restrooms. The blond, smiling father cradled his angelic looking son in his arms as he took in the black-clad group, with their dyed hair, pierced eyebrows, noses and lips. Many would have walked past this lot as hastily as possible, trying not to make eye contact as they did so. Not Vidar. Filled with the love of his day of worship, full of the missionary zeal that is part of the Jehovah's Witness teachings, he instead stopped to ask these teenagers who had so clearly lost their way: 'Do you believe in Jesus?'

No, Natasha told him, she didn't. He had never answered any of her prayers when she was little.

As the discussion continued, Delfina and Tabitha wandered up. Tabitha reached up her hand and offered Natasha and Karen a chocolate sweet called a Hershey's Kiss.

By now, all six of the Pikeville teens were standing around the Lillelid family. They were getting a bit tired of hearing another religious lecture, impatient to get back on the road. At some point, Joe Risner produced one of the guns they'd brought with them.

'I hate to do you this way,' he said. 'But we are going to have to take you with us for your van.'

He motioned with the weapon for the Lillelid family to walk back to their vehicle and get inside. As they did so, Vidar's mind flashed towards possible future scenarios. He begged the young man to take his car keys and his wallet and let the Lillelid's stay behind in the rest stop. Risner turned a deaf ear to his pleas. He made Vidar get into the driver's seat while he rode literal shotgun. Delfina and Tabitha were ushered into the back of the vehicle, where they crouched in fear next to Jason Bryant, Karen and Natasha. Ed Mullins and Crystal Sturgill followed behind the van in Joe's Chevy.

By now, the terrified children had begun to cry, and Delfina tried to comfort them by singing them lullabies. Joe told her in no uncertain terms to shut up. Then ominously, directed her husband first onto the interstate, then onto a secluded road at the next exit.

Last exit

What exactly happened next is disputed between Jason Bryant and the rest of the gang. In the statements given by Natasha, Joe, Karen, Crystal and Ed, Jason took control of the situation once both vehicles had stopped on Payne Hollow Lane, a small gravel road out of sight of the highway.

Joe, who was brandishing the .9mm, said that he handed his weapon to Natasha at that point, telling her he couldn't go through with what he knew was about to happen. Natasha claimed that she placed the weapon on the floor of the Dodge, while Jason, who had the .25, ordered the Lillelids out of their van and made them walk over to the edge of the ditch at the side of the track.

Vidar and Delfina were by now pleading for their lives and especially the lives of their children, promising they would not call the authorities if only they would just leave them alive. Natasha and Karen added their voices to these pleas, telling Jason to let the Lillelids go. This wasn't like the slick movie they had imagined in their heads. No one was looking like a heroic outsider here. These people were just too…innocent.

'You won't be able to tell them what we look like,' Natasha apparently said.

'Yes,' Delfina replied, 'All kids look the same these days.'

But, according to the others, Jason refused. They claim that he told the quaking Vidar that God doesn't like a liar, that he knew the man would call the police the first moment he could. But he promised he wouldn't hurt the children.

No one tried to get his weapon off him or make him calm down. Natasha and Karen said they simply returned to the van, where Joe was still sitting, his head in his hands.

Then a barrage of shots filled the air.

Shortly afterwards, Jason walked back to the van.

'They're still fucking alive,' he said, grabbing the other gun from the floor of the Dodge.

He emptied the contents of that gun into the Lillelid family.

Jason contends a different scenario. It was Joe, he testified, who ordered the Lillelids out of the ditch and told them to stand by the ditch. Joe who first shot Vidar with the .25 and then slapped Ed on the shoulder, a signal that he should join in. A hail of gunfire ensued, during which time, Jason said, he kept his eyes screwed shut.

When it was over, Joe and Ed ordered the others back to the van, where the gang laughed and bragged to each other about what had just happened. They turned on the radio to try and hear some Marilyn Manson. But the radio didn't work.

The damage done

What can be verified is the testimony of the forensic pathologist Dr Cleland Blake, who informed the court of the extent of the victims' injuries.

Vidar Lillelid, aged 34, received a total of six gunshot wounds, one to the right side of his head and five to his chest. In Dr Blake's opinion, the first shot entered the victim's right eye, travelled through his temple and exited in front of his right ear. The pathologist was of the opinion that this shot came from the .9mm weapon and would have caused a loss of consciousness. Dr Blake believed that Vidar fell to the ground lying on his back and was shot three times in the upper side of his chest with the same weapon, so that the wounds formed the shape of an equilateral triangle – perhaps related to the black magic ritual at the Colley Motel. A further gunshot wound just below his right nipple was consistent with a .25 calibre wound. There was a graze laceration on the victim's right forearm where a bullet had skimmed the surface of his skin.

Delfina Lillelid, aged 28, was shot eight times. All eight bullets were recovered; six were from a .9mm and two were from a .25. In Dr Blake's opinion, the first of these shots was fired by the .9mm and shattered the bone in her left arm. The second shot, from the same weapon, shattered the thigh of her left leg. Although these wounds would have caused her severe pain, the pathologist believed that they would not have killed her but she would no longer have been able to stand afterwards.

Delfina was shot an additional six times while she lay helpless on her back. The first three shots struck the side of her abdomen, and, in Dr Blake's assessment, deliberately formed the same triangular pattern as those wounds inflicted on Vidar. The three shots pierced her stomach, leaving a four- to five-inch tear, and travelled through her pancreas, spleen, left kidney and left adrenal. A final .9mm entry wound was located in the mid-section of Delfina's abdomen, just above her navel. There was a further .25 gunshot wound under her left armpit, another to her left side, and she had abrasions on her right calf. Dr Blake testified that none of Delfina's wounds were immediately fatal and she could have been conscious for as long as 25 minutes before she died.

Six-year-old Tabitha Lillelid was shot once in the head by a small calibre weapon. The bullet entered her head on the left side, travelled downward, and exited behind her right ear, causing immediate brain death. Her organs, however, continued to function until her death, one day after the shootings.

Two-year-old Peter Lillelid was shot twice with a small calibre weapon. One shot entered behind his right ear and exited near his right eye. A second gunshot penetrated his body from the back and exited through his chest. Somehow, Peter survived. Eleven days after the shootings, doctors had to remove his damaged eye. He remained in hospital for 17 days before being transferred to a rehabilitation centre in Knoxville.

The Lillelids' suffering didn't end there. When, after the shootings, Joe had apparently come to his senses enough to remove the license plate and registration from his Chevy, which he abandoned at the scene, he ran the family over. He said it was accidental, a response to an order from Jason to turn the vehicle around.

The bodies of Vidar and Delfina were discovered by the police only hours later, with their children still clutched in their arms.

Mexico or bust

With everybody now inside the Lillelids' van, the gang knew they would have to change their plans. New Orleans was out of the question now. They would have to try and cross the border into Mexico before the police caught up with them. In Mexico, they believed, they would be safe from extradition.

First they drove the Lillelids' van to a gas station where they bought a map and then headed south. When they reached the border, any visions of escaping like Wild West bandits into the South American badlands were abruptly curtailed by the fact that none of them had thought to bring their passports. However, despite this setback, they did eventually manage to somehow sneak their way over the border.

In Mexico, something else happened that the two conflicting sides diverge on. Somehow, Jason received gunshot wounds to his arm and leg.

What Jason says was that, while fleeing the scene of the crime, the rest of the gang had been doing some thinking. If they were caught and found guilty of first-degree murder, they could all be given the death penalty. All of them except Jason. He was only 14 years old and could not be given an adult sentence. Therefore, Jason said, Joe asked him to take the blame. When he hesitated, the other boy shot him in the hand and the leg.

The other five tell it another way. Jason shot himself, they claimed, so that he could make out he had attacked the Lillelids in self-defence.

Whatever they were all scheming, it wasn't going to amount to anything, except for the obvious physical pain caused to Jason. The Dodge had only got 12 miles over the border when it was flagged down by Mexican cops. Passport-less, the gang claimed they were lost, a story that didn't wash very well with their interrogators. They were ordered out of the vehicle while a search was carried out.

When they found a knife and a photo album belonging to the Lillelid family, the Mexicans ordered the six back to the Arizona borders and the custody of the United States police. There was no running away from this now. Only one day after the murders, on 7th April, the gang were arrested, the stolen van impounded.

Among the heart-breaking artefacts the police recovered were Tabitha's Hello Kitty diary lock on a chain, which Karen had around her neck, and a photo of the little girl that Natasha had put in her wallet, along with her stash of bloody razor blades. On the back of it was written, in Vidar's hand: 'Tabitha Lillelid...Summer 1995...My favorite girl.'

The reports of the Lillelid's murder had already shocked America. Now, as the news of the arrest hit the headlines nationwide, six nooses were dangled from a gallows erected outside a Knoxville convenience store.

'Burn in Hell, murderers!'

The gang were initially held at the Cochise County Jail in Arizona. Jason was sent to the Southeast Medical Center for treatment to his gunshot wounds and he and Karen, the two youngest members of the gang, mounted a futile attempt not to be extradited back to Greene County, Tennessee – the jurisdiction in which the crime had been committed – to be charged. The press buzz for the story was deafening; in this respect the story was indeed taking on the proportions of the plot of Natural Born Killers. And as the six languished in their cells, refusing to talk to the detectives, Tabitha Lillelid's life-support machine was turned off.

Her brother continued to fight for survival in hospital while hundreds of people, most of whom had never known the couple in life, went to pay their respects to the Lillelids at a funeral service at West Knoxville Kingdom Hall of Jehovah's Witnesses on 12th April. The job of preparing the Lillelids for burial had been a difficult one for the staff of the Weaver Funeral Home. 'When we put that little girl in the casket, we cried like babies,' attendant Tommy Petty told the press.

The case provoked a nationwide outpouring of such grief. As Vidar and Delfina's families met for the first time in the worst of possible circumstances, the public donated thousands of dollars to help with expenses and set up a trust fund for Peter. Yet even as the maternal and paternal grandparents united in their grief, a painful custody dispute over who would raise Peter soon threatened to divide them.

In Greene County, a Governor's warrant was being prepared that would force the extradition of the accused. On 15th April, Natasha, Crystal, Joe and Ed were transported in separate vehicles to Green County Detention Center. Word of their return spread like wildfire through downtown Greeneville, and a hostile mob of over a hundred people had soon assembled outside the jail. When the accused finally arrived the words, 'Burn in Hell, murderers!' 'Baby killers!' and 'You'll fry!' rang through their ears.

On 16th April, all six were charged with murder. District Attorney General Berkeley Bell judged the public mood just right when he filed notice that he would be seeking the death penalty against the four adults. Journalists covering the case from Scandinavia scrambled for pictures of Tennessee's electric chair.

Natasha fanned the flames still more when, two days after the arraignment, she told a reporter from the Associated Press how she was on a demonic mission to incite a youth rebellion against the Christian orthodoxy. She said she wanted to inspire: 'the children of America and the world to rise up against their parents and cast off their bondage.' She warned of an imminent apocalypse in which she and two other antichrists would re-order the world. 'Evil will become greater than it already is and will rule everything,' she prophesied. 'Satan will aid me.'

Conspiracy theories

The next day, Natasha's lawyer Eric Conn was removed from the trial at the insistence of General Sessions Judge James Carter for allowing this interview to take place, and also for releasing extracts from her diary alluding to Satanism to the press. With the statements of the four already causing concern, attorney Thomas Brady also withdrew from the case on the advice of other lawyers. It had been made public by then that one of the lawyers was concerned that Jason was being fitted up by the others to take the rap as he alone could avoid the death penalty.

On 25th April, Peter Lillelid was transferred from intensive care at the UT Medical Centre in Knoxville to a recovery unit at the nearby Patricia Neal Rehabilitation Hospital. Four days later, the battle for custody over the infant began, putting private family matters on painful display in a four-day hearing at Knoxville County Chancery Court. Eventually, Chancellor Frederick McDonald decided, to grant custody to Peter's paternal aunt Randi Heier because, he decided, the medical treatment he could receive in her Stockholm home would be better than that available if he stayed with his maternal grandmother in Miami. Peter had been fitted with an artificial eye, but had been promised state-of-the-art therapy to help him regain the ability to walk, which had been lost by the bullet that went into his back. He left for Sweden with his new guardians on 7th July.

In the meantime, Jason and Karen had finally been extradited from Arizona, and faced the Greeneville Court on 15th May to determine whether they should be tried as adults. The preliminary hearings rumbled on another two months. On 15th July, the booking officer with Cochise County Sheriff's Department, Shawn Ferrall, told the court about conversations he had with Joe and Ed shortly after their arrest. Ferrall testified that during normal booking procedures, Joe asked him, 'What usually happens to people who have done what I did?' then tearfully went on to say he wished he hadn't done what he did to those people. Ferrall also testified that Ed told him 'I'm a killer,' while he sat in his holding cell and asked if he thought he would get the death penalty. When Ferrall repeated his testimony at the court two days later, Joe's father stood up and said: 'Best to your family, son.' Plain-clothes police quickly whisked him out of the building.

On 18th July it was decided that all six defendants would be tried as adults. On 6th September, they all pleaded not guilty. But after DA Bell decided that the death penalty he had sought against them would be 'in name only' and would actually translate as life imprisonment without possibility of parole, they all changed their tune. Just before the trial was about to begin, on 20th February 1998, the six pleaded guilty. Bell told reporters that had the case gone to trial the state would have contended that Jason Bryant was the sole shooter.

Before sentencing, the two camps got to have their say in court.

Boys don't cry

Jason Bryant was the only one who didn't cry when he took the stand. 'We was basically raised up that you show emotion, you're weak,' he later explained. But his dry-eyed account elicited little public sympathy; on the contrary, it made him look just like the cold-eyed killer the others said he was. Natasha's lawyer Robert Cupp furthered that none of the others had been in any significant trouble until they encountered this 14-year-old demon, as if all of this was Jason's doing.

While true in terms of any involvement with the law, it was hardly the case.

'I just didn't know how to make it stop,' sobbed Natasha as she took the stand to tell her side of events. Apart from pointing the finger at Jason, a lot of Natasha's testimony was spent talking down the Satanic comments she had made while being represented by Eric Conn – despite the fact that when the judge removed Conn from the case, Natasha filed a suit to try and get him reinstated. Now, in a more sensible attempt by replacement lawyers Cupp and Stacy Street to prove their client had mental health problems, Madonna Wallen testified to her daughter's grim upbringing and her time in the psychiatric hospital.

Karen's testimony corroborated Natasha's account of the killings. She added the grim detail that while Tabitha lay screaming over her mother's fallen body, Jason put a gun to her head and fired.

What really happened down that lonely stretch of gravel track will probably remain forever unclear, the dark, ugly secret that binds the six youngsters for the rest of their lives. But whatever story they came up with was not going to elicit any sympathy from a public itching to use those Knoxville nooses.

On Friday, 13th March, Judge James Beckner handed down the maximum sentence to all six. DA Bell endorsed his decision. Never before, he said, had a case convinced him so thoroughly that there was real 'spiritual evil' loose in the world.

And now, a lifetime of incarceration awaited the six-six-sixers who had unleashed these dark forces.

However, not everybody agreed that this case was the straightforward battle between good and evil that it had been presented as. Forensic psychologist Dr Helen Smith became deeply concerned with what the whole episode had actually revealed – that the system of support for mentally ill and abused children in America simply wasn't working. She set about making a TV documentary, *Six*, in a bold attempt to foster a deeper understanding of what had made these kids behave the way they did.

Searching for clues

Helen Smith's take on the dynamic of the group concurs with the popular opinion that Natasha was the centre of attention, the one that held the six together. Jason, whether he was the sole shooter or not, was definitely her patsy. 'In research, we usually see that girls want to hire somebody to do their dirty work,' she told the website Suicide Girls in an in-depth interview about the documentary and the case. 'I think that Natasha found Jason, who had very aggressive tendencies and was very impulsive, and would do anything...girls who want to act out aggressively often find boys to do that, and then they can say they're not responsible. That's what [all the girls in this case] said, "Well the guys did it, we're not involved." But they are involved. To me, instigating a murder is just as bad.'

While Dr Smith believes that the punishments meted out to the six fit the crime, she still believed that the case warranted an investigation that went beyond the individuals involved. Like Michael Moore did with *Bowling for Columbine*, she posed the question of what it was about American society in particular that fostered such violent youth culture.

Was it down to the easy access of guns? 'I don't think that really plays a part. People have access to guns all the time and they're not running around killing anyone. Thirty years ago, people had guns over their mantel. I think it's a cultural phenomenon. In Japan there are more suicides than there are homicides in the US, it's just the cultural thing to do, you blame yourself if you're in Japan. In the United States you don't blame yourself, you have a sense of entitlement – by God, it's everybody else's fault. If McDonald's made your coffee too hot you sue them and you blame them. Here, if you've got problems, somebody did something to you, you just take 'em down. You can never be a victim, and if you are one, take everyone down with you. Get revenge on everyone.'

How much did the instability of these kids' backgrounds contribute to their attitudes? Weren't the parents to blame as much as society's prevailing attitudes? 'Everybody wants to put the blame on the parents because that's the easy scapegoat. We have to take responsibility, both as a society and as individuals for what's happening. Or we have to say as a society that we're not going to deal with it, if people are violent we'll take the chance that they're going to go out and kill people.

'What are we willing to do for parents who can't deal with their kids? Are we willing to help out through mental health programmes? Through residential treatment for them? Or are we just going to let their dangerous offspring loose in society?'

Zero tolerance

However, Dr Smith was realistic that the chances of implementing better safeguards and support systems were slim: 'The minute you suggest anything that costs money nobody wants to deal with it.'

In the years since Natasha Cornett cast her horned shadow across America there has been a strengthening of opinion against the liberal stance taken by Helen Smith. Zero-tolerance – the banning of bringing anything that could be conceived of as a weapon into the schoolroom – has become the preferred method of dealing with potential Natashas or Rod Ferrells. As Dr Smith points out, zero-tolerance doesn't cost anything – and neither does it provide anything. The violence of frustrated, angry, abused youth has gone on.

On 1st October 1997, 16-year-old 'Adolph Hitler fan' Luke Woodham, stabbed his mother, his former girlfriend and another classmate at his school in Pearl, Mississippi. 'I killed because people like me are mistreated every day,' he said. 'I did this to show society: Push us and we'll push you.'

On 1st December 1997, 14-year-old 'suspected Satanist' Michael Carneal opened fire on a prayer group at his school in Paducah, Kentucky, killing three girls.

On 21st May 1998, 15-year-old 'Marilyn Manson fan' Kip Kinkel, who had often complained to his uninterested teachers about the voices in his head, killed his parents then came to school in Springfield, Oregan with a semiautomatic rifle. He killed two and wounded eight others.

On 20th April 1999, the infamous 'trenchcoat mafia', 17-year-old Eric Harris and 18-year-old Dylan Klebold, massacred 13 fellow students before taking their own lives at the Columbine High School in Littleton, Colorado.

On 22nd March 2005, 16-year-old 'Adolf Hitler admirer' Jeff Weise shot dead his grandfather, eight others and then himself at the Red Lake High School in Red Lake, Minnesota.

By the time you read this, there is bound to have been more.

Chapter Eleven

⌒

Manuela and Daniel Ruda: A German Vampire in London (2001)

Love you to death

Manuela Bartel said that the Devil had called for her when she was only 14. She sold her soul to him at 21 after she had entered a vampire underworld in London, learning how to drink blood from another person's neck without severing an artery. When she returned to her native Germany, she sought out her perfect partner and found him in the personal ads of a Black Metal magazine.

'Pitch black vampire seeks princess of darkness who hates everything and everyone,' wrote 24-year-old car mechanic Daniel Ruda. Manuela was instantly entranced and responded under her alias Allegra, after Lord Byron's doomed, illegitimate daughter. They were married a year later, on the sixth day of the sixth month, 2001.

Bound up in sado-masochistic fervour, obsessed by vampirism and united in what a court psychiatrist later deemed 'severe narcissistic personality disturbances' they sealed their love with death one month after their wedding – stabbing 33-year-old Frank Hackert 66 times in a Satanic rite. Afterwards they drank his blood and then hit the road, leaving his body in their black-painted lair. Here police later found it with a scalpel protruding from the stomach and a pentagram carved in the chest, among their collection of human skulls and the coffin in which Manuela slept.

The case brought some disturbing trends amongst young people in Germany and neighbouring Italy back into the spotlight – and highlighted the links between gothic, occult, Black Metal and far-Right organisations. The name Hendrik Möbus was once more in the news – fleeing the murder scene, the Rudas had gone on a pilgrimage to Sondershausen to visit the desecrated grave of Sandro Beyer. They may have had even more sinister ideas in mind than just paying their respects to the boy's killer.

Once apprehended, the appearances of the killer couple in court were even more bizarre than the standards set by Richard Ramirez. Claiming that they were acting on commands from a lower authority, they denied murder and spent the trial rolling their eyes, sticking their tongues out and making rude gestures to the court. The couple continued hamming it up for the cameras even as sentences were passed down. They had already attracted a throng of admirers, known in German as 'Gruftis' (meaning 'crypt') who dotted the courtroom wearing black and holding roses in Gothic homage.

Passing judgement, Judge Arnjo Kersting-Tombroke said that said so much fan mail had been sent to the Rudas during the case that he was worried about the 'limitless stupidity' of so many members of the public. Even Daniel's lawyer, Hans Reinhardt, admitted to being deeply troubled by the ultimate motive of his client. As he told Britain's Channel 4 news: 'He says, "I want to get on stage, I want that everybody knows me...I want to be as famous as Charles Manson and so I have to kill someone".'

A difficult birth

Manuela Bartel didn't come into this world the easy way. She was born with the umbilical cord wrapped around her neck, almost strangling her before she had time to draw her first breath. An only child, she was, by all accounts, brought up in a loving, working class home by her railway worker father and housewife mother in the small town of Witten, in the industrial Ruhr valley in west Germany. Manuela never registered any complaints about her family. 'I was not allowed everything,' she later recalled, 'but I had good parents. They never struck me. They were always there for me.'

Even the local priest, Father Franz Josef Hagermann, remembers the youngster whom he prepared for her first Communion as a shy, reserved 10-year-old, who went to church every Sunday and had total faith in God. Perhaps because of her natural timidity and the fact she had no brothers or sisters, Manuela didn't have many friends, but she loved animals, collecting a menagerie at home which must have stretched her father's limited wages – birds, hamsters, guinea pigs, a dog, a rabbit and even a pony.

But when she reached puberty, Manuela's moodswings hit hard. She started feeling not just different from everyone else, but that she was somehow trapped in the wrong body. As her feelings of alienation increased, she was sent to see a counsellor, but withdrew from treatment after only one session, apparently fearing that if the shrink could figure out what was really going on in her mind, he would have her committed.

It could have been that, like Natasha Cornett, Manuela was showing the first signs of psychiatric illness. Certainly, it was at the same age, 13, that she started to cast around for another form of self-expression that made her feel more comfortable. She started dropping out of school to hang out with older kids in the town centre, kids who wore black and pierced their lips, ears and eyebrows, kids who listened to 'Dark Wave' music – Black Metal, Goth and neo-folk. She shocked her parents by dying her hair, emulating the black garb and darker habits of the other bored Witten kids.

Kids that already had drug habits in all likelihood too – by the age of 14, Manuela knew how to get hold of enough heroin to attempt suicide with an overdose. She had managed to do well enough at school to be selected for a place in the local gymnasium, the equivalent of a UK grammar school, where she was supposed to be studying for university. But her mental state had spiralled along with her eccentric appearance and she dropped out shortly after her first term started. After her suicide attempt, Manuela would later tell the court at her murder trial, she heard Satan call her.

Over the sea to Skye

At the age of 16, Manuela ran away from home, travelling first to the nearest big city, Hanover. Then, in the summer of 1996, she left for London, in the company of other like-minded teenagers, who flock to the English capital in their droves to take in such delights as Camden Market, the biggest Goth retail outlet in Europe, and legendary clubs such as Camden's Full Tilt at the Electric Ballroom and Islington's Slimelight.

From contacts she made here, she somehow managed to get herself a summer job in the remote Scottish Highlands, as a chambermaid in a hotel in Kyleakin, the 'Gateway to Skye' that at the time was the ferry point to the neighbouring island. Manuela loved the bleak, forbidding landscape there: the low clouds that swept over the mountains that towered over the town, and the desolate graveyards where she could walk at night.

Feeling at home in this new environment Manuela made friends with a local eccentric, Tom Leppard, known as the Leopard Man of Skye. A 62-year-old former soldier who is also a practising Catholic, Leppard has spent years transforming his appearance into that of the spotted big cat for which he is named, having 99.9 per cent of his skin tattooed with the animal's markings. He holds the Guinness World Record for being the world's most tattooed man and lives in a cave on the Isle of Skye, where he can go about the business of being a human big cat without fear of intrusion or ridicule.

Manuela paid four visits to Leppard's home that August and was fascinated by his way of life, how he had shunned society completely to live as an animal, only venturing across to Kyleakin when he needed provisions. She may well have encountered fetishists known as 'furbies' while in London; they tend to congregate in Camden's Devonshire Arms goth pub as well as at fetish clubs. These are usually fairly young teenagers experimenting with dressing up as animals, usually big cats, wolves or other nocturnal creatures suitable for Goth admiration. As well as being an extension of dressing up, the culture of 'furbies' constitute a fairly popular sexual fetish, with annual conventions and plenty of Internet sites. But Tom Leppard was not a part of this scene. He turned himself into an approximation of the animal he most identified with in order to keep his distance from other people.

In a rare interview with the BBC, Leppard described his outlook: 'As far as I'm concerned, if there is a paradise on Earth, I'm in it. You're welcome to what you've got. I'll keep this.' Gentle Tom's outlook was at odds with Manuela's darkly troubled soul, but she continued to seek his advice even after she left Scotland, sending him letters as she waited to go on trial. She admitted what she had done, but could not tell Leppard the reason why. He told Sky News: 'I said you can't just hate, you've got to have something to hate. You can't hate this, or hate that without a reason. And she never answered the question.'

Vampires in London

When the summer season was over in Kyleakin, Manuela returned to London, where she soon got herself a bar job at the Slimelight club in Islington and fell in with the local vampire crowd. In Manuela's mind, these were actually real vampires; she would later tell the court that the club, one of the oldest established Goth hang-outs in London, was frequented by 'both vampires and human beings'. She could tell the vampires apart from the mere mortals because 'they shunned the light', though how she could make this distinction out in the dimly-lit confines of the cavernous bunker of a club is hard to say.

In her new circle, Manuela began to attend what she called 'bite parties', which took place at night in cemeteries. '[We would] have a perfectly normal chat and drink some blood,' she later recalled. 'We drank blood together, from willing donors. You can't drink from the arteries, no-one is allowed that.' Manuela learned how to bite into someone's neck without severing the artery. She filed her canine teeth down so they were as sharp as possible. Later, back in Germany, she would have these removed completely and replaced with long animal fangs.

The 'donors' she talked about were contacted through the Internet; they traded blood for sexual kicks. 'Men were always trotting after me in London,' Manuela boasted. 'I made them pay for their affections – with their blood. That's all I wanted from them – to drink their blood. They were my blood donors.' On the fetish scene, it is quite hard even for experts to distinguish between sado-masochists looking for some role-play or people who genuinely see themselves as vampires. Despite – or maybe because – of the dangers of AIDS and other blood-borne diseases, vampire dominatrixes had become all the rage in big-city brothels by the late Nineties.

Manuela realised she had the right qualities to make a successful dominatrix – which was just as well, because straight sex repelled her anyway. She practised her skills with the whip along with her Transylvanian trials: 'I also slept on graves and even allowed myself to be buried in a grave to test the feeling,' she claimed.

Transformation and dedication

When Manuela eventually returned to Witten in 1997, it did indeed seem that she had somehow 'crossed over'. The shy, lonely girl she had once been was replaced with a PVC-clad dominatrix in kinky boots and enough hairspray to dent the ozone layer, who was soon pictured dragging one of her slaves through a graveyard on the end of a dogchain in the newspaper *Stern*. In the accompanying article on emergent youth culture Manuela stoked up business: 'I will gladly whip and bind you!'

However, Dracula's daughter was still living something of a bizarre double life, working in a bakery by day and studying Aleister Crowley by night in her black-painted bedroom. Her family despaired of her provocative behaviour and even weirder appearance. Manuela shaved off her eyebrows and drew in their place stark, black vertical lines. She had her lips pierced, her fangs installed and she covered her skin in Satanic tattoos. She started to claim that the daylight physically hurt her and again, she said, she heard the voice of Satan calling to her. She set up in her own apartment in Witten that was kitted-out with the tools of the dominatrix trade, as well as the coffin she acquired to sleep in.

Like Natasha Cornett and Rod Ferrell, Manuela had also begun self-harming. She had livid scars on her arms, face, neck and legs that she wore as proud decorations, the markings of where she had feasted on her own blood. She began referring to herself as Allegra, convinced that Byron's daughter had not died of a fever in a French nunnery at the age of five, but had been instead sacrificed to Satan by her libertine father.

Finally, on 31st October 1999 – the Satanic festival of Samhain as well as Halloween – Manuela signed her soul over to Satan in a solemn blood vow. As she put it: 'I placed myself in, and swore myself to, the service of our Lord, his will to perform.'

Satan rewarded his loyal daughter by sending her soulmate to her.

Call me Sundown

Like Manuela, Daniel Ruda came from a normal, working class Witten family. His father worked at a chemical plant while his housewife mother looked after Daniel and his sisters at home. Daniel always resented his sisters and spent most of his childhood trying to attract more attention from his mother than they did. He always seemed to be seeking the limelight and acting in increasingly aggressive ways to achieve it.

Although he was a strong student at primary school, by the time he reached his teenage years Daniel's results were slipping. Resentful of the perceived injustices of his life, he began to retreat into a fantasy world, dreaming of becoming a vampire monster that would snap off the heads of humans and drink their blood. He claimed that he had first developed a taste for 'the metallic, salty taste' of blood when he was only 12, and by the age of 14 was receiving messages from a demon called Samiel who would command him to act out Satanic instructions.

Daniel got his hands on a copy of *The Satanic Bible*, and liked what he read there. He also became fascinated with Charles Manson and the power he had wielded over his cult 'family'. Daniel got to thinking that maybe he could become Germany's equivalent to America's prize bogeyman. He started to cut himself in order to drink his own blood and told people that his name was Sundown.

As with Hendrik Möbus, it was only a thin line that separated Daniel's interest in the occult with a similar thirst for Right-wing politics. At his trial a former friend, 28-year-old Frank Lewa, testified that he had first met Daniel on the local far-Right/skinhead scene and that Daniel was far from a casual observer of this illegal milieu. In the 1998 German general election, Daniel had been out canvassing for the

National-Democratic Party of Germany (NPD), a far-Right party that was banned shortly afterwards from standing for parliament on the basis that it was trying to undermine the country's constitutional government. After his first foray into extremist politics, Daniel apparently moved away from the skinhead scene and into the Black Metal world, forming a band called the Bloodsucking Freaks. He also made a pilgrimage to Great Britain in his early twenties, visiting the same clubs and graveyards his future wife had been haunting.

Daniel told the court that his meeting with Manuela had been preordained by the demon Samiel, who ordered him to find his soulmate and marry her on the 6th June, then to consummate their union in a murder-suicide pact on the sixth day of the following month. This would spell out the Number of the Beast – 666 – and enable Daniel and his bride to take their place in Hell together.

When Allegra saw Sundown's message in the pages of a Black Metal magazine in August 2000 she wrote him a long letter, expressing her loved for *the beauty of the night, expired ruins of cemeteries illuminated by the full moon*. She assured her suitor that she was in total agreement with him on the worthlessness of humankind and the need to shun the daylight. They had their first date in the graveyard of the nearby Ruhr valley city of Recklinghasen and immediately fell madly in love.

Their courtship consisted of driving through the night in Daniel's Opel Vectra, visiting cemeteries to make animal sacrifices and meeting with other 'vampires' and 'Satanists' in clubs and over the Internet. Even after they had married, the Rudas rejected the 'terrestrial lust' of straight sex, acting out bizarre S&M scenarios instead. It seems that experiencing pain was as vital to Daniel as meting it out was to Manuela. The last Frank Lewa heard from Daniel was a note he sent to him shortly before the murder of Frank Hackert. Daniel and Lewa had argued at a party a few days earlier, and in the note, Daniel referred to his former friend as 'Judas'. He enclosed a picture of himself covered in blood and apparently hanging from hooks on the ceiling of his flat. He was pointing two gas pistols at the camera.

Death comes to dinner

Daniel and Manuela claimed that the only reason they had taken part in such a Christian concept as marriage was to legally ensure that their remains would be buried together. For, according to Daniel's Satanic orders, the murder they must now carry out would be followed by the taking of their own lives. Only then could they become united in death to serve Satan for all eternity. Manuela further believed the suicide would free her from her hated mortal shackles and turn her into the vampire she had desired to be since her early teens.

'We had to kill,' she later told the court. 'We couldn't go to Hell unless we did.'

She was so serious in her beliefs that she sent her parents a last will and testament in July 2001, bidding them farewell and asking that she be buried in the coffin she was presently using as her bed in her Witten apartment. '*I am not of this world,*' she told them. '*I must liberate my soul from the mortal flesh.*' It would be this letter that alerted the police to what the newlywed Rudas had done.

Daniel and Manuela had already picked out a victim for sacrifice. Frank Hackert worked with Daniel at a car parts dealership in the city of Herten. Known to his friends as 'Hacki', Frank was an easy-going, funny, and well-liked man of 33, who loved the music of The Beatles and took Christianity seriously enough to have once considered joining a monastery. He was one of Daniel's best friends at work and one of the most popular figures at the dealership. He was, in short, everything the Rudas were not – sunny, outgoing and carefree. Although the Rudas had managed to fall out with nearly everyone they knew, Frank remained a trusted friend who didn't pass judgement on their strange appearances. His reward was a vicious, demeaning death.

'He was always so funny,' Daniel would later tell the court. 'We thought he would be the perfect court jester for Satan.'

So they invited him over on the night of 7th July 2001, for what they told him was a party. On the afternoon before, Daniel claimed that Satan had taken over his body and therefore his perceptions of what came next were hazy. Manuela could remember far more. She said she and Daniel spent the afternoon 'just hanging out' together. She took a rest in her coffin for a short while before they wrote their 'farewell' letters to their families and then went to pick up Frank in Daniel's car at 6pm.

As soon as the three of them arrived back at Manuela's flat, she claimed that she could feel the presence of 'a strange force' and other beings in the room.

'We were no longer alone,' she said.

'The knife was glowing'

As the three sat chatting on the sofa, Manuela says she saw her husband undergo a transformation. 'We were sitting on the couch the whole time, then my husband stood up,' she recalled in the courtroom. Daniel left the room and then returned, brandishing a hammer, surrounded by a 'flickering aura'. 'He had terrible, glowing eyes and he hit out with the hammer. Frank stood up and said something, or wanted to say something. The knife was glowing and a voice told me, "Stab him in the heart!"'

Manuela didn't just strike once. According to the coroner's report, Frank Hackert was stabbed 66 times, and the forensics expert who testified to the court said that the couple had used many different instruments to inflict the multiple wounds upon their supposed friend. Police confiscated one short knife, one carpet cutter and a machete.

'He then sank down. I saw a light flickering around him,' Manuela testified. 'That was the sign that his soul had departed for the underworld. We said a prayer to Satan. We were empowered and alone.'

When Frank could no longer move, they used a scalpel to carve a Pentagram into his chest, drained off his blood and drank it from a bowl as another offering to their dark lord.

Disappointingly for Manuela, this ritual had not automatically turned her into a vampire. The couple slit the veins in Frank's arms in preparation for committing suicide themselves. But when the time came, it seemed they could not bring themselves to carry out the last part of their Satanic command. 'We were exhausted and we wanted to die ourselves,' Manuela explained. 'But the visitation was too short. We could no longer kill ourselves.'

Detective Franz Sobolewski, who had interrogated the couple after their arrest, gave the court a different view of the killer couple's state of mind. He said that Frank had actually been killed by a single hammer blow to the head and the rest of the wounds had been inflicted in a spontaneous frenzy afterwards. After they had calmed down, reality dawned on the Rudas. 'Suddenly, they realised that killing someone is not that simple, that it was monstrous and brutal,' Sobolewski testified. 'They didn't want to repeat that with themselves. They did not have the courage.'

He said that while repeating the story to him in custody, Manuela had sobbed that 'Satan has deserted me', saying she would willingly take it all back. She was incredibly upset that she had not become a vampire, 'because as a vampire, I would not have needed the streets'.

Unable to carry out their original plan to bleed to death, the couple later said they had considered two other methods of doing away with themselves. One was to drive to Denmark where they would be legally able to buy a gun, and then shoot themselves. This hardly sounds like a convincing or logical plan. Yet more improbably still, the other was to fill the boot of Daniel's car with diesel canisters and drive into a headlong collision with a lorry.

Possibly, killing themselves was never the Rudas' intention. For in their hurry to leave the scene of the crime, they left in Manuela's flat a list of 16 names, which police believe were the couple's next intended victims. Among them was the name of Cornelia Beyer – the mother of Hendrik Möbus' teenage murder victim.

Heading East

The Rudas loaded up Daniel's car with a few of their belongings and headed not to Denmark, but east to Thuringia, into Möbus country. Perhaps, using Daniel's old contacts on the Death Metal/far-Right scene or their other Internet play pals, they thought they might find sanctuary in the former East Germany.

On 9th July, Manuela's letter to her parents arrived. They were understandably alarmed by its contents and feared their troubled daughter had finally snapped. When they were unable to contact her by phone, they called the police and followed apprehensively behind them to Manuela's apartment. There were no lights on, but they could clearly make out a phrase, written in English in blood red paint on the window: *'Where Satan lives!'*

As the Bartels waited outside, police uncovered the grisly scene through the unlocked front door. Manuela's apartment looked like a cross between a brothel and a horror movie. The carpet was black, the walls painted blood red and grey and decorated with swastikas and upside-down crosses, Satanic slogans and Pentagrams. Handcuffs hung from a chain from the ceiling, along with a metal collar and rivet belts for bondage and suspension. The couple's ornaments included stones stolen from graveyards and the sites of concentration camps, a human mask fitted with the horns of an animal, cemetery lights and rows of imitation human skulls.

The whole room was splattered with blood. Next to Manuela's open coffin lay the butchered body of Frank Hackert, surrounded by an arsenal of knives, axes and machetes.

Public prosecutor Dieter Justinsky would later tell the court that: 'I have never, ever seen such a picture of cruelty and depravity before. They simply had a lust for murder. Both believed in Satan, they worshipped him.'

Meanwhile, the honeymoon killers had been travelling across Germany, drawing out some cash for their travels in Hanover, and having the brakes checked and the wheels changed on their car. Such precautions hardly suggest a suicide flight. Nor does the fact that on 12th July, on reaching the eastern German city of Jena in Thuringia, Daniel went into a department store and bought himself a chainsaw. He was recognised and reported, and shortly afterwards the Rudas were apprehended at a roadblock. Once in police custody, they promptly confessed to Hackert's murder.

During their flight, the police found out that the Rudas had indeed paid their respects to Sondershausen, but had been unable to locate the exact grave they wished to desecrate. Perhaps they were planning a return visit with the chainsaw. They had also visited the town of Apold, where Möbus' brother Ronald continues to do record label business. But apparently there had been no one willing to shelter the renegade couple in the underworld of the East. Perhaps there had been too much trouble down there already.

But with Manuela providing the grand spectacle at their trial in January 2002, with an upside down cross painted in mascara on the side of her shaven head, the attentions of the press firmly focused on her outrageous Satanic claims. Only a few commentators explored the links between Satanism, Black Metal and Fascism that continued to flourish in Germany.

They used dark forces

One exception was *Observer* journalist John Hooper, who made the connection between the Rudas' flight to Thuringia and the story of Hendrik Möbus in an article published in the British Sunday paper in November 2002. Concerned that the far Right was co-opting Gothic music to infiltrate with their ideas, he travelled to Germany and spoke to many participants in the music scene, the police and concerned monitoring groups.

Indeed, he found that by using Black Metal and neo-pagan folk, the far Right had far more success infiltrating Goth culture than any other area they'd tried – and they'd tried a few. Echoing the intentions of William Pierce's American organisation, one of the architects of this trend, Simone Satzger, partner of the leading right-wing agitator Roland Bubick, wrote that that the far Right's strategy was: 'to open up contemporary cultural and political phenomena to use them for our own purposes'.

Reinhard Boos, the Saxonian director of the Verfassungsschutz, the organisation charged with protecting Germany from a Nazi revival, spoke to Hooper about the level of threat the far Right posed. 'The Gothic scene is not to be confused with Right Wing extremism,' he pointed out. 'But there are some groups that use symbols which refer to Right Wing extremism and they do it mainly for provocation. Very, very few of them do it to support Right Wing groups. On the other hand, the Right Wing extremists know that there are people who can be useful to them, so some of them try to win them over for their own aims. It is not a plan by a few [people] that is carried out in a clear, structured way. Those who think it is a good idea do so of their own accord.' However, Boos still took the threat seriously, 'because it opens people's heads to extreme Right Wing thought.'

Different experts put different figures on how many young people they thought had got caught up in this world. Ingolf Christiansen, author of a book on Satanism and commissioner for ideological issues at the Lutheran Protestant Church in Hanover, estimated there were between 3,000 and 7,000 followers of 'Satanism' with neo-Nazi links. 'That's a conservative estimate,' he added. 'I see a rising tendency. The Internet is helping to spread it. It is driven by increasing brutalization in all areas and a corresponding loss of values.'

Alfred Schobert, a lecturer at the Duisberg Institute of Language and Social Research, took a similar view to Reinhard Boos in his 1998 academic investigation into the infiltration of the Gothic scene by the far Right. 'It is not about recruiting in the short term. It is about [producing] an overall reversal that picks up on and distorts the prevailing mood.'

The aims are the same as William Pierces's, he said. That by gaining access to the minds of the thousands of young people in Europe who are interested in Goth and Black Metal music, the far Right can encourage them to accept that certain beliefs and symbols are acceptable and indeed desirable. Then they can achieve what Schobert believes is their mid-term goal, 'the removal of the taboos that attach to Nazi symbols and racist-nationalist ideology'.

Marks of the Beast

Indeed, similar crimes to those of the Rudas' and Möbus', tainted with the brush of Black Metal, had been occurring not just in Germany but in neighbouring Italy. In March 2002, the death toll from Satanist-related killings and suicides in Germany reached 30, when a 16-year-old boy from Wenden slit his parents' throats after they banned him from going to a Satanic club. Local police said that the boy's parents had been concerned about the company their son was keeping, in a group of teenagers who held drinking parties in local graveyards. They had recently dragged him from a church spire during a Sunday service as he waved a knife and shouted, 'Satan! Satan!' to worshippers below, and had been disgusted to find he'd had a Pentagram tattooed on one arm.

When they found the boy, amid a scene of 'indescribable horror', the police said the young Satanist had slit his parents throats while they slept, then watched them bleed to death before making himself a meal of fried potatoes and sausages.

Two weeks before that, a couple who had met on the Internet for a 'death chat' jumped from the 23rd floor of a block of flats in Berlin, taking their pet cat with them. Their suicide notes stated that they were offering themselves up as 'Satanic sacrifices'. This followed another suicide jump by two girls off the infamous Goeltzaschtal Bridge at Reichenbach in Saxony, apparently in homage to the three boys that had killed themselves there in a Satanic pact in August 2000, as described in Chapter 7.

Music for the Black Masses

Over in Italy, another Black Metal band went on a murderous rampage in 1998, in a case so complex it wouldn't finally come to trial until April 2005. Mario Maccione was sentenced to 19 years for his part in the murders of 19-year-old Fabio Tollis and 16-year-old Chaira Marino, brutally assaulted and then buried alive in the woods near Milan in January 1998. Tollis and Marino had fallen in with a Black Metal band called the Beasts of Satan, of which Maccione was a member, and they were apparently sacrificed to the Dark Lord. Maccione's fellow Beast, Massimiliano Magni, was acquitted due to lack of evidence, although the band were also suspected of being behind another 11 murders which fit the same MO. The lead singer of the Beasts, Andrew Volpe, had been previously sentenced to 30 years for the killing of his ex-girlfriend Mariangela Penzotta in 2004. She was shot in the mouth and then buried.

In a case that grabbed worldwide headlines and stoked the fury already directed towards Marilyn Manson for the Columbine shootings, three young girls from the small town of Chiavenna in Italy connived to kill a nun in June 2000. Sister Maria Laura Mainetti, 61, was known for her work with prostitutes and drug addicts. When her body was found with repeated stab wounds and a blow to the head, it was assumed that it was probably the work of one of her outreach charges.

But when three teenage girls confessed to luring Sister Mainetti from her convent and murdering her 'for a game' the real outrage was let loose. It was discovered that Ambra, Veronica and Milena, all aged between 16 and 17, had a burgeoning interest in Satanism and diaries full of song lyrics by Marilyn Manson in their possession. The three girls had made a blood pact some months earlier that they would make a sacrifice for Satan, deciding on Sister Mainetti over the local priest because 'Father Ambrogio was too fat'.

One of the girls, Ambra, was deemed mentally ill and sent to a reform house, the other two to prison. Marilyn Manson was banned from entering Italy shortly afterwards. 'It is not the Satanism of Charles Manson [that we are most worried about] but that of his namesake Marilyn Manson,' stated Italy's chief exorcist, Fr Gabriele Amorth. 'Not of the black masses but of Black Metal music.'

Oh what a circus

But the Pope's man was looking at the wrong Manson, just as his counterparts were in America. It was to Charles, not Marilyn, that the Rudas were drawn, just as so many youthful Satanic killers had been before, and soon Daniel's admiration for the cult killer would be made public in court.

It didn't take long for the German authorities to fix a date for the hearing. Once in captivity, the couple were examined by three of Germany's top psychiatric consultants as they were kept isolated for 192 days before the trail began in the west German city of Bochum.

Manuela was apparently a well-behaved prisoner but Daniel had to be placed in a special isolation cell for his own protection – he had begun slashing himself with his own sharpened nails in order to keep up his special diet of his own blood.

The trial began on 10th January 2002, and quickly became a global three-ring circus. The judge allowed in more than 100 of the world's press photographers, news teams and journalists and the galleries were packed with Gruftis, skinheads and prurient spectators desperate to get a glimpse of these ungodly folk heroes. Manuela and Daniel acted as ghoulish ringmasters to the show, laughing and mugging for the cameras, flashing Satanic signs and sticking their tongues out. If they had shown any remorse under questioning, it was completely absent from this very public freakshow.

Daniel made his debut in court wearing a *Nosferatu* T-shirt and several fresh lacerations from his nails over his lips. Seeing his throng of admirers assembled around the room he raised his arms and gave the sign of horns. 'My people!' he cried out. But Mrs Ruda was determined not to let her husband steal the show. She got up at four in the morning each day to prepare a new look – a target painted on the side of her head; green, black and red nail varnish painted over her long talons; white and black make-up a mask against the world. Her off-the-shoulder tops revealed flesh heavily tattooed with Satanic symbols.

Across the room from this parade of studied insolence sat Hermann and Doris Hackert, the parents of the victim.

On the second day of the trial, Manuela's attorney Siegmund Benecken petitioned Judge Kersting-Tombroke on his client's behalf, asking if the courtroom lights could be turned down and the windows blacked out. 'She cannot stand the light,' he claimed. 'She sleeps all day and comes out only at night.' He furthered that 'suffering' the light would put an added strain on Manuela, causing her headaches that caused her undue duress. The Judge denied his request but gave permission for Manuela to wear sunglasses for the duration of proceedings, which added to her air of aloofness as she sat, chewing gum, pouting and grinning away to the audience.

'It was in his best interest'

Since Manuela had already confessed to killing Hackert, she declined to answer any questions in court, but Benecken did get her to outline her state of mind by asking how she reacted to the charge of murder.

'We are not murderers,' she replied. 'It wasn't meant in a bad way. We wanted to release his soul from the hateful flesh, so that he can serve Satan. It was in his own best interest. We only followed orders.'

She insisted that she and her husband liked their victim, and that his killing was nothing personal. 'Hacki is still here,' she said as his parents watched, clearly stunned. Later Doris would comment, her eyes full of tears: 'I came here each day to try and find some kind of remorse or sorrow in their eyes. I found nothing.'

The couple had entered pleas of not guilty, despite conceding that they had committed the crime; their defence was based on diminished responsibility. They had only been acting on orders, they said.

In his written statement, Daniel spoke of himself as an instrument acting on another's will. 'If I kill a person with my car and half his bloody head is left on my bumpers, it's not the car that goes to jail. It is the driver who is evil, not the car. I have nothing to repent because I did nothing.'

There followed testimony by the psychiatric consultants who had examined the Rudas in jail. Professor Norbert Leygraf, one of the most outstanding forensic psychologists in the country, agreed unanimously with the opinion of his colleagues that both Daniel and Manuela had severe narcissistic personality disorder, which, he said, is better understood as a character defect than a mental illness. Professor Leygraf considered that therapy sufficient to render the pair harmless would take over 10 years, but he couldn't rule out that this therapy could also be completely futile – neither of the pair had ever developed any feelings of guilt and perhaps they never would be able to.

Michael Emde, representing the Hackerts, was sceptical of how 'disturbed' the Rudas really were. He told *Stern*: 'I was told that the defendants behaved quite normally outside the court. This strong make-up, the cruel haircut, showing these signs of the Devil with their fingers and making faces, all this has been instigated and supported by this massive media presence.'

'Nothing mystical happened here'

The trial came to an end and sentencing was passed down on 1st February 2002. Both remained quiet as they sat before the judge, Daniel staring menacingly at Doris Hackert, Manuela chewing away on her gum. In his summing up, Judge Kersting-Tombroke opined: 'This case was not about Satanism. It was about a crime committed by two people with severe disorders. Nothing mystical or cult-like happened here, just simple, base murder.' But they were human beings, not monsters, and society had a duty to try and cure them, he continued. Despite the prosecution's request that the pair be sent to a maximum-security prison, he decided that Manuela should be sentenced to 13 years in a secure mental facility and Daniel to 15 years. His decision provoked uproar in the courtroom.

Defiant to the last, Manuela's final gesture was to make a Satanic sign with her little and index fingers and inch-long black nails. Daniel stuck his tongue out and pulled a demented face, captured for posterity by the news agencies' cameras. The couple hammed it up all the way out of the court, giving each other a last kiss goodbye on the steps.

Silently, the Hackerts sat holding hands opposite the killers. Interviewed directly after the verdict was passed down, Hermann

Hackert told reporters sadly that: 'At the beginning I did not want to go to the trial but now I'm glad that we sat eye-to-eye. Now I understand that they are bad people, but people – not devils, and absolutely unsound of mind.'

Violently unstable fantasists, Manuela and Daniel Ruda were like two unmanned trains speeding towards each other with unstoppable force. Had they never got together, would infamy have followed? Manuela is quite repentant from her treatment centre. 'Believe me, I'm not proud of what I've done, and now I know I've been wrong all the time,' she told Sondra London for *True Vampires*. 'I'm not the fucking weirdo you might have expected to meet.'

Still more unnerving to contemplate is what might have followed if the couple had not been apprehended with their chainsaw in Thuringia. Would Daniel have gone through with his dream of a Manson-like atrocity? The belief-systems the couple had independently reached gave their union a sense of fate and purpose when they eventually did meet. They egged each other on to the ultimate crossing-over a human being can make – the taking of another's life. Yet even as they did so, the myths and legends they had woven into their minds as higher truths unravelled spectacularly. Dark forces were certainly at work here – but not of the supernatural kind.

Chapter Twelve

Allan Menzies: Queen of the Damned's Consort (2003)

Killer Queen

Queen of the Damned, Michael Ryner's 2002 film adaptation of Anne Rice's cult vampire novel, is remembered mostly for being the last performance of doomed R&B singer Aaliyah, who died in a plane crash shortly after filming her role as the vampire queen Akasha. But the film's bad luck didn't end with the premature death of its leading lady at the age of only 22. A year later it was to claim another victim, working its way into the testimony of a disturbed young man called Allan Menzies, who claimed to be under the spell of Akasha when he stabbed to death his best friend and left his body on high and lonely Scottish moors.

The film itself was hardly a horror classic, or indeed particularly faithful to its source material. Ryner's cursory summary of Rice's *The Vampire Chronicles* skimmed over the Queen of the Damned conjured by her original author, a radical feminist who believed that as the world's suffering had been caused in the main part by men, then men must die for their sins. Aaliyah's Egyptian queen and original vampire is portrayed as an equal-opportunities killer with a deadly beautiful face, the über-goddess of the underworld who is awoken from a centuries-long sleep by the music of the vampire Lestat, who has decided to become a Marilyn Manson-style rock star.

Ryner shamelessly went after the Gothic buck in his attempt to replicate the success of Neil Jordan's 1994 Rice-approved *Interview With The Vampire*, picking up Lestat's saga where that story left off, but leaving out the attention to detail, storytelling and fantastical, otherworldly atmosphere of which Jordan is such a master.

However, *Queen of the Damned* would end up having another kind of pulling power for its adolescent fan-base, one it shared with another recent cult horror movie, Alex Proyas' 1994 *The Crow*. That dark, Gothic fairytale starred a young actor in a breakthrough role – Bruce Lee's son Brandon – who was killed filming a stunt scene, when a gun that should have been loaded only with blanks inexplicably contained live ammo. Ironically, both Aaliyah and Brandon Lee had played lead roles in which they came back from the dead, yet neither would be alive to see the finished cut. Like *The Crow*, *Queen of the Damned* had the notoriety of opening as a 'curse movie'.

In a film that deals with immortality as a central theme, this shocking imposition of real life should really serve as a caution against believing in myths and fairytales. But not to Allan Menzies. In his repeated testimonies to the police, Menzies, an unpopular loner with a history of severe behavioral problems, said that he believed the film that he had watched so obsessively had given him the key to gaining eternal life.

The secret was murder.

Black Christmas

Christmas 2002 was not a merry one for the French-McKendrick family of Fauldhouse, not a Christmas that any family should have to go through. But when 53-year-old widow Sandra French last said good-bye to her 21-year-old son, Thomas McKendrick, on 11th December, nothing seemed to be out of the ordinary.

Thomas, a big, broad young man with a fair complexion and a shaved head, did not seem like the sort of person who'd attract any trouble. He wasn't a flamboyant character, more of a quiet outdoorsman, who liked to spend time hunting with his ferrets in the disused Levenseat quarry in neighbouring Breich. That was what Sandra had assumed her unemployed son would be doing that day; he was dressed for it in blue jeans and sturdy black boots. There wasn't much else to do in Fauldhouse, a tiny village that lies high up in the moors in the southwest corner of West Lothian, roughly halfway between Glasgow and Edinburgh.

Winter night falls swiftly in that part of the world. The sun set at 3.39 that afternoon, putting paid to any further outdoor pursuits. But the hours drew on and Thomas didn't return home. Sandra and her daughter, Sandra Mary McKendrick, went to bed without hearing his key in the door, his footsteps in the hallway. The telephone kept the silence. The minutes ticked by, long and cold as the winter outside. They stretched to hours. They stretched to days.

Christmas, which was also Sandra Mary's birthday, came and went with Thomas' presents still sitting under the tree unwrapped. Neither woman could bring herself to celebrate without knowing where their

Thomas was. 'We just sat and listened for him coming through the door,' Sandra told the police. 'None of us had the heart to do anything else.'

He wasn't home by Hogmany either, and there was no way Thomas had gone out prepared to stay away from home for so long. The weather was hostile – icy cold with lashing storms that got steadily worse over the Christmas period. He had been due to collect his income support payment the week he had disappeared and now there was another one waiting for him. Fauldhouse was such a small place too, but no one said they had seen him.

'The situation is just getting worse and I'm so anxious waiting for him to come home. No one has seen or heard anything from him, including his friends. It's like he has vanished into thin air,' said a distraught Sandra, the morning of 3rd January, when specialist police teams were brought in to scour Levenseat quarry. 'If anyone has seen him or knows what has happened to him, could they please get in touch and bring him back home.'

But one of Thomas' friends, one who had known him since they were both four years old, hadn't been telling the truth. Allan Menzies, or 'Leon' as he preferred to call himself these days, knew exactly where Thomas was.

He'd even approached Sandra at the local supermarket a few days after her son had disappeared to ask her what was the best way to get rid of bloodstains.

His comments would soon come back to haunt Mrs French. On 4th January, the police turned up a bag of the clothes Thomas had been wearing the last time his mother saw him.

Two weeks later, combing the woods behind the local community centre, Police Constable Kenneth Gray came to a clearing and noticed something that looked odd. As he approached, he realised what he was looking at, 'a hand and forearm sticking out of the ground'.

It was Thomas McKendrick's body, lying in a shallow grave. Injuries to the corpse showed every sign that he had met his end with extreme violence. And on the same day that he was formally identified, the cops had made their arrest.

An accident waiting to happen

When Detective Constable Robert Lowe accompanied Allan Menzies to his charge hearing at Linlithgow Sheriff Court, the 21-year-old said something so bizarre it shocked the 37-year-old policeman to the core.

'He said, "I'm going to get 20 to 25 [years] for this, for doing him with a hammer and a Bowie knife, but I have got his soul. I drank his blood and ate a bit of his head. There was blood everywhere and I buried him up the woods".'

Menzies showed no particular emotion as he relayed his confession. It was as if he had just been discussing the weather.

But Allan Menzies had always been a boy with problems, and a history of dark, brooding moods exploding into violent rage. This wasn't the first time he'd seen the inside of a police cell either.

Menzies had been bullied at school. Shy and unpopular, he had been quickly singled out by his classmates at Whitburn Academy as a figure of fun. When, at the age of 14, he was beaten up in the school playground, Menzies brooded on this humiliation and began to plot revenge. He took a knife into school and stabbed the boy who had bullied him right in front of his shocked classmates.

At Menzies' original trial in 1996, his defence counsel Edgar Prais QC said that his client had acted this way to defend his own schoolyard credibility: 'It was important to his self-esteem that he re-establish himself among his peers,' he told the court. He also revealed that in the wake of the stabbing, Menzies had twice tried to kill himself by taking an overdose and once left home carrying a noose, saying that he was going out to die.

He got three years in a detention centre for this crime, then returned to Fauldhouse to live with his mother in Lanrigg Avenue. For Menzies, the prospect of returning to the village that had reviled him was a bleak one. At 17, he was unwilling to go back to school and instead struck up a close friendship with another boy who had been ostracised by his peers, Thomas McKendrick. Thomas' father was dead and Allan's was estranged from his mother, although they both continued to live in Fauldhouse. The two young men shared an interest in horror movies, which for Menzies, quickly developed into a serious obsession.

At Menzies' trial, a former friend of Thomas', 21-year-old Stuart Unwin, gave an account of Menzies that described a man who had always been disturbingly intense. Unwin, a security guard, said that Menzies had been obsessed with vampires since the age of 18, and he also admired serial killers and Nazis. To illustrate his point, Unwin described Menzies' fevered enthusiasm upon hearing a news report about the ritualistic murder of a pensioner from Anglesey, North Wales, in October 2001.

He told the court: 'The next-door neighbour of a pensioner killed the woman and ate parts of her anatomy and drank her blood and claimed to be a vampire. I described the killer as "a bit of a fruitcake" but Menzies had a certain amount of respect for the guy. At one point, he said it would have been a waste if he had just killed the woman and cut her apart and did not drink the blood.'

Unwin added that about a month after the report of the Anglesey murder, Menzies asked his friends to call him 'Vamp'.

One of the many artefacts police had collected from Menzies' house that led them to arrest him was a *True Crime* magazine account of the Anglesey case. It had disturbing similarities to what Allan did next.

Hell comes to the Valleys

In July 2002, five months before Menzies' killer outburst, a 17-year-old art student from Llanfairpwll, Anglesey, was given a 12-year sentence for stabbing a 90-year-old woman to death and then removing her heart and drinking her blood. It was described by the 60 officers of the North Wales police who worked it as 'the most callous and brutal' case they had ever seen.

Matthew Hardman had been an art student at the Coleg Menai college when he carried out the attack. He lived only yards away from his victim, Mabel Leyshon, and had even once been her paperboy. Mabel was a much-loved woman, confident and independent despite her advancing age, and what happened to her shattered not just her own small community but sent waves of revulsion out to the rest of Britain when it was featured on the BBC1 programme *Crimewatch* – which was probably where Menzies heard about it first.

Hardman broke into Mabel Leyshon's house by smashing a window. He found the old lady watching television in her favourite chair and set upon her with a knife, stabbing her 22 times, until she was dead.

He then moved her body to another chair and placed two pokers in a cross formation at her feet. Harman proceeded to cut out Mabel's heart, wrap it in newspaper and place it on a silver platter. He retrieved a saucepan from his victim's kitchen which he filled full of blood from her leg, before drinking the contents. Finally, he placed the heart on top of the saucepan, next to her body.

During Hardman's 14-day-long trial at Mold Crown Court, it emerged that the defendant had an interest in vampires, the occult and the quest for eternal life. In his sketchy testimony, Hardman claimed he had been smoking marijuana at the time of the offence, which rendered his recollections hazy. But when it got down to it, the young man was motivated by a deep-seated rage that he seemed to have channelled through a vampire fixation.

'It was just something inside me, my genes started going crazy,' he told the court. 'I could not stop myself going crazy. I was holding back anger as if it had been bottled up inside me – like an adrenalin rush, only 60 million times more than that.'

Such emotions Allan Menzies could well identify with.

Hardman feigned memory loss at the testimonies of several of his college mates, who recalled him saying that vampires usually killed old women. Nor could he remember that he had once asked a German student, who he thought was a vampire, to bite him so that he could become one too. But everyone who the police had spoken to told them the same thing – Hardman was obsessed with vampires and believed he could live forever if he became one of them. Hardman denied murder – denied, indeed that he had even entered Mabel's house – and attempted to appeal his sentence, a motion denied by the judge.

The Hardman case had such an effect on those officers who worked it that they were later given commendations in recognition of their professionalism and dedication by the North Wales Police Chief Constable, Richard Brunstrom. Brunstrom said: 'In difficult circumstances, the officers were presented with psychological and emotional challenges and managed to catch and convict the offender. It was a particularly difficult investigation because of the awful circumstances. It was an unpleasant case, which the officers had to get very close to – in terms of dealing with the relatives and the appalling scene itself.

'We are human beings just like anybody else but have to retain a sense of professional detachment. We cannot collapse in horror and recoil – it was a psychological challenge.' To underline his seriousness, he added: 'A commendation like this is not common and is a prize to be cherished. If you get it, you have earned it.'

Yet to Allan Menzies, Matthew Hardman was the hero here. Psychologists studying Menzies before his own trial would later find that the two of them had a great deal in common.

The hit man and her

Like Matthew Hardman, Menzies had problems with the truth. When he had to defend his decision to brutally murder the only real friend he'd ever had, he flipped that blame back on Thomas. Thomas had lent him the video of *Queen of the Damned*. Thomas had let Akasha into

Allan's mind. 'I wish I'd never seen that fucking video!' he would later scream to the police.

But from most accounts, all Thomas had done was support Allan through his many times of crisis. In an early attempt to get away from Fauldhouse, Menzies had tried to join the army after his discharge from the Juvenile Detention Centre. Thomas had come with him and consoled his friend when, unsurprisingly, his application had been turned down. Allan's reaction was to stash the slight down in the grudge drawer in his mind and transform his rejection into a fantasy revenge. He watched Luc Besson's 1994 film *Léon* – in which Jean Reno plays a hit man – over and over again on video. He even went to have his name changed by deed poll to Leon Menzies. Perhaps he thought he would get back at the army by becoming the deadliest assassin they had ever seen.

The idea of sneaking around would have appealed to him, as confronting the truth was anathema to the young man. Six days after the police had discovered the bag of Thomas McKendrick's clothes, they paid his best friend a visit on 10th January. Menzies was at that time living with his father, Thomas, and their relationship had come under a lot of recent strain from what Thomas Menzies would later describe as Allan's increasingly bizarre behaviour.

They found Allan in possession of the *Queen of the Damned* video and a book by Anne Rice, *Blood and Gold*, which is the part of the *Vampire Chronicles* on which the film was based. Inside the novel were handwritten notes, including the eyebrow-raising lines: *I have chosen my fate to become a vampire. Blood is much too precious to be wasted on humans. The blood is the life I have drunk the blood and it shall be mine for I have seen horror. The master will come for me and he has promised to make me immortal for I will do as they command. The errand boy signed vamp.*

The police also noted the *True Crime* article on Matthew Hardman, entitled *Satanic Slaughter*, and the videocassette of *Léon*. They asked Menzies when he had last seen his friend Thomas. He said it had been on 11th December but claimed, 'I never harmed him. The day he left my house he was still breathing.' He added that he had phoned Thomas twice after that. He said he did not know what had happened and agreed it was 'a mystery'.

But then, following the same pattern as he had after his non-fatal schoolyard stabbing, as soon as the police had left, Menzies downed a handful of prescription drugs.

His father found him unconscious and rushed him to hospital. When Menzies came around, he called home and castigated Thomas Menzies for letting him live.

The police had seen enough. They sent consultant psychiatrist James Hendry to question the young miscreant in hospital, and as soon as he was fit enough, they arrested Allan Menzies.

Written in blood

On the way to be charged, Menzies made his shocking admission to DC Lowe, adding that he had used a wheelie bin to take McKendrick's body out to the woods. His next comment suggested that he'd had time to think of a contingency plan while he lay in hospital. He told the Detective Constable he would plead guilty if he could 'get Carstairs', meaning the state hospital for mentally disturbed criminals. From that moment on, like so many before him, the guilty man proceeded to try and convince everyone else he was mad and not bad, that somehow, none of this was his fault.

The facts spoke for themselves. The autopsy on Thomas McKendrick had revealed an astonishing amount of violence – he had been stabbed 42 times and received ten hammer blows to his head.

Menzies' explaination?

'He should never have insulted my bird.'

In lengthy interviews with Detective Constable Gary Boyd and PC Kenneth Gray, Menzies claimed that he had watched the *Queen of the Damned* video Thomas McKendrick had lent him in August 2002 'about 100 times'. He had played songs from the soundtrack over and over again until it sent him 'quite literally mad'.

'I'd get up at five in the morning and have it on for three hours and it would never be off,' he said. 'I would go to bed and could never get the thought of being a vampire out of my mind. I was addicted to watching it.'

As a result, he believed he had become possessed by Akasha, who had appeared to him in his bedroom and told him to go and collect souls for her. It hadn't been Menzies himself who killed McKendrick, but his alter-ego Vamp. He added: 'I thought if there really is a God, I'd sacrifice this life for the next. This life is short, I'm 21, no future, so I figured I'd sell my soul for this life to be reborn in the next, which now seems mad even to me.'

DC Gray told Menzies that they had found Thomas McKendrick's blood soaked into the floorboards of Allan's bedroom. 'Well, you should watch who you insult in life,' was their suspect's reaction.

While he was under arrest, Menzies continued to act as if he was under a vampire's spell. From Saughton prison, he sent letters back to his father's address, addressed to Thomas on the envelope but to Akasha within. He signed them *Vamp* in what appeared to be his own blood. In one he told the fictional Egyptian queen, '*Everything is going well and I will kill for you again soon. These humans are nothing but animals, fodder for us.*'

At home with a killer

Thomas Menzies was asked about his son's mental state in the weeks leading up to the murder. He said that Allan had become withdrawn, shunning normal conversation and spending hours in his bedroom, talking and even shouting to himself. He watched the same films over and over again; first it had been *Léon*, then the hit man was replaced with *Queen of the Damned*. Menzies Senior estimated that Allan watched the videos up to three times a day. When he wasn't thus engaged, he was also addicted to playing violent games on his console.

'He started to watch more horror films, films that were a bit bloodthirsty,' Mr Menzies revealed. 'I thought it was a bit strange, but that was like Allan. All his games were about fighting.' Thomas, who worked as a joiner, admitted that he had found it more and more difficult to communicate with his son in recent years. 'His character had changed, the way he went about things. He had become more withdrawn into himself. He would not speak as much. All Allan's talk was about vampires, the games and blood. It was not normal conversation.'

He would testify in court that he agreed his son probably had a split personality.

'Yes, one his own personality and the other a character in a film,' said Mr Menzies, adding, 'I could hear him talking to himself in his room. It didn't make much sense. Sometimes, he would be shouting. I thought he was talking to friends but when he came downstairs, he was by himself.' Apparently, these monologues could last for up to two hours.

Square-eyed Allan offered the court a plea of culpable homicide for reasons of diminished responsibility. The crown rejected his plea. Dr James Hendry, the psychiatrist who had examined the prisoner in hospital immediately after his overdose and later in jail, thought that although Menzies had 'a very vivid fantasy life' he was not mentally ill. He stopped short of accusing Allan of feigning mental illness to try and escape a murder charge, saying that the bizarre Akasha stories were, 'a combination of his fantasies about vampires and his attempt to explain his behaviour at the time of the offence'.

Others were more suspicious. Thomas Menzies would be forced on oath to deny that there was any collusion between himself and his son as to the stories they told the police. He denied also that he helped his son dispose of the body, concealed Thomas McKendrick's clothing or put a wheelie bin in a pond. 'I didn't cover up no crime,' he stated, 'I had no involvement at all.' When he came home to find blood all over his house, he said that Allan had told him he cut himself using a tin-opener.

The self-styled Vamp would stand trial for murder in Edinburgh High Court on 30th September 2003, where another consultant psychiatrist would raise some issues with Dr Hendry's diagnosis.

The offer of eternal life

When Sandra French faced her son's killer across the courtroom she was forced to hear only his account of Thomas McKendrick's last moments on earth. And Allan Menzies stuck firm to his stories throughout the trial.

Akasha, said Menzies, had visited him in his bedroom and offered him eternal life if he would kill for her. He prepared himself for his life as a vampire by getting used to a new diet: 'I had started going to the shop and buying ox liver and eating it raw and even drinking the blood out of it just for the sake of it.' But why, when the moment came, had he chosen to take the life of his oldest and most trusted friend?

Because, said Menzies, Thomas had made an insulting comment about Akasha as the two of them stood in his kitchen on the fateful morning of 11th December. And as he did so, the Vampire Queen materialised before him.

'It was the look on her face,' Allan told the jury. 'She was not pleased. Then, she turned her back on me. I thought it was because Thomas had insulted her and I let him away with it. When she turned her back on me, I felt I had let her down. At the end of the day, I knew I would have to murder somebody anyway, so…if you did not murder somebody you could not become a vampire.'

Menzies said that he had left out a Bowie knife in the kitchen, along with some ox liver that he was going to feed his ferrets. When he saw the look on Akasha's face, 'I picked up the Bowie knife and stabbed [Thomas] in the neck three or four times.'

He recalled stabbing McKendrick in the face, shoulders and back before reaching for a hammer that he knew was in one of the kitchen drawers. At this point, showing superhuman reserves of his own, Thomas apparently started to run upstairs to Allan's bedroom. Which was as far as he got before Menzies set about him with the implement, smashing over the back of the head. Thomas then fell to the floor.

Realising that his friend was dead, Menzies commenced with the next part of his ritual. He described drinking two cups full of Thomas' blood and eating a fragment of his skull. 'I looked in the mirror to make sure my teeth were covered with his blood,' he added.

Now, he said, he believed he was a vampire, and eternal life was his.

But if that was the case, asked the sceptical prosecution, why had he taken an overdose of pills after the police had first questioned him?

'That was to get to the other life quicker,' was his nonsensical explanation. 'That was when I would get rewarded.' He added that Akasha had come to visit him while he was held on remand in Carstairs State Hospital. 'People tried to tell me she was not real and I could not see her, but that's bullshit.'

The prosecution's psychiatrist, Dr Derek Chiswick considered this testimony and did not entirely agree with Dr Hendry.

The great pretender?

At this point, Dr Chiswick raised the possibility that Menzies' vampire fantasies were a cunning ruse. He agreed that the accused was 'an emotionally disturbed young man' and had a psychopathic personality disorder. 'I suspect his enjoyment of violence is the principal factor in the prolonged and excessively violent nature of this crime,' he opined, adding that Menzies' interest in inflicting pain was part of this disorder, but not a feature of mental illness.

When asked what purpose Allan's vampire fantasies served, he replied: 'It does occur to me that one possibility is that they are manufactured to avoid conviction for a crime of murder. The other possibility is that they are used by him to psychologically cope with an appalling and horrific act of violence.'

His reasons for thinking this were clear. In the 48 hours Menzies had spent in hospital after taking his overdose, he had made no mention of Akasha or these fantasies.

'They have developed over time and it makes me suspicious that the first option, that these have been manufactured, is a real one that has to be taken seriously,' said Dr Chiswick.

Another person who had visited Allan in hospital during that time was his aunt, Sandra Hamilton. On 8th October, she told the court that Menzies had offered her a different excuse for the killing.

'He told me he had killed Thomas,' she said. 'He said he battered his head in with a hammer, then he cut him up and drank his blood. He said he had done it to get back at God, because God had been getting at him.'

And to his aunt, Menzies offered his only words of remorse for his crime. 'He said if he ever got out he could not go back to Fauldhouse because he could not look at Thomas' mother, knowing he had killed her son.'

Mrs Hamilton, 39, of Armdale, West Lothian, filled in some more dark details of Allan's troubled past. 'He was always strange,' she recalled, going on to tell the court of how he had previously attacked a member of his own family with a knife.

'He had been having a fight…He had attacked somebody with a knife. I did say he was going to kill somebody – he would kill somebody and end up in Carstairs.'

When it came time for the final statements in the trial, Menzies' defence team brought in another psychiatrist as an expert witness. Dr Alexander Cooper, a retired psychiatric consultant, told the court that, in his opinion, Menzies had a severe and violent antisocial personality disorder when he killed Thomas McKendrick, which had caused him to develop a split personality and to hear voices in his head. It tied in with Menzies' defence and went against the opinions of the other psychiatrists who had studied the killer.

Unsurprisingly, the jury didn't buy it.

At the end of the eight-day trial, they found Allan Menzies guilty of murder. He was sentenced to life imprisonment with the recommendation that he serve at least 18 years before being considered for parole. The Judge, Roderick MacDonald, said: 'Three psychologists have diagnosed you as a psychopath. In my opinion, you are an evil, violent and highly dangerous man who is not fit to be at liberty. You subjected Thomas McKendrick to a savage and merciless attack. You totally lack remorse.'

Outside the court, a tearful Sandra French told reporters: 'We are pleased with the verdict.' She had no doubt that Menzies had been fabricating the circumstances of the killing to the court.

'It was all an act. He was using the vampire claims to try and get away with murder and he has failed.'

Thomas' sister, Sandra Mary added: 'I would just like to say we are very pleased with the verdict and he is not going to do it again. He got what he deserved. I believed he was not mentally ill all along – it was just an act.'

Thomas Menzies left the court without a word, leaving his son's defence solicitor Aamar Anwar with the last words concerning the controversy. 'The continued taboo and lack of understanding or support of schizophrenia and mental health in our community can only mean tragedies like this case are more likely to happen and not less,' he warned.

Dark habits in the UK

Thomas Menzies could not bear to stay in the house in which his son had committed so foul a crime. He put his former home up for sale days after Allan had been sent down to start his sentence, telling the press: 'I've looked in the door of Allan's bedroom and I know there's still blood on the floor. I just can't bring myself to go in. The thought of what happened here is just too much to bear.'

But even as he attempted to make a break with the past, yet another vampire case was hitting national UK headlines. On the very day that Allan Menzies had been sentenced, another trial had begun in Hampshire, in the south of England, where two young men were accused of waging a three-month-long campaign of intimidation against their local vicar.

Scott Bower, 26, and Ben Lewis, 25, along with Lewis' 19-year-old girlfriend Natalie Gibson, had been targeting the Reverend Christopher Rowberry, his wife, Karen, and children, Hannah, 15, and Simon, 17, for abuse in the small village of Eling Hill, near Totton. They had made scores of terrifying phonecalls to the family and had spent nights hiding in the graveyard howling like wolves, throwing fireworks at the vicarage and leaving obscene pictures on the parish noticeboard.

What made this case so unnerving right after that of Allan Menzies' was Lewis' boast to the police: 'I'm a vampire and proud.'

Police had found pictures of Bower and Lewis apparently drinking each other's blood when they raided Lewis' home. The pair dressed in Gothic black clothing and had a keen interest in vampirism, subscribing to bloodsucker fanzines such as *Crimson*, for which Lewis had also submitted articles. In one, he repeated a line familiar to devotees of Anne Rice and the jury in the Menzies trial alike: 'I am beyond the earthly understandings of humans because I am a reincarnated vampire.'

The clearly unimpressed Judge John Boggis QC sentenced both men to six months' imprisonment and handed Gibson, who was pregnant with Lewis' child, a suspended 12 months sentence. He commented: 'This is a case of repeated victimisation of a man who showed you tolerance and understanding, the effect of which was to drive a wedge of fear into his family. The distress of his wife was clear for all to see. I hope you are truly ashamed of what you did but it is clear from the pre-sentence reports that you are not.'

Another wave of Satanic panic had crossed the Atlantic. Just as America had tried to fathom what was turning its troubled teens into wannabe vampires, just as Germany had tried to cope with the evil spirits it had unwittingly invited over the threshold of the fallen Berlin Wall, now the British Isles, from which the great figures of Gothic literature had first sprung, had to ask itself – what is happening to our children?

Dracula AD2003

In the autumn of 2003 it was not just in secret societies and fringe Gothic clubs that vampires were thriving in the UK. You only had to turn on your TV to see the top-rating US show *Buffy The Vampire Slayer* grabbing the peak time slots and a mesmerised teenage audience. Opening at the cinemas, homegrown star Kate Beckinsale took the lead role as a beautiful vampire warrior in the film *Underworld*, while action hero Wesley Snipes reprised his successful 1989 role to continue battling the bloodsuckers in *Blade II*. Vampires were all around us. They were the top form of kids' entertainment.

Even Hammer Studios, the home of British horror that had first given the world Christopher Lee as the most iconic Count Dracula, announced they were resuming their business in low-budget horror production in August 2003. In a joint venture with Australia's Pictures in Paradise productions, the Studios announced they were set to deliver a slate of six new movies over the next five years 'for a worldwide teen audience'. Up until this point, Hammer hadn't made a new movie for nearly 30 years.

'We are moving towards another high point in vampirism,' considered the aptly-named Dr Glenice Byron of Stirling University, a lecturer on the UK's only post-graduate course in the Gothic Imagination. In an article in *The Observer* in October 2003, journalist Stephen Khan tried to nail down the links between the mainstream Gothic revival and the recent spate of 'vampire' crime cases. Dr Byron told him, 'I don't think the general public are aware of the extent to which it permeates our culture. On the Internet it's an entire culture...'

To get a criminologist's perspective, Khan turned to the Edinburgh-based forensic psychologist Ian Stephen, on whom the hit TV series *Cracker* was based. What did he think was going on in the mind of Allan Menzies?

'So many teenagers become obsessed with parts of culture like this young man. It's very difficult for parents to pick up these changes from normal interests to something that can become quite scary,' Stephen pointed out. He then outlined the sado-masochistic urges inherent in the vampire mythology, and how they were apt to be interpreted by youthful dabblers like Menzies. 'The cult of vampirism is to do with power and dominance, using blood to give you energy and immortality. If someone had ridiculed [Menzies], he may have needed to compensate for this – something like vampirism may have given him what he was looking for.'

'A fine bogey tale'

Allan Menzies was not much longer for this world anyway. At 7.50 in the morning of Monday 15th November 2004, the 23-year-old was found hanged in his cell at Shotts Prison, Lanarkshire. He had finally succumbed to those desires of self-immolation that had seemed as strong as his urges to inflict pain on others throughout his short and violent life.

Menzies had always been corrupted by his inner rage and the time in which he lived offered him artistic conduits to channel it into. They were Hollywood films that fetishised the outsider, from Jean Reno's cool, world-weary depiction of the hired gun whose soul is saved by a precocious little girl, to Aaliyah's glamorous beauty as the ultimate killer.

However, the artistic creation of a soul divided in torment that he probably most resembles has his roots in the same Scottish soil, and was rendered over a hundred years previously. One of the greatest novels ever to cross horror, crime and psychiatry was written in 1886 by the Edinburgh-born Robert Louis Stevenson.

The Strange Case of Dr Jekyll and Mr Hyde, the story of a doctor who creates a potion that splits him into two people, a barbaric murderer and a genteel intellectual, came to Stevenson in an opium-induced nightmare. Woken by his screams, his wife Fanny shook him into consciousness only for him to rebuke her: 'Why did you wake me?

I was dreaming a fine bogey tale.'

When daybreak came, Stevenson began to write his story like a man possessed. When Fanny dismissed his initial draft – 30,000 words produced in three days – he angrily threw the manuscript in the fire and began again. He produced a further 64,000 words in six days flat, copied the entire thing out once more in two days and put it in the post to his publisher the next. Even by the high-achieving standards of the Victorian day, Stevenson's output was remarkable. What he created was a landmark in English literature, a novel that introduced a new phrase into the language and was used as a text in churches before it formed the template of a plethora of horror movies, both literal adaptations and interpretations.

Whether Menzies had a split personality or not, he had a savage beast lurking under his thin skin, a Mr Hyde who had burst more powerfully out of him on 11th December 2002 than any imaginary vampire queen. In the end, not even his best friend could stand in the way of the rage that had been building up inside the mocked and marginalised Menzies for so long.

It was clear from the testimony of Stuart Unwin that Menzies had longed for people to fear him, and from his father that his fantasy world was breaking through into his reality. The films he watched over and over again may have actually had the opposite effect of what is generally assumed. Instead of firing his fantasies, they may have temporarily provided him with a different way of seeing himself, as a cool loner who mocked the confines of the real world. But in his own, isolated village there was nothing cool about him at all. Fantasy could not reinforce the reality that he was seen as a loser, a maniac.

The dam he had been building around himself since he came out of Juvenile Detention was going to break sooner or later, whatever he had watched. When it did, all Hell was truly let loose on Fauldhouse.

But if Scotland thought this was an isolated case of Satanic juvenile delinquency, then it was soon going to have to think again. In a grim reprise to Aamar Anwar's words, there was another one coming. Coming down fast...

Chapter Thirteen

Luke Mitchell: When the Levee Breaks (2003)

Sign of the Times

As far as showstoppers go, the case of Luke Mitchell and Jodi Jones seems to bring the elements of every other case studied in this book to one singularly dramatic climax. While the bizarre fantasies of Allan Menzies may have sounded a warning shot that all was not too bonny in Scotland, that case simply didn't have the right combination of elements to really capture the popular imagination. Luke Mitchell's story, however, had them all:

A disturbed adolescent from a split family with a strange closeness to his own mother doesn't so much dabble as drop headfirst into a chronic drug habit. He listens to Marilyn Manson, dresses all in black and worries the teachers at his Roman Catholic school with his essays on the glory of Satanism. He starts going out with two almost identical 14-year-old girls virtually simultaneously – then viciously kills one of them in an apparently ritualistic recreation of Los Angeles' most infamous unsolved crime, the 'Black Dahlia' murder. He cunningly and cold-bloodedly leads her family straight to her corpse, then continues to play mindgames with the police, with the assistance of his sinister mother, until he is eventually arrested. And all at the age of 14.

Sex, drugs, Satan and a child-on-child killer, ripping away the life of the trusting young girl who loved him; a girl who had had more than her fair share of problems already. This was as much of an era-defining crime for the UK as The Moors Murders, The Yorkshire Ripper and Fred and Rosemary West.

It would provide the longest ever single-assailant court case in Scottish history, lasting two months, in which not only Mitchell ended up in the dock but the whole swathe of youth culture and youth problems around him. A case that saw two of Scotland's top QCs, Allan Turnbull and Donald Findlay, coming to bitter blows about how professionally the trial was being handled. A case in which police were shown to have acted against the rules of normal investigations to ensure their suspect's arrest, and in which the press were only too happy to collude with their foregone conclusions, resulting in that UK speciality – trial by tabloid. It ended in Mitchell being convicted of murder and sent down for 20 years.

This case is troubling for different reasons from all the others recorded in this book. For Luke Mitchell is the only person to have been charged, tried, judged and sentenced without there being one shred of physical evidence against him.

On Dead-End Street

A satellite to the town of Dalkeith, Jodi Jones' home of Easthouses is a former mining village on the outskirts of Edinburgh. The community here used to be closeknit, traditional – before the bitter, year-long miners' strike of 1984/5, when the Thatcher government closed down the industry. Easthouses colliery was shut in 1985. The Lady Victoria mine in nearby Newtongrange, once the showpiece of the Scottish coalfields, soon followed suit and has since been turned into a museum. The last remaining local coalface, Bilston Glen, was closed down in 1989, following a flood.

As in many of the suddenly redundant mine-working communities in Scotland, Wales and the north of England, crime and depression levels soared along with the abrupt and vicious end of a centuries-old way of life. Twenty years after the strike, Easthouses seemed at a loss. There was one corner shop but two off-licences, an estate agents and a roofing firm keeping the place afloat. Similar to the trade in alcohol, the only business that was really booming was the illegal trade in cannabis to schoolkids, something that Luke Mitchell was deeply involved in.

Easthouses and its neighbouring village Newtongrange would have probably remained just obscure little places, unwelcome reminders of the price paid for the decade of greed. But used and abused towns have a history of getting their revenge on the wider world. Like Pikeville in Kentucky, like Sondershausen in Germany, poverty, boredom and ignorance conspire to spawn monsters and let them loose on those societies that refuse to acknowledge responsibility. To rub their noses in everything that has gone wrong.

So it was on the night of 30th June 2003, when a murder took place along a lane which joins the two villages, known as Roan's Dyke. A murder so horrifying it shocked even hardened pathologists, criminologists, judges and policemen who thought they had seen it all. An outrage that burned its way into a nation's consciousness and reunited a fracturing community under the worst possible circumstances.

Jodi Jones, a bright, popular 14-year-old girl, was found lying dead in woodland just off Roan's Dyke, only a few hundred yards away from her front door. Her throat had been slashed up to twenty times, her body undressed and trussed up with her own trousers. Her breasts, abdomen and face had been further slashed with the knife, her eyelids slit off and her mouth cut open.

The search party that found her there were her grandmother Alice Walker, 67, her sister Janine, 19, and her fiancé Steven Kelly, 21, as well as Jodi's boyfriend Luke Mitchell, 14, who first made the grim discovery.

According to the family's testimony, which would vary from their first statements to those later made in court, while the family members went to pieces on the spot, Luke retained an eerie calm. A calm that didn't seem to be shaken even when the questions of the police got serious over the course of the coming days and charges were eventually laid against him. It was this detachedness, coupled with the fact he seemed to have gone directly to the spot where Jodi was, that lay at the heart of the prosecution's case against him.

Luke Mitchell didn't deal in normal emotions, everyone said. He didn't even seem to react when he was being found guilty in court 18 months later. But then, Luke Mitchell was not a normal kid.

A mother's touch

Luke Mitchell was born on 24th July 1988, the younger of two sons. His brother Shane had arrived eight years earlier in 1980, the same year his parents Corinne and Philip married in Corstorphine Old Church in Edinburgh. The couple had settled in a semi-detached house in Newbattle, where they seemed just like any other family. Philip was an electrician and Corinne ran the caravan dealership business begun by her adoptive father Richard Guetta. She was a successful businesswoman and an accomplished horsewoman, who kept a number of animals at the local stables over the years.

Corinne and Philip divorced in 1999, when Luke was 10. Corinne kept the house and the boys and was able to buy her ex-husband out of the mortgage as part of the divorce settlement. Luke still saw his father, who moved to Livingstone, West Lothian, on weekends, but relations between the split couple were described as 'strained' and 'tense'. Certainly, it didn't take long from the time that Philip moved out for

Luke's behaviour to start degenerating. Without a strong paternal presence in the house, Luke began to grow wild and people looked askance at his mother.

Corinne always stood out from the crowd, especially in a small community like Newbattle. She dressed flamboyantly, in gypsy style, a nod to her adoptive parents Richard and Ruby, who were from a travelling background. Corinne always said she knew nothing of her real parents and never wanted to know. She was happy with what she had and where she was.

The pictures of her splashed all over the papers at the time of Luke's trial showed her wearing a different look; she appeared more like a contemporary of her son on the Goth scene than a Romany. This reflected another couple of stories that would circulate about Corinne and her younger son, that she had lost control of him and that she had more than a 'normal' relationship with him. Certainly it looked as though Corinne was dressing just like Luke's girlfriends.

Yet before Luke was convicted, plenty of Corinne's neighbours described her as a likeable, hardworking woman who had done her best to provide for her sons a smart, respectable start in life. These stories changed dramatically after the trial, although there were some who declined to be named for obvious reasons, that continued to tell the papers that Corinne had always been a good neighbour, her sons a credit to her. That they couldn't imagine such a likeable young man as Luke committing so hideous a crime.

However, tales of Corinne's weirdness vastly outweighed such endorsements. One repeated endlessly was from an unattributed former babysitter who had looked after Luke and Shane when they were small: 'Corinne was really weird with the boys. She liked to dress them just like herself when they were young. If she wore leg warmers, they were put in leg warmers.'

And Corinne's conniving would provide two massive blows in the prosecution's case against her son – that she made up an alibi for Luke's whereabouts at the time of Jodi's murder and forced her other son Shane to collude in it, and that she proved her untrustworthiness by taking Luke to a tattooists in Edinburgh on 7th October 2003, with a false ID saying that he was 18 and of legal age to have such an adornment.

Then there were the other things, the things that reinforced the notion that Luke was a weirdo and Corinne was an unfit mother. The evidence was pretty hard to argue with: by the age of 14, Luke was openly dealing drugs, with a set of scales and weights in his bedroom and testimony from half his schoolmates that he supplied them. He had a massive collection of knives, some of which were bought for him by Corinne as presents. And he lived in a squalid bedroom with a vile and unnatural collection under the bed – bottles of his own urine.

About a girl

Jodi Jones started seeing Luke Mitchell in March 2003. Like so many other ill-fated couples in this book, Jodi and Luke bonded over a love of a certain type of music, a budding cannabis habit, a history of self-harm and the pain they felt over the loss of their fathers – though in Jodi's case this was much more intense. Her parents hadn't split up. Her father had actually taken his own life.

The Jones family – parents Judith and Jimmy, son Joseph, daughters Janine and Jodi, were all living in Mayfield at the home of Jimmy's mother when the tragedy happened. Judith and Joseph, then only 15, had found Jimmy hanging from a tree in the garden in 1988. Not only did the family have to deal with this sudden, devastating blow, but the paranoia Joseph was already being treated for exacerbated after his shocking find.

'It was quite difficult at times,' Judith Jones recalled. 'It became quite frustrating at times for all of us.'

Judith and her children moved to a new home in Parkhead Place, Easthouses but Janine didn't like it there. She missed her friends and her grandmother and eventually Judith allowed her to move back, letting Jodi visit her sister on weekends. When Judith eventually met another man, Allen Ovens, the family reunited to live together in Easthouses.

Concurrent to all this upheaval, Jodi was also moving from primary to secondary school. It must have seemed to her that her childhood had been brutally ended overnight. Judith estimated it took Jodi a year to settle at her new school, to come back out of her shell and start getting the good results she'd been achieving before her father's death.

Jodi found some strength to get through her ordeal in the music and writing of Kurt Cobain, the Nirvana singer who died in 1994. Cobain, who came from a hugely troubled and dysfunctional family, probably wrote more movingly about the thrills and pains of adolescence than any rock singer before or since, and uniquely amongst his macho contemporaries had a very pro-feminist outlook.

Cobain was officially deemed to have killed himself, which has left him enshrined in youth culture history as a doomed icon, worshipped still by new generations of kids like Jodi and Luke who were too young to ever have seen Nirvana play. Yet Kurt was no nihilistic pretty boy like Sid Vicious or Jim Morrison. He came from a very similar place to kids like Natasha Cornett and Rod Ferrell – only Cobain had a place to channel his rage: music. Which is why his body of work remains so powerful to so many alienated teens. Nirvana probably did a lot to help Jodi through her worst moments.

A lot was made of the fact that Jodi had a particular Cobain line written on her bedroom wall: *'The finest day I ever had was when tomorrow never came,'* taken from his posthumously published journals, when it appeared in an early draft of the song that made him globally famous, 'Smells Like Teen Spirit'. The suicide inference was clearly on Jodi's mind. She wrote her own poem, entitled *Burn Your Wings in Hell*, which went: *When the world around you falls and becomes shit, take the knife, all your pain can be taken by one slit, slit of your wrists, be free, be happy, just like me.*

Yet when Jodi met Luke she thought she had found her soulmate, the one to help her overcome the traumas of the past. She wrote her thoughts down in her own journal, which was later read out in court, something Judith said would have 'mortified' Jodi. The poignancy of her words is haunting; even as she praises her new boyfriend, the fear of being left alone again is never far behind her:

God, I think I would die if he finished with me. When I am not with him, I want to be. When I am with him, I am happy. He is the only person who makes me forget about most of the shit in my life. Sometimes when I cannot forget, he helps make me feel better. If I am crying, he hugs me and strokes my face. He is just so sweet. No matter what he says, I believe him and that's really dangerous. I will have to be very careful. I have had my trust broken too many times.

Jodi had no idea that her 'sweet' boyfriend was already cheating on her as she wrote these lines. On her last night on earth, she went off to meet Luke Mitchell high on love and happiness.

A message of hope

The night of 30th June was the first time Jodi had been allowed out for some time, ever since her mother had discovered two things about her daughter that dumbfounded her. One was that she had been having sex with Luke. The other was that Jodi had been smoking cannabis. 'I was really, really shocked,' Judith recalled. 'I smoke and Jodi would not even pass the ashtray or touch my cigarettes.'

But smoking dope was *de rigeur* among the pupils of St David's and it wasn't Luke who had introduced her to the drug. Schoolfriends testified she had often joined a group of pupils to toke joints in her lunch hour at a nearby park known as the China Gardens before she had got together with Mitchell. Everyone would later agree that all this drug-taking was a bad thing. But no one asked why it was so prevalent to be considered completely normal by Dalkeith's teenage population – even those studying at a Roman Catholic school, even those considered bright and responsible by their teachers. Which even if Luke wasn't, Jodi was.

When Judith made her discovery, she punished Jodi by grounding her between 4pm and 6pm on weeknights, making her do household chores as penance. But on the night of 30th June, Judith had decided that her daughter had done her time. When Jodi got home at around 4.05 that evening, Judith told her, 'That's you hen, you're free to go out now.'

Delighted, Jodi borrowed her mother's phone to send a text message to Luke, arranging to meet him about an hour later. Her own phone had broken and had yet to be repaired. She changed into an outfit that included a T-shirt borrowed from Janine, and chatted to Judith and Joseph as her mum prepared lasagne for the family's tea. Before Jodi left, Judith played a record that was symbolic of the family's long journey through the sadness of the past, Rod Stewart's 'Never Give Up on a Dream'. Jimmy Jones had been a big fan of the singer and that particular song held a lot of meaning for Judith. She wanted her children to hear the lyrics because she thought they held an important message. 'I played it to them because they had been through a lot over the years – it is quite a beautiful track, it is a hopeful song.'

Jodi was ready to leave at about 4.50pm. 'That's me off now, Mum,' she said, giving Judith a kiss. As she went towards the front door, she remembered the lasagne, her favourite. 'Mind and keep me some,' she called out.

Half an hour later, Jodi was dead.

She's not there

Judith Jones only started to get worried when her daughter had not returned home for her 10pm curfew. Because Jodi's phone was broken, she sent a text message to Luke's instead, at around 10.40. He called back immediately to say he hadn't seen Jodi all night.

Judith knew something was badly wrong. 'I said [to him] I just want the truth,' she later recalled. 'Tell me if she is with you. I won't care. I just want to know.'

But Luke continued to reiterate that he hadn't seen Jodi.

Judith began to ring round other family members and also called the police. An impromptu search party was put together; Janine and her fiancé Steven together with grandmother Alice Walker met up with Luke on Roan's Path, where Judith was sure Jodi had been headed. She had assumed that was where she had arranged to meet Luke – Judith had often warned her youngest daughter not to walk down that path alone, even in the broad daylight of a midsummer afternoon.

What happened next was so disputed between the two parties that a reconstruction of the lane was assembled in Edinburgh High Court so that the witnesses could recreate their movements in front of the jury. Judge Lord Nimmo Smith even took the unprecedented step of taking the jury out to visit the scene, in the cold daylight of 8th December 2004. What he was most keen for them to see was a V-shaped section of the wall behind which Jodi's body was found, so that they could better understand the evidence when it came.

Janine, Steven and Alice say they set out along the path at 11pm, carrying torches. They soon met up with Luke coming the other way, also with a torch and his German Shepherd dog, Mia. Alice asked Luke if he had seen anything, to which he replied, 'no'. He seemed, she recalled, his normal self, not panic-stricken like the family were. He led them back down the way they had come, while Alice called out Jodi's name. When they got to the V-shaped break, he suddenly handed his dog to Mrs Walker and vaulted over the wall. Moments later he shouted out that he had found something.

Steven Kelly followed him over. He came back white and shaking, mumbled that he didn't quite know what it was that they had found and began to vomit. When he had to recall this moment in court and was presented with a photo of the crime scene, Steven fled the room in tears. Alice went to have a look and let out a piercing scream when she saw what was lying there.

In her original statement to the police, Janine said that 'everyone was in hysterics' at this point. In court, she claimed the police had misrepresented her. Everyone was in hysterics – except Luke. Luke remained completely calm when faced with the dead and mutilated body of his girlfriend.

Mitchell himself told a different story of how he led the others to his terrible find.

Alice Walker remembered that Luke had told her Mia was 'a sniffer dog' when they first met along the lane, and had asked if they had anything of Jodi's with them so that he could give her the scent. When she replied that they didn't, Luke ordered the dog anyway: 'Seek Jodi, look for Jodi'.

Mitchell himself told the court: 'I carried on walking around the bend. The dog was on the lead. There was a V-shaped gap in the wall and I carried on a few yards past it. Mia stopped, put her nose in the air and paws up on the wall. I said: 'I think she's found something'.

'I went back to the V in the wall and offered to go over the wall. I climbed over. I turned left and followed the path for about six yards. I had to pass a big oak tree. I shone my torch and I saw this white thing that stuck out in the light. It looked like legs. After I saw these legs I took another step and I could see there was a body there.

'I could see her head facing up the way – there was blood on the neck. The legs were facing the wall. I could see it was female and that she was naked. I recognised the face – it looked like Jodi.'

Under suspicion

Detective Chief Superintendent Craig Dobbie, who led the murder enquiry, later told the press that it took three days of interviews and over 3,000 statements before Luke Mitchell emerged as their prime suspect. Those statements had presented a pretty bleak picture of the 14-year-old.

Firstly, there were the drugs. Schoolfriends told the police that Mitchell smoked cannabis 'pretty much every day', and that he usually carried a knife with him to cut the resin down. He told psychiatrists that his consumption went up to 300 joints a week after Jodi's death, an amount few believed possible. To consume the amount he did, Luke would have had to have stumped up £50 a week for his habit. The conclusion reached as to how he could afford that was that he was also dealing it to his peers.

Then there were the knives. Mitchell had been in the Army Cadets and his detachment commander Matthew Muraska told of the day in the summer of 2002 when he had to remove a particularly alarming weapon from the 13-year-old Luke.

'It was about six or seven inches long, a lock-type knife with a pointed blade. I held it up so all the cadets could see. I said that I never, ever wanted to see a knife like that in the Army Cadet Force...a knife such as that was made for one purpose and one purpose only.'

There was Luke's fantasy life too. He had made remarks to

schoolfriends that he thought it would be funny to 'get stoned and kill' someone. He stubbed cigarettes out on his palms and carved 666 into his arm 'for a laugh'. His English teacher, Geraldine Mackie, had grown increasingly concerned that one of her former star pupils was experiencing a steep decline at the beginning of 2003. That January, he had handed in an essay to her that was supposed to be a short story about the end of the world.

What he had written instead was: *If God forgives everyone then why the need to be sent to hell. If you ask me God is just a futile excuse, at most, for a bunch of fools to go around annoying others who want nothing to do with him. Are these people insane? Open your eyes. People like you need satanic people like me to keep the balance.*

Mrs Mackie reported Luke to guidance staff. When he gave in his next assignment, a critique on a poem about euthanasia, the vengeful Mitchell used the piece to goad her for her interference: *Whose business is it other than my own if I cut myself? Just because I am more violent than others, does that justify some pompous git of a teacher to refer me to a psychologist? Just because I have chosen to follow the teachings of Satan does not mean I need psychiatric help.*

But being an antisocial Satanic stoner didn't automatically make him a killer. The key question was: where was Luke at the time of Jodi's death? Hadn't she arranged to meet him on Roan's Dyke at the exact time she was killed?

Luke said he had been at home between 5 and 5.45pm, making dinner for Corinne and Shane, and was backed up by statements to the same effect by his family. But, when questioned under oath, Shane's story crumbled. Server records showed that the computer the elder Mitchell brother had in his bedroom had been used for downloading pornography between the times he said he had seen Luke cooking. When confronted with this, and with a picture of Jodi's mutilated body in court, Shane broke down.

He admitted that he had been alone in the house, masturbating over Internet porn at the times he'd said he'd seen his brother, that his original statement to the police had basically been dictated to him by Corinne. But he was so shaken by events he had gone along with it. Corrine steadfastly refused to admit she was lying about these times. It was enough to suggest to anyone that the Mitchells were a shady, unsavoury lot – enough to suggest they were capable of covering up a crime as terrible as murder.

Where there's smoke...

Yet if Luke was the killer, his genetic fingerprints would surely be the irrefutable way of proving it. Immediately after Jodi's body had been found, Luke was examined by Dr Kranti Hiremath, the forensic medical examiner at Dalkeith police station, in the early hours of 1st July. She had found no injuries on him that could have been inflicted in the last 12 hours, which would have been expected if a violent struggle had taken place. She also took fingernail scrapings from Luke to send for DNA testing. The clothes he was wearing went with them, along with the bottles of urine later found in his room. At the same time, Jodi's clothes and shoes were also being examined.

A prolific amount of work was carried out on all these items, at the pioneering Forensic Science Service Lab in Wetherby, West Yorkshire. It should have given the police everything they needed.

There was no match between them. No traces of Luke on Jodi. No traces of Jodi on Luke.

DNA expert Jonathan Whitaker told the court that his lab specialised in examining traces which were very small in order to make comparisons, and outlined what they called the 'Low Copy Number' test. He said that although the lab found DNA that did not come from Jodi on one of her trainers found at the scene, it could not possibly have come from Luke Mitchell.

If Luke was the killer, his DNA should have been all over the crime scene. But the police had not taken good care with what they had.

The first forensic scientist did not arrive to examine the body until eight hours after Jodi had been found – eight hours in which it had rained and no tent had been erected over the scene. Derek Scrimger examined the site at 8am on 1st July. A colleague of his had been dispatched earlier, he told the court, but she had a bad back and couldn't climb over the wall on Roan's Dyke. He agreed that a substantial amount of rain had fallen over the night, which had affected the areas of bloodstaining. Not only that, but Jodi's body and the articles of her strewn clothing had been moved before Scrimger even got there. It was not, as he agreed in court 'an ideally managed crime scene'.

The weapon used to kill Jodi was also never recovered – and the police had allowed the council to go ahead and empty all the bins in the area the morning of 1st July.

The prosecution offered another reason why the crucial DNA was missing – the clothes that Luke had worn when he murdered his girlfriend had gone up in smoke, in a woodburning stove the Mitchells had in their garden and used for barbecues. Several of the neighbours reported seeing smoke drifting over their garden walls at around 6.30 to 7pm and then later at about 9pm that evening, something most of them didn't consider unusual. However, one neighbour, George Ramage, did notice that with the smoke came a peculiar smell that was neither sausages nor wood. 'If that's food,' he remembered remarking to his wife, 'then I wouldn't want to be eating it.'

LA Story

It wasn't until August 2003 that the police questioned Luke again, and this time they warned him he was under a caution. They raided his house again, and also his father's. But the items recovered from his bedroom in Corinne's residence, which would be used in court as compelling, if controversial, evidence were found later, on the day of his arrest.

Firstly, they found a leather knife pouch bearing the inscription '*JJ 1989–2003*', underneath which was written Jodi's favourite Cobain quote and the numbers 666. The suggestion was that this empty pouch had once contained the weapon used to kill Jodi and had been subsequently adorned in a manner that celebrated this fact.

Secondly, they took away a number of records, DVDs and other articles by and about Marilyn Manson. What the court would be later asked to consider in relation to Manson was not among these items. It was instead research carried out by the prosecution's team via the Internet. On the singer's homepage they had come across a series of paintings Manson had rendered of Elizabeth Short, otherwise known as The Black Dahlia.

This 1949 unsolved murder in which a beautiful starlet was tortured, cut in half, drained of blood and then dumped in full daylight, haunts Los Angeles to this day. It has been the subject of countless novels, including James Ellroy's *noir* masterpiece, and a legion of true crime books purporting to have solved the mystery.

What interested the prosecution in the Jodi Jones case was the way Manson had depicted the horrific mutilations Short had suffered post-mortem – her mouth had been gashed from ear to ear and her breast slashed. Her torso had been completely severed at the waist.

Jodi Jones had received post-mortem knife wounds to her face, breast and stomach. The prosecution invited the jury to connect the two cases, to consider that Jodi had been killed and mutilated in some unspeakable homage to The Black Dahlia.

Professor Anthony Busuttil, the pathologist who carried out a post-mortem examination on Jodi's body on 1st July 2003, opined in court that there were 'major similarities' between the two cases when being questioned by Allan Turnbull for the prosecution. However, when cross-questioned by Mitchell's defender, Donald Findlay, he amended this view to 'major dissimilarities'.

TV tributes

By the time Jodi was buried, on 3rd September 2003, Luke was under such suspicion that Judith Jones asked him to stay away from the funeral. Instead, with the help of Corinne, he staged his own tribute to his lost love – on Sky TV.

Interviewed by Jim Matthews, Luke was filmed at his home, with his mother standing by his side. He started out by reading a poem he had penned for Jodi, which included the lines:

'Goodbye Jodi, please can you say what happened, please tell us who it was, who took your life so cruelly for no apparent cause. You have so much to give us, you live life your own way, whoever did this to you should just be put away.'

He then faced the question that was on everyone's mind – was he the killer?

'No, never,' he stated. 'I wouldn't think of it. I mean, in all the time we were going out, we never had one argument at all. Never fell out or anything.'

He said the weeks since Jodi's death had been worse than a nightmare, but, 'at least you woke from a nightmare'.

He was asked what had been the worst aspect. With Corinne's arm around his shoulder, he said it was finding Jodi's body. 'All the rest of it, the police and accusations and things, I couldn't care about...I just want to find out what happened and who did it.'

Jim Matthews asked if he thought the finger was being pointed at him. Luke opined there was a 'trial by media' and that while the police had other suspects, he seemed to be the only person mentioned by name.

He was also saddened at being told to stay away from the funeral. He had been dreading it, but had wanted to go, and he thought it would have been a media circus even without him. Instead, he had written his poem. 'If I couldn't say goodbye at the funeral, I had to say goodbye at some point.'

Later, Luke was pictured with his mother, taking flowers to Jodi's grave and smoking a cigarette, which hardly improved his public image. When she found out, an angry Judith Jones returned his wreath. The whole community was outraged by what they saw as Mitchell's mockery, resulting in Luke being barred from returning to school after the holidays, despite furious protests from Corinne and threats of legal action.

Still the police didn't have enough evidence to charge him. So they cast around for more witnesses to help them – and uncovered another bizarre strand of Luke Mitchell's secret life.

Dead Ringers

At the same time that Luke was going out with Jodi, he had another girlfriend, Kimberly Thompson, of Kenmore, Perthshire, whom he had met in the summer of 2002 when she had been holidaying in the Newbattle area. They had continued to visit each other during school holidays ever since, and as far as she was concerned, Luke was her boyfriend.

When Kimberly showed up in court on New Year's Eve 2004 to testify, Judith Jones had to leave the room. Kimberly looked virtually identical to Jodi.

Kimberly described Luke in similar tones to Jodi's diary. He was 'gentle, funny, kind and affectionate' – but she was shocked to find out that he had been two-timing her. Luke obviously kept his secrets well.

Seemingly, there was another girlfriend too. On 21st January 2005, the day the jury returned their verdict, the Scottish *Evening News* ran an interview with a girl who didn't want to be named, who said she had gone out with Luke for about five months in 2003. She described how Luke had pressed a Swiss Army knife to her throat in their local youth club hall, saying: 'Don't move or I'll gut you.'

'At first I thought he was just mucking about, but then I started to feel threatened,' she told reporter Chris Mooney. 'He had grabbed me round the neck with his arm and held the knife at my throat, saying he was going to cut me and stuff like that.' The 'pretty 14-year-old' added that she had finished with Luke shortly afterwards, in May 2003 and had little contact with him since, but that he had threatened her friends when he saw them in the street. When asked what she had thought when she saw Mitchell accused of murder, she replied: 'At first, I never thought he could have done it. But, as all the stuff started to come together, I started to think it was possible, that he could do this, because of the way he acted and what he'd done to me.'

Strangely, the next day, the *Evening News'* sister paper *The Scotsman* ran a similar interview with a girl called Cara Van Nuil, aged 16. It was not clear if the reporter, Angie Brown, actually spoke directly to Cara as every quotation from her was prefaced with the words 'she told friends'. In this version of what seems like the same story, Cara had been going out with Luke for a few months when, at an Army Cadet meeting in Bonnyrigg 'not long before' 30th June, he pulled a penknife on her.

'He grabbed me and turned me round,' she is reported to have 'told friends'. 'He had one arm across the top of my chest with his hand on my shoulder to hold me tightly against him. His other hand had a knife which he had pressed against my throat. I felt really scared and uncomfortable by the way he was acting and the way he held me.

'I tried to push him away but he aggressively held on to me so I started to get a bit nervous and scared. He then suddenly stopped and said he was only joking.'

The report then went on to describe another act of violence – in the woods at Roan's Dyke. Mitchell had again apparently become suddenly aggressive and had 'forced her arm up her back and twisted her body into positions which she said caused her pain'. Cara again 'told friends' that: 'He started play fighting with me but he started hurting me by pushing my arm up my back really hard. I told him he was hurting me and he said, "Shut up or I'll kill you".'

But it wasn't until Luke Mitchell was charged with murder in April 2004 that she 'confided in family and friends', but obviously not the police, these deeply worrying stories.

There are several inconsistencies in these two reports. But inconsistencies were legion in this case. And they never got in the way of a good conviction.

Was it or wasn't it?

In the end, all the police had to place Luke Mitchell at the scene at the right time were conflicting witness statements of a person or persons sighted at Roan's Dyke around the appropriate timeframe. Jodi Jones' death was estimated at 5pm. The prosecution brought the following witnesses into court:

Adriana Bryson, 26, saw a couple standing at the entrance to the pathway just after 4.45pm on 30th June. She didn't know either Jodi or Luke and was unable to identify either as the pair she spotted. She recalled that the male had 'a lot of hair' and told police he resembled

'Shaggy out of *Scooby Doo*' and appeared to be in his early 20s. The police then showed her a series of 12 photographs from which she picked out Luke Mitchell – who was the only person of the 12 depicted with longish hair. Mitchell's hair at the time was reddish blonde and touching his shoulders, a little longer than a grown-out Beatle cut.

When she took the stand to give evidence and was asked whether Mitchell was indeed the person she saw, Bryson replied: 'I cannot say'.

Rosemary Fleming, a 49-year-old council worker, spotted a young boy leaning on the gate at the top of Roan's Dyke as she drove past at around 5.42pm on 30th June. She remarked to her passenger, her sister-in-law Lorraine Fleming, 46, that: 'he looks as if he's been up to no good'. When she heard about Jodi's murder she had been sufficiently worried enough by the youth's demeanour to contact the police. In court, she pointed out Luke as the person she had seen.

Carole Heatlie, 46, was also driving past the same spot at 6.05pm when she saw a long-haired young man emerge from the pathway and then seemingly draw back when he noticed her car. She pointed to Luke in the dock and said: 'he looks very similar'.

Photography student Alan Holbourn, 18, said he had seen Mitchell in this place at 5.55 or 6pm. He was cycling past with friends, and although he didn't know Luke, his companions Dean Houston and Grant Elliot both went to St David's and could positively identify him.

But – and this is where things become really troubling – when the police began their initial investigations, they were told by several witnesses living next to Roan's Dyke that they had heard and seen two youths riding and pushing a very noisy moped on the path that day at around 5pm, the exact time of the murder. One of those youths was described as having long, curly, ginger hair. Police went on TV asking to hear from anyone who fitted this description.

Riders on the path

Five days after the murder, a teenager came forward. He was Jodi Jones' second cousin and the person who supplied Luke Mitchell with his cannabis. John Ferris and his cousin Gordon Dickie had been riding a moped along Roan's Dyke at 5pm that afternoon, had even stopped at the V-shaped intersection in the wall. By the time Ferris went to the police, he had cut off all his long, distinctive, curly ginger hair. He had also 'fallen out' with the Jones family.

When he gave his initial statement, he said he had been on the path at 4.30 on the afternoon of 30th June, which was before Jodi had left her home. When cross-questioned by Donald Findlay in court, Ferris, then 18, explained the half-hour discrepancy between the time he originally stated and the time he'd actually been seen by saying that the last clock he'd checked had been telling the wrong time.

But he did admit 'a rather substantial list of coincidences'. That he was in the place where Jodi was murdered at the time she would have been walking along the path, yet he hadn't seen her or heard anything untoward. That he had stopped his moped at the V-shape in the wall. That he had actually been due to go to the Jones' house later that night but had suddenly decided against it.

When Gordon Dickie gave a statement to police on 7th July, he mentioned that he and Ferris had been talking about Luke Mitchell in the days after Jodi's death. He said: 'John and I have been talking about everything and realised we had came up the Roan's Dyke path about the time Jodi possibly went missing. We kept thinking about everything and talking about Luke.'

Challenged by Findlay, the pair denied colluding in their stories to attempt to frame Luke Mitchell or being the actual murderers of Jodi Jones. After they had given their evidence, they were never mentioned in the press again.

'Blown to hell'

It wasn't until October 2003 that Detective Superintendent Dobbie believed he had enough evidence to report Luke to the Procurator Fiscal (the Scottish equivalent of the Crown Prosecution Service) for a circumstantial case. After they had carried out their own investigations and interviews, a warrant was issued for Luke's arrest in April 2004.

When they came for Luke on 7.30pm 14th April, the police found him in his bedroom. Detective Sergeant David Gordon told the court: 'He stood up beside the bed, fully clothed. It was explained he was being arrested for the murder of Jodi Jones and that he was not obliged to say anything. Asked if he understood, he nodded.'

Other newspaper reports had Corinne in Luke's bedroom with him, 'comforting him' because he 'couldn't sleep'.

Mitchell was searched and three separate quantities of cannabis were found in his trouser pockets.

However, no attempt was made to contact the then 15-year-old's solicitor as is normal practice. In a further break with protocol, the police took his photograph and showed it to Adriana Bryson, when they should have held an identity parade. Though, as Donald Findlay pointed out, when pictures of Luke appeared in the papers the day after his arrest, his last chance of getting a fair ID parade were 'blown to hell and back'.

Instead, detectives worked on grilling a confession out of their suspect. Detective Constable Stephen Quinn asked Luke what he had been doing on the night Jodi was killed. He said that after he had received a text from Jodi he had left his house at 5.45 and gone to wait for her at the bus stop on the edge of the housing estate where he lived. He had hung about there for a while, before looking down the Roan's Dyke path to see if she was on her way. He had checked his mobile constantly for messages so he knew what the time was. He also mentioned seeing his school friends on their bikes, and them asking if he was 'waiting for his bird'.

Luke said he waited 45 minutes for Jodi, by which time he had grown anxious – it should only have taken her 25 minutes to reach him. But he jumbled up his answers as to what he did next, firstly saying that he didn't want to worry Judith by calling her, then saying that he did call, only to be told that Jodi had already left. He gave long pauses between his answers and when asked why he hadn't called again when Jodi still didn't arrive he replied: 'Because I assumed that she might have stopped to talk to somebody or to muck around with someone else.'

What about calling later, after her 10pm curfew, to ask why she hadn't appeared? Because, Luke reasoned, he could quite easily have asked her the next day. When the police persisted with the same question, Mitchell became angry and started swearing, saying: '...she did not have her fucking mobile because it was broken. How the fuck should I know who she was likely to meet?'

Yet DS Dobbie would later describe Luke's interview style as utterly collected. 'He was totally in control of himself and challenged the abilities and authority of the police. It was almost like taunts. He had the mental ability to sit and take control of the interview and that's incredible from someone who has not previously been part of the criminal process, or not come from a criminal family. He was not fazed or shocked or panicking. I have never seen someone so cool and calm and who needed to control the situation.'

Speaking to *Scotland on Sunday* two days after the trial had ended, Dobbie also offered up his opinion of the one thing missing from the picture so far – Luke's motive. The superintendent suggested that Jodi had found out about Kimberly, and this had led to an argument on Roan's Dyke that quickly escalated into murder. He was quick to bring in Marilyn Manson as a possible influence, and the newspapers were quick to mutate the Elizabeth Short paintings the prosecution found on Manson's website into a 'DVD about the Black Dahlia killing' that Luke had supposedly bought. Actually, the DVD was a film called *Doppelherz* that came free with the Manson album *The Golden Age of the Grotesque* and had nothing to do with the Black Dahlia case whatsoever.

There was also something jarring about Dobbie's hypothesis. If Jodi Jones had left to angrily confront her boyfriend over his two-timing, why had she been so happy and carefree when she left her house that evening?

Spectres in the dock

In the end, Scotland's finest advocate could do nothing to defend Luke Mitchell from popular opinion and the outrage generated by Jodi's vile and violent end. After 24 hours of deliberations, the jury found him guilty of murder and supplying cannabis. The other charge that had been brought against him at the start of the trial, possession of a knife or knives, had been dropped, as had a movement to charge Corinne with conspiring to pervert the course of justice.

It was the most high-profile loss of Donald Findlay's career, which caused a lot of gloating in the Scottish press. Findlay had a reputation for defending the bad guy and using Scotland's unique 'not proven' verdict to get them off. His previous successes had included gangsters and controversial murder suspects, so for many, this was the flamboyant QC finally getting his just deserts. But to the letter of the law, Findlay was right. There was a higher standard of proof required to find his client guilty than was provided in this case.

However, it was clear Luke Mitchell had not been alone in the dock. With him were the spectres of folk nightmares old and new. Child-killing, the most ancient and dread – many was the psychologist quick to compare the 'cold-blooded, calculating' Mitchell with Britain's most notorious mini-murderer, Mary Bell, who was only ten years old when she killed two little boys of three and four in Newcastle in 1968. Mary Bell is still such a hate figure in the United Kingdom that one book that took a realistic look at her life and crimes, Gitta Sereny's *Cries Unheard,* ignited a firestorm upon its publication in 1998, mainly because Sereny had paid Bell, now living under an assumed name with a court order keeping the press away from her. Sereny did not excuse Bell's crimes. But she did point out that Bell had a mother who hated her, forced her into child prostitution and attempted to kill her, lose her or give her away on numerous occasions – so it was pretty impossible for her to ever have behaved like a 'normal' 10-year-old.

The public did not want to hear the mitigating circumstances of Mary Bell's life, just as they didn't want to hear that the case against Luke Mitchell was by no means watertight. On 11th February 2005, Lord Nimmo Smith sentenced Mitchell to at least 20 years. 'Looking back over the evidence I still cannot fathom what led you to do what you did,' he said, while Luke stared into the distance, betraying no emotion. The Judge expressed concern that Mitchell's chronic cannabis habit could have 'seriously damaged' his mental processes: 'In your case I think that it may well have contributed to your being unable to make the distinction between fantasy and reality,' he opined. He also noted that 'with hindsight' Mitchell's unconventional upbringing may have also affected him.

But Lord Nimmo Smith was also convinced by the prosecution's argument that Marilyn Manson's paintings were an influence, as was Mitchell's professed Satanism:

'I do not think that your interest in Satanism can be ignored as mere adolescent rebellion. I think it is a sign that you found evil attractive and that you thought there might be a kind of perverted glamour in doing something wicked,' the Judge said.

'If you were older, I would have no difficulty in deciding that the seriousness of the offence merited the imposition of a punishment part among the longest that there have been. It is only your age that has led me to decide that a lesser period will be appropriate...20 years.'

Other shades circled the courtroom that day, but perhaps only Donald Findlay could perceive them. Shadows of other long-held and shameful British traditions: witch hunting, scapegoating, police desperate for a conviction not paying attention to the fine details of the facts before them. No one wanting to consider for one possible moment that maybe they could be wrong. Jodi was avenged that day, everyone agreed. Everyone said so, from the pizza delivery boy who thought Luke was rude, to the woman who served teas at the local café. And they had somehow all known, all along, that Luke Mitchell was a natural born killer who had to be purged from their society.

Endless, Nameless

Following his sentencing, Luke Mitchell was taken to Polmont Young Offenders' Institute, where he is expected to stay until he is 21 and can be transferred to an adult jail. 'Cold-hearted' Luke was placed on suicide watch when he arrived. He has since complained that prison guards spat in his food and kept him awake all night by kicking on his door, but these complaints 'were not being given a serious grading' according to the authorities. The papers were more interested in the sackfuls of mail he reportedly receives from 'sick goth' admirers.

On 15th February 2005 Mitchell lodged an appeal against his sentence with Donald Findlay standing by him: 'so long as that young man maintains to me he did not kill Jodi, the fight to clear his name will go on,' said the QC.

Apparently, Luke sleeps with a picture of Jodi under his pillow.

Jodi sleeps in a darker, colder place, the words of Kurt Cobain on her headstone: *'Come as you are/As you were/As I'd want you to be/As a friend/As a friend.'* Her story has since been taken up by another American punk band. In May 2005, New Yorkers The Killers announced they had written a song about the teenager, entitled 'Where Is She?'. Singer Brandon Flowers said he had seen the case come to an end on the news while on tour in Scotland and had written his tribute from Judith Jones' point of view. 'It affected me deeply and got me thinking about how awful it must feel to be the parent of a missing child, how powerless a person must feel in such a dreadful situation,' he told *NME*. Yet it didn't seem to have crossed his mind that Judith could have found this a bit insensitive coming from a band revelling in a name like The Killers.

It will probably take a year before Mitchell's appeal will be heard. No one from the Crown Office wants to comment on it. In Easthouses, the general feeling is summed up by one nameless local: 'Hopefully they've got the right man, and hopefully the mother can move on now. But people here will not forget this.'

Corinne Mitchell has had her property attacked several times now and is no longer welcome in the environs of Dalkeith. It is doubtful she or Shane will have much of a life if they stay there.

At the time of writing, Britain seems to be experiencing a wave of youth-on-youth crime. On 8th June 2005, three teenagers were being questioned over the death of a 15-year-old girl in Bradford, West Yorkshire. On the same day, the Crime Reduction Bill was published, giving teachers more powers to tackle violence in classrooms and bringing the age at which knives can be purchased up to 18. This followed calls from teacher's unions for the government to take action against gangs of violent youths who bring knives, firearms and drugs into schools without fear of reprisal.

Only a week before, a 12-year-old girl was arrested and charged with grievous bodily harm and attempting to pervert the course of justice in nearby Dewsbury, West Yorkshire, after a 5-year-old boy was taken from his garden into a nearby park and was found later wandering around in a distressed daze with horrific ligature injuries around neck.

With the tabloids taking their usual inflammatory stand on the issue of 'yob' violence it would seem that, at this moment in time, society's greatest fear is a dope-smoking, knife-wielding schoolchild.

Which is why, distressing as the case may be, it is so important to try and strip away the hysteria surrounding it and look instead at the hard facts.

Without a doubt, Lord Nimmo Smith was right when he described the death of Jodi Jones as 'one of the worst cases of murder of a single victim to have come before the court in many years'. No one would want to diminish the pain meted out to the Jones family nor the suffering that Jodi went through.

But the Luke Mitchell case is bedevilled by errors, doubt and deliberate misrepresentation. It is, of course, possible that despite this not being the best police work in history, Mitchell could have been a 14-year-old psycho, his fantasies inflamed by the monstrous amount of drugs he was consuming at a time when the brain is developing and therefore at its most vulnerable. It is also possible that his relationship with Corinne was not a normal one; Luke's letters from prison apparently tell of his obsessive urge to have sex all the time – as we have seen with Rod Ferrell and Natasha Cornett, children who are sexualised too early in life can become nymphomaniacs. There is a huge temptation on society's part when a crime like this occurs to conclude that, if the right man went down, then the methods that got him there are irrelevant.

Yet there could only be one thing worse than this murder itself, one final insult to the memory of Jodi Jones – and that would be that the local weirdo was made a scapegoat for it, because he ticked all the right boxes.

Leaving the real killer or killers still out there, free to carry on the Devil's work.

Afterword

How to keep the Devil from the door

If we are serious about stopping Satan from getting his claws on impressionable children then we cannot fight him with garlic and a Bible. Just like Robert Ressler's study on indicators for serial killers, the contemplation of these cases reveal very similar links between our killers, factors which cannot be explained away by simple good and evil.

Because these criminals were all very young, this book set out to explore the touted link between popular culture and criminality for the precise reason that 'youth culture' has been the media's favourite weapon of choice in trying to comprehend them. Yet as we have seen, books, films and pop music were most certainly not the root of their deviancy.

The fact these killers had deliberately chosen the Left-hand path as a revolt against society tells us very clearly that society is failing to connect with young people. As our fears of teenage crime have mushroomed, we need to take a sober and unhysterical look at just what it is that has gone wrong.

The Root of all Evil

The first and most damning of all circumstances that most of these criminals have in common is an appalling upbringing. They were victims long before they were victimisers; many were trapped in circles of abuse that had afflicted previous generations of their families. This is why they should not be viewed in isolation as aberrant but seen instead as the very severe symptoms of a deep societal malaise. These criminals were once all vulnerable children. Satan did not create them out of thin air as witches and monsters, vampires and bogeymen. They were bred in the heart of our societies and conditions that caused them to grow up bad were direct results of public policy.

One of the most prescient comments on this was made by the Rev Johannes Richter in Chapter 7. With a very clear view of where trouble was pouring into the former East Germany, he summarised the problems faced across the world: 'The only reality many young people know is the virtual reality they exerience electronically. It's a reality without values, a reality where parental neglect has become acceptable, a reality that glorifies brutality, waffles about human rights but disdains human dignity.'

He is describing the legacy of the Reagan/Thatcher years, of the powerful State and God. America and Britain have followed a model of politics over the past three decades that has trumpeted values of decency yet at the same time ruthlessly dismantled community, shrilled evangelical Christianity yet promoted the rights of the individual over those of society. Above all, these have been the politics of selfishness. Which is virtually the exact philosophy that you will find in Anton La Vey's *Satanic Bible*.

The breakdown of community

Western society has fractured over the past 30 years. The effects of globalisation, begun in the Reagan/Thatcher years, have not just been catastrophic for the Third World but have had a malign influence on our own, much richer societies.

For instance, the decampment of the car industry from the Midwest of America to cheaper, Mexican climes and the destruction of the coal industry in Britain have had pernicious repercussions. Where communities have been broken, crime, drugs and helplessness have poured in. With Trades Unions smashed, America and Britain now have the worst working conditions in the Western world. Children suffer keenly from the imposition of low wages, long hours and few paid holidays on their parents. And when you take away any safety nets of a Welfare State and a decent, free education, you stop those children from having any ladder to climb back up again.

Luke Mitchell and Allan Menzies were both brought up in former industrial towns now fallen on hard times. So were Rod Ferrell and Natasha Cornett. The inequalities between the standard of living in East and West Germany generated a mushrooming of the dreaded Nazism in the depressed East that found a potent focus in Hendrik Möbus. Predators like William Pierce are always circling, waiting to take advantage of disaffected young people for their own dubious ends.

The displacement of communities also takes away tradional support structures for the poor. Extended families are broken when you have to relocate to find work. Even the basic family unit of a father, a mother and children has been eroded to the point of near-obsolescence in an amazingly short space of time. None of our killers come from a stable background. Many of their parents were single teenagers themselves when they had them. Grandparents were often in direct ideological conflict with their offspring, causing a plethora of mixed messages to be passed over the playpen, often along stark, religious lines. How could these infants decide for themselves what was right or wrong?

The other institutions that once bonded societies have also come unstuck. The churches in Britain are empty; in America they are fronted by rabid capitalists in cassocks.

No wonder the Devil is laughing.

The electronic nanny

Professionals working in the rehabilitation of young offenders have noted that, increasingly, their charges find it almost impossible to separate fantasy from reality. Some of them think that films are acted out in real time, with real people, not actors. Some of them think that when they are stealing a car, for instance, and taking it for a joyride, they are taking part in a film, or a computer game, of their own making.

That's because many of them have never known much other than the electronic reality provided by computer games and TV sets, DVDs and videos. Precisely because parental neglect has become, if not acceptable, than increasingly necessary for monetary survival, that the little screen has been left to foster these children while their parents or, more likely, parent, have more pressing concerns.

Only recently, it seems, have we started to wake up to the fact that children cannot rear themselves from in front of a TV screen. Recent studies in the States have drawn definite links between the amount of time babies and young children spend in front of the television and the likelihood of them suffering from Attention Deficiency Hyperactivity Disorder (ADHD), the plague of our modern youth.

Food for thought

More basic still, the recent UK television campaign by TV chef Jamie Oliver to bring attention to children's real dietary needs has revealed horrendous pictures of what Oliver rightly calls 'abuse' on the dining table. Children brought up on diets of sugar-loaded pop and fat-saturated, processed food with none of the vital nutritional requirements for them to grow up healthy both physically and mentally are legion. This is the other key player in the ADHD epidemic.

Margaret Thatcher was not just the 'milk snatcher' of infamy; her government also replaced nutritonally balanced school meals, vital to those children who relied on them for their only stable source of nutrition, with American-style canteens full of burgers and chips. Now the children of the Eighties, whom this first affected, are bringing up their own children to be obese, hyperactive and often profoundly disturbed. And, two decades into the cycle, the Labour government have only just been shamed into doing something about the state of what we feed our children by a TV chef.

Remember Richard Ramirez as a child, drinking cola and eating sugar-laden cereal in front of the TV? Remember Rod Ferrell dining exclusively on junk food as his teenage mania increased? Are they so very different from millions of children growing up today?

Vacant glamour

The teenage years are the most painful of our lives, and if children are brought up without basic love, self-respect and decency, they are going to be more troublesome still. In the latter part of this book, we have seen alienated teenagers repeatedly replacing 'straight' society with elaborate fantasies based on myths of vampires and eternal life. The Rudas, the Kentucky Vampire clans and Allan Menzies all shared a sense that they were already doomed, already excluded. The fantasies they constructed for themselves were preferable to the real world they lived in, for only by dressing up as the monsters society has feared since ancient days could they feel a measure of power and self-worth.

Popular culture used to provide a more vibrant outlet for self-expression in the young. The 'do-it-yourself' ethos of punk was an updated version of the hippy ideal that communities can be created from the disaffected to a positive end. The teenagers of this era had more of a chance of a decent education and a solid upbringing and their ideas flourished. Rage and unjustice could be channelled through creative means.

Todays teenagers have role models that are more 'pretty vacant' than even Johnny Rotten could have imagined. Realising that youth culture meant mega bucks, the music industry has steadily become a modern manufacturing business that aggresively sells the idea of beauty and riches as the only ideals worth having to those who can least attain them.

This has reached its apex in the cult of reality TV and celebrity magazines, where an entire generation of youngsters are willing to pubicly debase themselves in a hysterical attempt to grab their five minutes of all-important fame.

For fame is all, our children are told. Skill, talent, empathy and intelligence are left by the wayside. In the few cases where genuine talent has emerged of its own accord and directly connected with young peoples fears, hopes and dreams, it has either been grimly destroyed (like the tragic end of Kurt Cobain) or demonised (hello again, Marilyn Manson). Yet is it any wonder that teenagers would rather listen to the truths of Nirvana or Manson than the lies of *Pop Idol* or *Heat* magazine? Is it any wonder that the more powerfully they are physically distanced from society's ideal, the more they will revolt towards the opposite extreme?

Drugs, drink and self-immolation are rife. Yet if that rage could only be channelled into creative outlets then the young could empower themselves instead of destroying themselves. And everyone would be a lot happier.

But all around, the mass media, owned by the most powerful people on the planet, perform the same service that the Games did in Imperial Rome – distracting us from reality. Because, after all, who are our ultimate role models? Who is really responsible for the way we live today?

The biggest bully in the playground

Our leaders are not setting us a great example. At the time of writing, President George W Bush and Prime Minister Tony Blair are embroiled in a 'war of liberation' in Iraq that has led to the death of quarter of a million civilians and hundreds of young soliders. Most of the cannon fodder came from very similar backgrounds to our killers. Yet Bush and Blair are both avowed 'Christians', waging a war on an 'evil ideology' that apparently threatens our very way of life. If this is what is being done in the name of God then how are we ever to come to terms with such double standards?

The great comic Bill Hicks once succinctly compared American foreign policy with the 1953 Western *Shane*. Jack Palance, the epitome of Old West toughness, goads an innocent Mexican peasant into picking up a gun, only to shoot him dead with the words: 'You all saw him – he had a gun.' It is this glorification of brutality as somehow heroic that America has been busily exporting to the world since World War II.

But America, for all its pretentions of opportunity, fairness and rough-and-tumble common decency comes across as nothing so much as the most hormonal teenager in the playground. An angry adolescent who can never be separated from the Hollywood fantasy he has constructed in his head to block out the blatant untruths of his reality. Because he is also the biggest teenager in the playground, nobody can stand up to him – especially when Britain, who is older and should know better, is standing behind this posing cowboy, acting as the indulgent schoolmaster, using his head bully to keep any other troublesome young pups in line.

If you want to indict any form of culture in these crimes, then this American way is your chief offender. Is it any wonder that Anton La Vey used to frequently refer to his homeland as 'The United Satanic States of America'?

Listening in

If we want our children to behave, we have to set them a better standard. Look after them properly; help them to grow up with self-belief and the knowledge of how to cope in the big, bad world. Do not teach them that they should be out for themselves and no one else. That all scores should be settled with firearms. Or that the pinnacle of achievement is the amount of diamonds you own.

Satanic killers are the misguided spawn of problems that affect all of us, and preventing a further epidemic of such crimes requires society as a whole to act. Even if that requires us to look hard into our own dark places and admit that we have much to learn. For only by illuminating the social ills of injustice, poverty and ignorance can we truly ever banish the demons that are only too eager to prey on our most vulnerable.

It is ironic for his detractors that the most demonised public figure in this book, Marilyn Manson, also offers the best advice:

Listen to your children.

Bibliography

Chapter One

Books:

Do What Thou Wilt: A Life of Aleister Crowley by Lawrence Sutin (St Martin's Press)

Lucifer Rising by Gavin Baddeley (Plexus)

Turn Off Your Mind: The Mystic Sixties and The Dark Side of The Age of Aquarius by Gary Valentine Lachman (Sidgwick & Jackson)

The Garbage People by John Gilmore and Ron Kenner (Amok)

The Secret Life of a Satanist: The Authorised Biography of Anton La Vey by Blanche Barton (Mondo)

Articles:

'Look Back at Anger' by Sanjiv Bhattacharya, the *Observer* 22.8.04

'Kenneth Anger: Celluloid Sorcery and Psychedelic Satanism' by Mark Pilkington, *Fortean Times* 25.1.03

'Kenneth Anger' by Robert A Haller, Film in the Cities, February 1980

'Kenneth Anger' by Maximilian Le Cain, *www.sensesofcinema.com*

Chapter Two: David Berkowitz

Books:

Whoever Fights Monsters: My Twenty Years of Tracking Serial Killers for the FBI by Robert K Ressler and Tom Shachtman (St Martin's True Crime Library)

A Plague of Murder: The Rise and Rise of Serial Killing in the Modern Age by Colin Wilson (Robinson)

Multiple Murder and Demonic Possession by William D Tatum and Brian McConnell (The Book Guild Ltd)

Please Kill Me by Legs McNeil and Gillian McCain (Abacus)

Articles:

'Son of Sam' by Marilyn Bardsley, *www.thecrimelibrary.com*

Films:

Taxi Driver (Martin Scorsese, 1976)

Summer of Sam (Spike Lee, 1999)

Chapter Three: The Chicago Rippers

Books:

Deadly Thrills by Jaye Slade Fletcher (Onyx True Crime)

Articles:

'Homicidal Mania: The 15 Most Horrific Crimes to Shock America' by Bill Kelly, *www.cybersleuths.com*

'The Chicago Rippers' by Katherine Ramsland, *www.crimelibrary.com*

'Geraldo Rivera: Satanic Ritual Abuse and Recovered Memories' by BA Robertson, *www.religioustolerance.org*

'Satanic Panic: Update on the Sword of Horus' by GM Kelly, *The Newaoen Newsletter*, May 1989

Chapter Four: Richard Ramirez

Books:

The Night Stalker by Philip Carlo (Pinnacle True Crime)

The Serial Killers: A Study in the Psychology of Violence by Colin Wilson and Donald Seaman (True Crime)

Whoever Fights Monsters: My Twenty Years of Tracking Serial Killers for the FBI by Robert K Ressler and Tom Shachtman (St Martin's True Crime Library)

A Plague of Murder: The Rise and Rise of Serial Killing in the Modern Age by Colin Wilson (Robinson)

Articles:

'Richard Ramirez' by Anthony Bruno, *www.crimelibrary.com*

'Ramirez and Satan: Perfect Together?' by Katherine Ramsland, *www.crimelibrary.com*

Chapter Five: Tracey Wigginton and Lisa Ptaschinski

Books:

Death Cults: Murder, Mayhem and Mind Control, ed Jack Sargeant (Virgin True Crime)

Pig City: From the Saints to Savage Garden by Andrew Stafford (UQP)

Articles:

'Murder Casebook 83: The Vampire Killers' by David Jessel, Colin Wilson, James Morton and Bill Waddell, Marshall Cavendish partworks

'Lesbian Vampire Killer in Low Risk Jail', *Herald Sun*, 10.2.05

'How the Vampire Killer Became a Bachelor of Arts', *Nationwide News*, 9.6.02

'Student Drank Blood of Victim', *Sydney Morning Herald*, 31.01.90

'Versed in Vampires – After a Rich Vein' by Deb Verhoeven *The Age*, 9.4.93

'Dead, Deranged, Devious' by George Zdenkowski, *Sydney Morning Herald*, 4.9.92

'When the Victim Kills' by Elissa Blake, *The Age*, 11.12.96

'Bad Girls' by Katrina Fox, *LOTL*, October 2004

Chapter Six: Count Grishnackh

Books:

Lords of Chaos: The Bloody Rise of the Satanic Metal Underground by Michael Moynihan and Didrik Søderland (Feral House)

Lucifer Rising by Gavin Baddeley (Plexus)

Articles:

'Media Constructions of Satanism in Norway 1988–1997' by Asbjørn Dryendal, *Foaftale News*: Newsletter of the International Society for Contemporary Legend Research, February 1998

'The Nottingham UK Ritual Abuse Cases' by BA Robertson, *www.religioustolerance.org*

'MVMO Satanic Ritual Abuse (SRA) Hoax Lewis, Scotland' by BA Robertson, *www.religioustolerance.org*

'We Are But Slaves to the One With Horns' by Jason Arnopp, *Kerrang!*, 1992

'Into the Lion's Cage' by Stephen O'Malley, *Sounds of Death 5*, 1995

'Burzum Library: Life of Euro and Varg' by Ilde, *www.burzum.org*

'Varg escapes the Prison' by *Blabbermouth.net* and Metalstorm

'Interview with Varg Vikernes' by Admin, *www.doomish.com*

Chapter Seven: Hendrik Möbus

Books:

Lords of Chaos: The Bloody Rise of the Satanic Metal Underground by Michael Moynihan and Didrik Søderland (Feral House)

Articles:

'National Socialist Black Metal Leader Arrested in the US' by Devin Burghart and Justin Massa, *Searchlight,* October 2000

'My Seven Years of Stupidity, Lies and Ignorance' by Hendrik Möbus, October 2000

Möebus, Hendrik, *IDGR Encyclopedia right-wing extremism*

'Satanic Killer Must Serve Five Years in Prison', Deustche Press Association

Chapter Eight: Nico Claux

Books:
   True Vampires by Sondra London (Feral House)
   Apocalypse Culture II, ed Adam Parfrey (Feral House)
Documents:
   La Cour D'Assises de Paris, Nicolas Claux, 12.5.97
   First Amendment, Center Arts & Free Expression FAQ
Articles:
   'Vampire of Paris: The Story of Nicolas Claux' by David Lohr, *www.crimelibrary.com*
   'Interview with a Vampire' by Warren Schofield, *Bizarre* 51, October 2001
   'Nicolas Claux' by Laurent Courau, *laspirale.org*
   'How Black is Black Metal?' by Kevin Coogan, *Hitlist,* Feb/March 1999
   'Where Crime, Commerce and Art Collide' by Sam Handlin, *www.courttv.com*

Chapter Nine: The Kentucky Vampire Clan

Books:
   Children Who Kill: Profiles of Pre-Teen and Teenage Killers by Carol Anne Davis (Allison & Busby)
   True Vampires by Sondra London (Feral House)
Documents:
   Statement given by Rod Ferrell on Friday 28.11.96, Baton Rogue, LA
Articles:
   'Florida v Rod Ferrell "The Vampire Cult Slaying Case"', *www.courttv.com*
   'Vampire cult town shrinks under national spotlight', Associated Press
   'Teens Face Court Quietly by Lesley Clark', *Orlando Sentinal,* 12.8.96
   'Mother of 'vampire cult' pleads guilty', Associated Press, 15.9.97
   'Affaidavit: Girl plotted to kill folks' by Lisa Holewa, Associated Press
   'Rod Ferrell Trial to start on schedule', Associated Press, 24.1.98
   'Teen insists she never told cult to kill her parents', Associated Press, 8.15.98
   'Vampire Cult Trial to Begin Monday' by Mike Schnedier, Associated Press, 2.1.01
   'New Orleans Voodoo: Mystery, Magic, Murder' by Tony Thompson, *Bizarre* 4, Sept/Oct 1997

'Death sentence for cult leader reduced' by Jackie Hallifax, *Sun Sentinal*, 10.11.00

Chapter Ten: Natasha Cornett

Books:
True Vampires by Sondra London (Feral House)
Documents:
Court of Criminal Appeals of Tennessee at Knoxville October 1999 Session: Howell, Cornett, Bryant, Mullins, Risner, Sturgill v. Greene County
Articles:
'Report: Cornett planned killing spree', Associated Press, 31.10.97
'It's Not Evil Spirits That Make Teens Kill' by Dr Helen Smith, *Los Angeles Times*, 16.12.97
'A Blackened Rainbow: How do we make sense of the Lillelid murders?' by Jesse Fox Mayshark, Weekly Wire, 2.4.98, *http://weeklywire.com*
'Innocence Lost' by Gina Stafford, *Knoxville News*, 22.2.98
'The Lillelid Murders: So Preventable' by Stephanie Piper, *Tennessee Almnus Magazine*, Fall 2003
'Dr Helen Smith' by Keith Daniels, *www.suicidegirls.com*
'School killers: the list' by Katherine Ramsland, *www.crimelibrary.com*
Films:
Six (Dr Helen Smith, 2003)
Natural Born Killers (Oliver Stone, 1994)

Chapter Eleven: Manuela and Daniel Ruda

Books:
True Vampires by Sondra London (Feral House)
Articles:
'Flirting with Hitler' by John Hooper, *The Guardian*, 16.11.02
'Satanic killers tell of blood drinking rites' by Hannah Cleaver, *The Daily Telegraph*, 18.1.02
'Murder Suspects Express Sympathy for the Devil' by Karen Truscheit, *Frankfurter Allgemeine Zeitung*, 18.1.02
'Murder throws spotlight on Rise in Satanism' by David Crossland, Reuters, 31.1.02
'German Satanists jailed', BBC World News, 31.1.02
'Self-styled Vampire reveals British link', *The Guardian*, 1.2.02

'Vampire couple jailed for Satanic Murder' by Justin Rowlatt, *The Independent*, 1.2.02

'Satanic killers grin as they are locked away' by Allan Hall, *Irish Independent*, 1.2.02

'Blood-drinking devil worshippers face life for ritual Satanic killing' by John Hooper, *The Guardian*, 1.2.02

'Tour of Britain's bizarre underworld' by Vikram Dodd, *The Guardian*, 1.2.02

CESNUR Center for Studies on New Religions 2003 Annual Conference 9.4.03: Religion and Democracy: An Exchange of Experiences Between East and West

'From Black Masses to Black Metal: The Last Temptation of Satan' by Sandro Magister, *www.chiesa.com*

'Know thine enemy, by Simon Jeffrey and agencies', *The Guardian*, 17.2.05

www.marilynmanson.com

Chapter Twelve: Allan Menzies

Articles:

'Vampire Killers: Influenced by Fiction' by Katherine Ramsland, *www.crimelibrary.com*

The Scotsman Archive: Allan Menzies articles 3.1.03 to 15.11.04, *www.thescotsman.com*

'Murder accused had vampire "interest"', BBC News, 25.7.02

'Celebrity cult of vampires can turn into real life evil' by Stephen Khan, *The Observer*, 26.10.03

'Vampire fans "harassed vicar"', BBC News, 9.10.03

'"Vampires" jailed for harassing vicar', BBC News, 14.11.03

Films:

Queen of the Damned (Michael Ryner, 2002)

Chapter Thirteen: Luke Mitchell

Articles:

* The coverage in the UK press on the Luke Mitchell case was too phenomenal to list individually each article referenced by the author, but all sources can be found at the following online newspaper archives:

The Scotsman Archive: Luke Mitchell articles 18.11.04 to 15.2.05, *www.thescotsman.com*

The Times Archive: Luke Mitchell articles 18.11.04 to 15.2.05, *www.thetimes.com*

The Guardian Archive: Luke Mitchell articles 18.11.04 to 15.2.05, *www.theguardian.co.uk*

'Silent and defiant to the end, Luke Mitchell denied family of Jodi Jones the one answer they needed' by Liam McDougall, *The Sunday Herald*, 11.2.05

'Casting Light on Dark Science at Scene of Crime', *Edinburgh Evening News*, 13.2.05

Acknowledgements

The author would like to thank the following for their time, knowledge and translation skills: Petra Smith, Connor McLeod, Simon Crubellier, Augustus Thede-Haskell, Ronnie James Lavelle and Seigfried Klingenberg. And, for patience beyond the call of duty, my partner in crime, Mary.

3